The State of Public Finances 2015

STRATEGIES FOR BUDGETARY CONSOLIDATION AND REFORM IN OECD COUNTRIES

OECD
BETTER POLICIES FOR BETTER LIVES

This work is published under the responsibility of the Secretary-General of the OECD. The opinions expressed and arguments employed herein do not necessarily reflect the official views of OECD member countries.

This document and any map included herein are without prejudice to the status of or sovereignty over any territory, to the delimitation of international frontiers and boundaries and to the name of any territory, city or area.

Please cite this publication as:
OECD (2015), *The State of Public Finances 2015: Strategies for Budgetary Consolidation and Reform in OECD Countries*, OECD Publishing, Paris.
http://dx.doi.org/10.1787/9789264244290-en

ISBN 978-92-64-24424-5 (print)
ISBN 978-92-64-24429-0 (PDF)

The statistical data for Israel are supplied by and under the responsibility of the relevant Israeli authorities. The use of such data by the OECD is without prejudice to the status of the Golan Heights, East Jerusalem and Israeli settlements in the West Bank under the terms of international law.

Photo credits: Cover © masik0553 / Shutterstock.com

Corrigenda to OECD publications may be found on line at: *www.oecd.org/about/publishing/corrigenda.htm.*

Foreword

The *State of Public Finances 2015* provides a record of the strategies pursued by OECD countries to correct, consolidate and stabilise their public finances in the period to 2015, and in particular of how these strategies have evolved over the entire period of the economic and financial crisis from 2007-08 onwards. The report also provides an insight into the future plans for public finances over the coming years. Importantly, the report does not confine itself to the challenges of managing public finances, but encompasses a broad range of related policy themes including: the use of fiscal rules, the strategies adopted in various countries to sustain economic growth during fiscal consolidation, the developing role of independent fiscal institutions, how the role of parliaments and citizens in budgeting has been affected, and the degree to which fiscal consolidation has been accompanied by broader-based budgetary reforms.

In addition, the report includes a closer examination of how fiscal consolidation has affected human resource management within the public sector as well as in-depth analysis of public financial management and the co-ordination of fiscal relations across national and sub-national levels of government. These analyses provide deeper insights into how expenditure savings have driven reforms to traditional practices, and into the scope for extending the fiscal 'toolkit' available to policy makers by reference to good sectoral and regional budget practices.

The report draws heavily upon self-reporting from governments, with 32 of the 34 OECD countries having completed the survey that forms the core of the material in the country notes in Chapter 2. The position as set out in each country note generally reflects the position as of June 2015, and has not been updated to reflect political, economic and budgetary developments since that time. Chapter 3 of the report is based on self-reporting by members of the OECD Network on Fiscal Relations across Levels of Government. The material on human resource management is drawn from an analysis conducted for the OECD Working Party on Public Employment and Management. Fiscal data and economic data relating to OECD countries are derived respectively from the OECD National Account Statistics database and *OECD Economic Outlook No. 97* (May 2015), with key figures updated to reflect the OECD Interim Economic Outlook (September 2015). Thanks are due to the staff of member countries for their time and care in supplying survey material and in responding to follow-up queries.

This report was edited by Ronnie Downes and authored by Jaehyuk Choi, Ronnie Downes, Scherie Nicol and Annamária Tüske (Chapters 1 and 2), and by Claudia Hulbert and Camila Vammalle (chapter 3). Ms Hulbert is an independent consultant; all other authors are members of the OECD Budgeting & Public Expenditures Division at the Public Governance & Territorial Development Directorate of the OECD. Editorial and administrative support was provided by Bonifacio Agapin. The authors are grateful for support and advice received from other colleagues in the Directorate and in the Economics Department of the OECD.

Table of contents

Tables

Figures

Preface

by

Julian Kelly
HM Treasury and Chair of the OECD Working Party of Senior Budget Officials

Right across the OECD, public policy over the past decade has been dominated by the challenges of steering the public finances through troubled times. The fundamental national debate over resources – how they should be raised, allocated and prioritised – often takes precedence over sector-specific concerns, and most particularly when resources are under pressure and even shrinking.

Indeed, the severe economic shock and the accompanying pressure on public finances, as experienced by a large majority of OECD economies, have had a number of repercussions for public governance. The fact that the public finances veered so badly off course, often with negative impacts on people's living standards and traditional public entitlements, has undoubtedly undermined public confidence and trust in government and in policy-making. The question of supporting and restoring trust in government is thus a central organising theme of the OECD's work in recent years.

Budgeting itself, as a principal tool of policy making, has also come under closer scrutiny. It is understandable that citizens ask why public financial management processes did not guard, in a more effective way, against the vagaries of the economic cycle? One response to this legitimate challenge is set out in the OECD's recent Recommendation on Budgetary Governance, which spells out a number of simple, clear yet ambitious principles for how countries should manage their budgets and fiscal policy processes. The principles, to which all OECD countries have lent their wisdom and to which all can subscribe, emphasise the need for clear, credible fiscal-policy objectives, an open and accessible budget framework, and the need to identify and manage "fiscal risks" of the sort that have blown the national finances off course in many countries. This is closely intertwined with work, nationally and internationally, to re-think public policies, to make them more resilient, effective and affordable, and ultimately to promote sustainable, inclusive growth.

Against this background, this OECD report on *The State of Public Finances 2015* is a welcome and timely addition to the international library of policy makers and the interested public. What is distinctive about this publication is how it traces the fiscal impacts of the economic and financial crisis across the various OECD countries, and sketches the diverse range of policy approaches adopted in each country to respond analysis. What emerges is a rounded picture that effectively conveys some real insights into the practical challenges to which policy makers and politicians have had to respond.

The range of responses highlighted in the report is highly thought-provoking. It is notable how virtually all OECD countries have identified the need to protect and support economic growth, in the face of fiscal retrenchment, as a key priority; while the specific policy tools to achieve this objective have varied considerably from one country to another. It is also notable how countries have sought to diagnose the deficiencies in their budgetary frameworks, and address these apparent deficiencies in a number of ways: whether though new independent fiscal institutions, new fiscal rules (either simpler and clearer, or more complex, depending on the country and culture in each case), or more broad-based reforms across the various dimensions highlighted in the OECD's Recommendation.

Perhaps the most salient lesson is also the simplest, and in a way the least surprising. The challenge for policy makers is not to seek to avoid altogether the fiscal shocks and cyclical downturns, to which our economies are subject from time to time. The real challenge is to build resilience into our national frameworks, both to mitigate these fiscal shocks insofar as it is within our power, and to introduce greater agility and flexibility to allow our policies to adapt to these challenges, in proportion to their scale and gravity. As to fiscal resilience, this report underpins the wisdom of counter-cyclical fiscal policies as the norm – not as a mere ideal or aspiration – with fiscal rules or fiscal objectives designed to anchor this policy imperative. As to policy flexibility, the report gives a flavour of the varying expenditure, regulation, taxation and other responses adopted by OECD governments under each heading.

As a primer on perhaps the most important policy concern of recent times, *The State of Public Finances 2015* is also, perhaps, an entrée to the rich analysis and country-to-country dialogue being pursued by the OECD Senior Budget Officials, its various policy and regional networks, and indeed the expert policy communities working together to promote better policies for better lives.

Executive summary

For most countries in the OECD, 2015 is the seventh or eighth year of dealing with the budgetary consequences of the economic and financial crisis precipitated in 2008. These years have been marked by challenges of fiscal retrenchment on a scale and nature unprecedented in modern times.

Previous OECD publications (OECD, 2011, 2012) have tracked the fiscal policy responses adopted by OECD countries during the early years of the crisis (2007-12). This publication takes stock of how these policy responses have evolved and been re-shaped over more recent years (up to 2014/15). Some key findings from the overall analysis are summarised below.

- **The public finances of almost all OECD countries have been badly affected by the crisis, but to widely varying degrees**. In general, public finance deficits across the OECD deteriorated from an average -1.5% of GDP in 2007 to -8.3% in 2009. While the scale of the fiscal shock has remained relatively stable in many countries (e.g. Estonia, Germany, Korea, Sweden), there have been particularly acute deficit swings in certain countries (e.g. Ireland, Slovenia, New Zealand), reflecting the fallout from banking crises and other one-off events.
- **The policy responses adopted by OECD countries have not been uniform**. Some OECD countries (e.g. Ireland, Portugal) that were acutely affected by the crisis responded with rigorous and sustained fiscal correction. Other countries (e.g. Finland, Netherlands and Sweden) relied upon fiscal buffers in the early stages and have been less quick to address underlying fiscal weaknesses. Still others (e.g. France, Hungary and Slovak Republic) have sought to chart an intermediate course that balances a range of objectives.
- **The health of each country's fiscal position at the outset of the crisis strongly determines its current fiscal circumstances**. The long-standing economic argument in favour of "counter-cyclical" budgetary policies is borne out by the data, which shows that the countries that allowed their public finances to run at significant deficit before the fiscal crisis have the greatest level of fiscal consolidation still ahead of them. Conversely, those countries that ran a surplus in advance of the crisis are now in a better position to face the future, and have managed to protect their citizens from the most severe consequences of the crisis. It is notable that five of the OECD's seven largest economies –the exceptions being Canada and Germany – were all running very high deficits before the crisis in 2007. The fact that so few OECD countries were running a fiscal surplus prior to the crisis suggests that the policy tools currently available do not provide the right incentives for doing so. The tools for aligning political incentives with fiscal policy imperatives, across both political and economic "cycles", appear to be lacking in many OECD countries.
- **The different models of "fiscal rules" frameworks have not coped uniformly well with the crisis**. The European Union's Stability and Growth Pact, with its complex and hard-to-enforce provisions, proved largely ineffective in protecting

countries from the effects of the fiscal crisis. In response, the European Union has further strengthened elements of the economic governance framework – at the cost, however, of making them even more complex. Simple and clear fiscal anchors – e.g. the Swiss and German debt brake rules – appear to have been more effective in influencing effective fiscal management.

- Most OECD countries have attempted to **shield economic growth** from the adverse effects of fiscal correction, using various approaches. Some countries have adopted structural economic reforms, including labour market liberalisation, deregulation and red-tape reduction, while still pursuing fiscal correction. Other countries have eschewed the full rigours of fiscal "austerity" and consciously allowed space for fiscal stimulus. Still others have sought to combine the different strategies (e.g. Canada, France, Japan and the United Kingdom), with varying results: relatively little impact in correcting public finances in most cases, but stronger overall growth in the economy in some cases.
- **Independent fiscal institutions** (IFIs) **have proliferated** across the OECD area in response to the crisis, with 25 OECD countries now having some such arrangements in place, compared with only 9 in 2008. The functions of such bodies vary widely, ranging from technical advisory functions, to promoting enhancing transparency and accountability through parliament. However, the effectiveness of such bodies, and the usefulness of the various alternative models for their operation and structure, will be tested during the economic recovery phase, which is already under way in some OECD countries.
- Most countries have stepped up their efforts to increase the **transparency and accessibility** of budget documents and data, including through web portals, tablet apps and "citizens' budgets". Only a small number of OECD countries (including Australia, France and New Zealand) have taken steps to engage either parliament or citizens more fully in the budget policy cycle. Austria, Canada and Ireland are among those pursuing intensive, broad-based **budget reform**, but most countries have focused on particular dimensions of budgeting rather than adopt a more holistic or integrated approach.
- **Payroll costs,** which amount on average to 23.6% of overall public expenditures in the OECD, provide an interesting case study of how fiscal consolidation has been applied in practice. Countries have tried to reduce these costs by reforming employment (downsizing) and remuneration systems. Such austerity-related human resource management (HRM) measures have given rise to both good and bad effects on workplace attitudes.
- **Sub-national budgeting** has been an important dimension of the overall fiscal consolidation picture. Many sub-national governments (SNGs) have limited ability to respond to fiscal pressures and shocks, and governments have adopted a range of strategies in response to this. "Rainy day funds" are one popular approach to insulating SNG finances from the vagaries of the economic cycle, and may hold lessons for fiscal management at the national level.

Public finance management during the crisis: Policy responses and impacts

	fiscal Balances			fiscal consolidation			fiscal rules	status of IFI	support for economic growth	budget reform intensity	engaging parliament & citizens
	2007	*2009*	*2014*	*achieved 2009-2014*	*consolidation needs**	*planned 2015-16*					
Australia	1.9	-4.1	-2.2	▮▮	0		○	■		△	▷
Austria	-1.3	-5.3	-2.4	▮▮	▮▮▮▮	▮	●	■	◈	▲	-
Belgium	0.0	-5.5	-3.2	▮▮	▮▮▮▮	▮	●	■	◇	-	-
Canada	1.5	-4.5	-1.6	▮▮	▮▮▮▮	0	○	■	◈	▲	▷
Chile				0			○	□	◈	△	-
Czech Republic	-0.7	-5.5	-2.0	▮▮▮	▮	0	-	-	◈	-	▷
Denmark	5.0	-2.8	1.2	▮▮▮	▮▮▮		●	□	◆	△	-
Estonia	2.5	-2.2	0.6	▮▮	0	0	●	□	◇	-	-
Finland	5.1	-2.5	-3.2	0	▮▮▮▮	▮	●	□	◈	-	▷
France	-2.5	-7.2	-4.0	▮▮▮	▮▮▮▮	▮▮	◖	■	◆	△	-
Germany	0.3	-3.0	0.6	▮▮▮	▮	0	●	□	◈	-	▷
Greece	-6.7	-15.3	-3.6	▮▮▮▮	▮▮▮▮		●	□	◇		-
Hungary	-5.0	-4.6	-2.5	▮▮	▮▮▮▮	0	◖	■	◆	-	-
Iceland	5.1	-9.4	-0.2		0						
Ireland	0.3	-13.9	-4.1	▮▮▮▮	▮▮	0	●	■	◇	▲	▷
Israel	-0.6	-5.6	-3.7		▮▮▮						
Italy	-1.5	-5.3	-3.0	▮▮	▮▮▮▮	▮	◖	□	◆		▷
Japan	-2.1	-8.8	-7.7	▮	▮▮▮▮		○	-	‡	△	▷
Korea	4.2	-1.3	1.6	▮▮	0		○	■	◆	△	▷
Luxembourg	4.2	-0.5	0.6	▮	0	▮	●	□	-	-	▷
Mexico				0		▮	○	■	◆		
Netherlands	0.2	-5.5	-2.3	▮▮▮	▮▮▮	▮▮	●	■	◈	△	-
New Zealand	4.4	-2.9	1.4	▮▮▮	0	▮▮▮	○	-	◆	△	▷
Norway	17.1	10.3	9.1	0	0	0	●	-	-	-	-
Poland			-3.2	▮▮▮	▮▮	▮▮	●	-	◈	-	-
Portugal	-3.0	-9.8	-4.5	▮▮▮▮	▮▮▮▮	▮▮▮	●	■	◇	△	▷
Slovak Republic	-1.9	-7.9	-2.9	▮▮▮▮	▮▮	▮	●	■	◆	-	▷
Slovenia	-0.1	-6.1	-4.9	▮	▮▮▮▮	0	●	□	◈	-	-
Spain	2.0	-11.0	-5.8	▮▮▮▮	▮▮▮▮	▮▮▮	●	□	◇	△	▷
Sweden	3.3	-0.7	-1.9	0	▮	▮▮▮	●	■	-	-	-
Switzerland	0.9	0.8	0.2	0	0	▮	●	-	◈	-	-
Turkey				0			○	-	◈	△	-
United Kingdom	-3.0	-11.0	-5.3	▮▮▮▮	▮▮▮▮	▮▮▮	○	■	‡	△	▶
United States	-3.7	-12.8	-5.0	▮▮▮▮	▮▮▮▮	▮▮	○	■	‡	△	▷

LEGEND

0 no fiscal consolidation
▮ >0 and ≤1.5% of GDP consolidation (1.5< ▮▮ ≤ 3%, 3< ▮▮▮ ≤ 4.5%, 4.5%< ▮▮▮▮)
● Fiscal rules significantly determine fiscal policy course
◖ Fiscal rules significantly influence fiscal policy course but balanced with other objectives
○ Fiscal policy objectives are under control of government and/or parliament
- Fiscal policy course is not governed by fiscal rules or fiscal policy objectives at present
■ IFI has an established role in influencing budget forecasts / fiscal policy
□ IFI very recently established and/or with limited influence in budget forecasts / fiscal policy
- No IFI role
◆ fiscal stimulus measures and structural economic reforms
◈ fiscal stimulus measures (incl. relaxed / counter-cyclical fiscal policy stance and prioritisation of capital investment)
◇ structural economic reforms and/or reliance on stable position of public finances
‡ complex, multi-faceted approach to supporting economic growth
▲ reform activity intensive and/or broadly-based across various aspects of budgetary governance
△ reform activity moderate and/or focused on specific aspects of budgetary governance
- no significant focus on budgetary reform
▶ strong engagement of parliament and/or citizens in budgeting policy incl. policy formulation and accountability
▷ accessibility and transparency of budgetary information for parliament and/or citizens
- no particular initiatives to promote engagement / accessibility for parliament and/or citizens in budgeting

* OECD calculations: consolidation required to meet 60% debt-to-GDP level by 2030

Source: OECD (2015), *State of Public Finances Survey*.

Chapter 1

The state of public finances 2015: An overall perspective

This chapter presents the overall state of public finances in OECD countries with a particular focus on trends and policy responses between 2007 and 2014. The chapter presents the headline and underlying fiscal position and presents the various fiscal policy responses to the global economic and financial crisis, as well as the ongoing implications for fiscal policy in light of remaining fiscal challenges and country plans. The chapter includes a discussion of fiscal consolidation strategies, recent developments in fiscal rules, country strategies to protect and promote economic growth, the developing role of independent fiscal institutions and the broader range of related reforms in budgetary governance.

1. The economic and fiscal context for budgetary strategy in OECD countries

Economic situation in OECD countries

The prolonged economic and financial crisis that was precipitated in 2008 has had a profound effect on the economic dynamism of most OECD countries over the past seven years, and – as this report illustrates – upon the health of their public finances. Economic growth had appeared strong and robust across the OECD area in the run-up to the crisis, reaching 2.7% per annum in 2007, but the widespread and systemic shocks to the international economy stopped this growth in its tracks in 2008 and led to a sharp economic decline of 3.4% per annum in 2009. Since then, the global economy has been on a steady upward trajectory, albeit with different rates of recovery in different regions (and with the euro area in particular being relatively sluggish) (see Table 1.1 and Figure 1.1). The recent *OECD Economic Outlook* projects that global growth will strengthen during 2015 and 2016, but only to a modest extent relative to previous recoveries. The global recovery is underpinned by very supportive monetary conditions and lower oil prices, and the strength and intensity of fiscal consolidation has varied, as some OECD countries have sought to temper the pro-cyclical impact of fiscal retrenchment (see Section 4, Protecting and promoting economic growth: Country strategies).

It is notable that the risks to the outlook, and to future growth, are particularly uncertain at present, ranging from:

- the possible withdrawal – whether gradual or sharp – from the very accommodative monetary position across OECD countries and particularly in the United States
- the effects of a possible "hard landing" in China, an issue that has been brought into sharper focus as a result of market turbulence in mid-2015
- the resolution of Greece's difficulties within the euro area
- various geopolitical tensions and potential upheavals.

Box 1.1. **Note on methodology, definitions and sources**

Fiscal data and economic data are derived respectively from the *OECD National Accounts Statistics* (database), which uses the internationally recognised System of National Accounts, the *OECD Economic Outlook No. 97* (May 2015) and the *OECD Interim Economic Outlook* (Sep 2015). The country-specific economic summaries in Chapter 2 are also based on the *OECD Economic Outlook No.* 97 and the *OECD Interim Economic Outlook.* Data in relation to fiscal consolidation undertaken or proposed to be undertaken by countries, and on related budgetary governance issues, are based on country responses to the *OECD State of Public Finances Survey 2015.* Comparisons with previous fiscal consolidation plans use material from the OECD report, *Restoring Public Finances, 2012 Update.*

Several of the charts/presentations of fiscal data and economic data have appeared in the *OECD's Government at a Glance 2015* as well as the *OECD Economic Outlook No. 97.*

Note: OECD WA and UWA are weighted and unweighted averages.

Table 1.1. **The global recovery will gain momentum only slowly**

OECD area, unless noted otherwise

	Average 2011-12	2012	2013	2014	2015	2016
			Percent			
Real GDP growth[1]						
World[2]	3.9	3.3	3.3	3.3	3.1	3.8
OECD[2]	1.7	1.3	1.4	1.8	1.9	2.5
United States	1.7	2.3	2.2	2.4	2.0	2.8
Euro area	1.1	-0.8	-0.3	0.9	1.4	2.1
Japan	0.7	1.7	1.6	-0.1	0.7	1.4
Non-OECD[2]	6.7	5.2	5.1	4.7	4.2	4.9
China	10.6	7.7	7.7	7.4	6.8	6.7
Output gap[3]	0.1	-2.1	-2.2	-2.0	-1.9	-1.2
Unemployment rate[4]	6.9	7.9	7.9	7.3	6.9	6.6
Inflation[5]	2.1	1.9	1.3	1.5	0.7	1.7
Fiscal balance[6]	-4.4	-5.8	-4.2	-3.7	-3.1	-2.5
Memorandum items						
World trade growth	5.6	3.1	3.3	3.2	3.9	5.3

Notes:

1. Year-on-year increase; last three columns show the increase over a year earlier.
2. Moving nominal GDP weights, using purchasing power parities.
3. Percent of potential GDP.
4. Percent of labour force.
5. Private consumption deflator. Year-on-year increase; last three columns show the increase over a year earlier.
6. Percent of GDP.

Sources: OECD (2015a), "OECD Economic Outlook No. 97 (Edition 2015/1)", *OECD Economic Outlook: Statistics and Projections* (database), http://dx.doi.org/10.1787/data-00759-en; OECD (2015b), "OECD Interim Economic Outlook".

Figure 1.1. **Global growth is set to recover**

Quarter-on-quarter percentage changes at annual rates

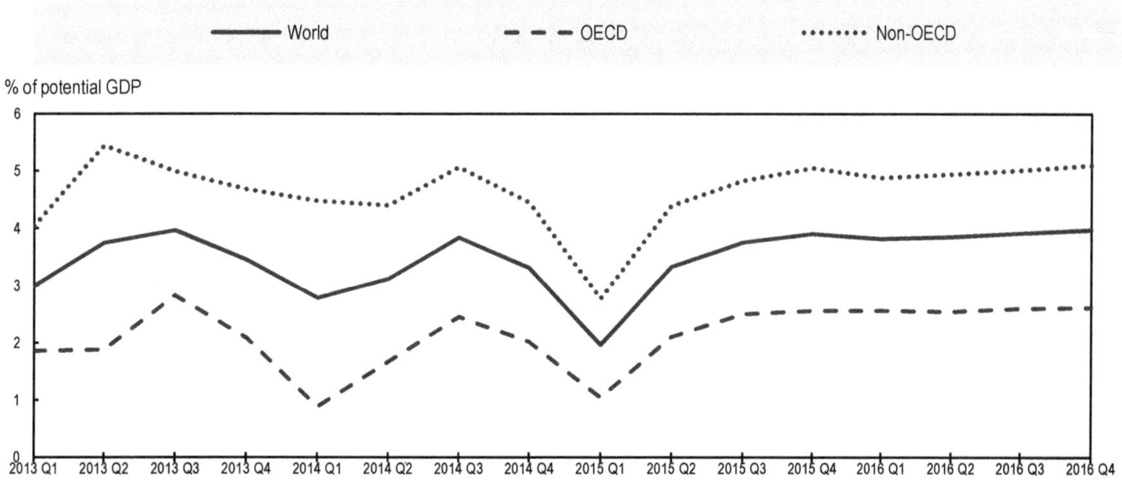

Note: Data is projected from 2015 Q2.

Source: OECD (2015a), "OECD Economic Outlook No. 97 (Edition 2015/1)", *OECD Economic Outlook: Statistics and Projections* (database), http://dx.doi.org/10.1787/data-00759-en.

StatLink http://dx.doi.org/ 10.1787/888933287890

Overall fiscal position in OECD countries

With regard to **fiscal balance of public finances,** in aggregate OECD countries were running a fiscal deficit of -1.5% of GDP (gross domestic product) just prior to the crisis in 2007 – a figure which swung to around -8% of GDP in 2009 and 2010, and has recovered slowly so that it remains -3.7% of GDP in 2014 (Figure 1.2). These average figures mask, however, some strong variations across countries, both with regard to their starting pre-crisis position (some countries - notably Denmark, Korea, New Zealand and Norway - had a strong fiscal surplus in 2007) and to the nature of their fiscal policy response, i.e. whether to focus upon strong fiscal correction (Ireland and Spain) or to seek to allow some space for fiscal counter-stimulus (Czech Republic, France and Hungary). The analysis later in this chapter shows how the different strategies have correlated with fiscal outcomes. It is notable that fiscal deficits have been improving across most OECD countries, albeit at varying rates over recent years.

Figure 1.2. **General government fiscal balance as a percentage of GDP 2007, 2009, 2013 and 2014**

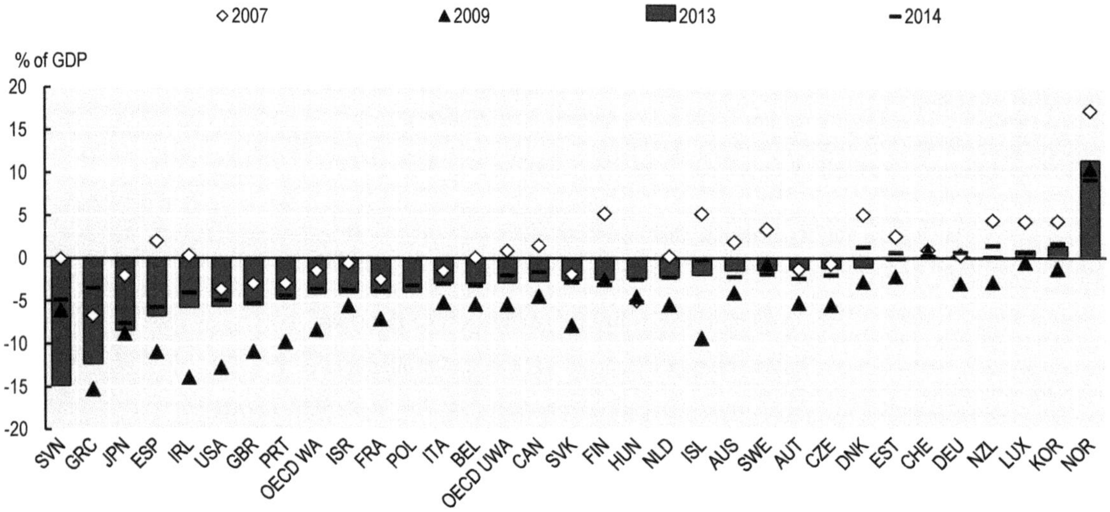

Source: OECD (2015a), "OECD Economic Outlook No. 97 (Edition 2015/1)", *OECD Economic Outlook: Statistics and Projections* (database), http://dx.doi.org/10.1787/data-00759-en.

StatLink http://dx.doi.org/10.1787/888933287906

With many OECD countries still showing a fiscal deficit, the **public debt position** continues to worsen (Figure 1.3). The average gross debt position across the OECD has risen from 80% of GDP in 2007 to 118% by 2013. The debt position worsened for all but three OECD countries over the period (Israel, Norway and Switzerland) and the figures for some OECD countries are particularly stark: Ireland's debt ratio increased by 109 percentage points from its pre-crisis level to its peak level in 2013, with increases of between 60-70 percentage points recorded in four OECD countries (Greece, Iceland, Portugal and Spain) over that period. While a small number of countries (Israel, Norway and Turkey) began to reduce their public debt level from 2009, trends since 2013 have begun to diverge, as some OECD countries (e.g. Czech Republic, Ireland and Slovak Republic) have seen a downward turn in the debt ratio, while in other countries (e.g. Italy, Slovenia and Spain) the debt level has continued to rise.

Figure 1.3. **General government debt as a percentage of GDP 2007, 2009, 2013 and 2014**

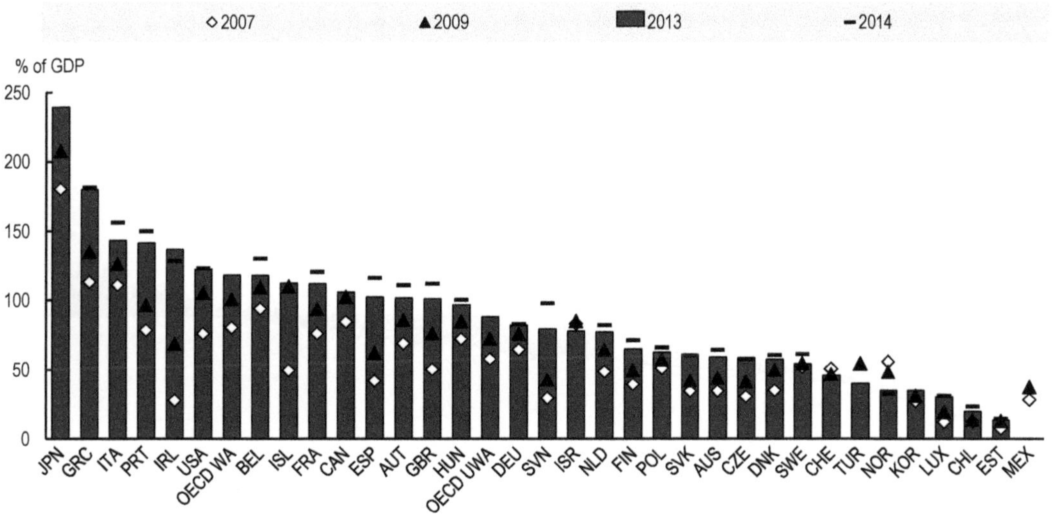

Sources: OECD (2015c), *OECD National Accounts Statistics* (database), http://dx.doi.org/10.1787/na-data-en; European Commission (2015), *Government Finance Statistics* (database), Eurostat, http://ec.europa.eu/Eurostat/web/government-finance-statistics/data/database.

StatLink http://dx.doi.org/10.1787/888933287914

The figures for **financial net worth** of general government (or net government debt), which reflect the gap between financial assets and liabilities held by governments, provide another perspective on the decline in public finances (Figure 1.4). In 2007, OECD countries, on average, recorded a negative financial net worth of -43.7% of GDP, and this figure has almost doubled to -73.7% in 2013, reflecting the impact of the financial crisis. The largest declines in financial net worth over the period have been experienced in Ireland (84.4 percentage points), Iceland (52.6 percentage points) and Spain (51.5 percentage points), reflecting, in particular, the impact of banking sector bail-outs and supports in those countries.

2. Public finance responses across OECD countries

Overview of fiscal policy responses

To form an assessment of the underlying position of the public finances and the scale of fiscal policy responses undertaken by countries, it is useful to examine the structural fiscal balance and the primary fiscal balance. The **structural fiscal balance** is the balance of expenditures and revenues, corrected for effects of the economic cycle and for one-off events, thereby illustrating the underlying strength of the public finance position. A growing structural surplus (or declining deficit) indicates a contractionary fiscal stance, whereas a growing structural deficit (or declining surplus) shows an expansionary stance. It should be noted, however, that the fiscal stance of the public sector is only one factor in the overall growth dynamic of an economy and thus of the public finances. In other words, running a structural fiscal deficit is not formally incompatible with a situation of weak growth and worsening public finances; and conversely running a structural surplus is not incompatible with achieving a growing economy and improving public finances. The overall trend and composition of the structural fiscal balance may also affect confidence levels which, in turn, feed into patterns of consumption and investment which directly affect growth.

Figure 1.4. **General government financial net worth as a percentage of GDP 2007, 2009, 2013 and 2014**

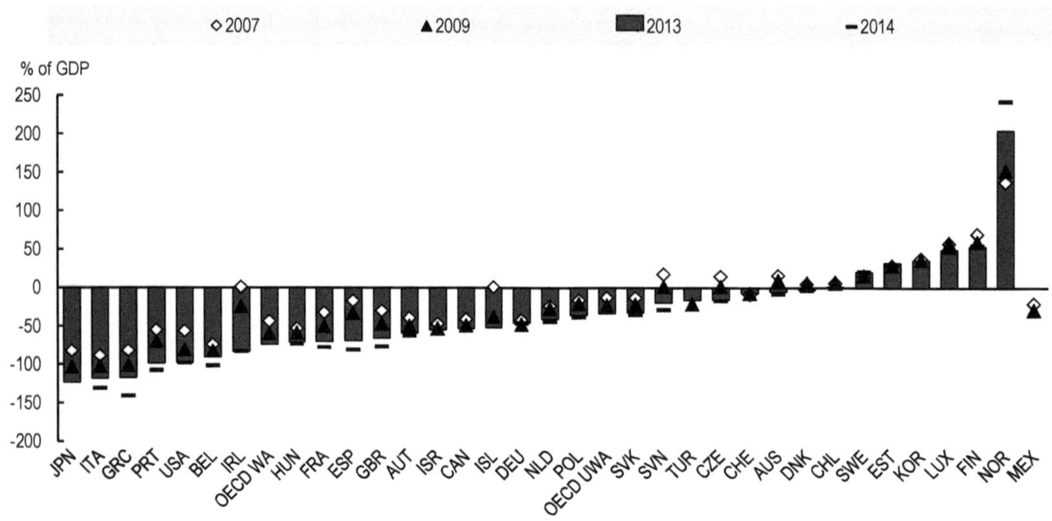

Sources: OECD (2015c), *OECD National Accounts Statistics* (database), http://dx.doi.org/10.1787/na-data-en; European Commission (2015), *Government Finance Statistics* (database), Eurostat, http://ec.europa.eu/Eurostat/web/government-finance-statistics/data/database.

StatLink http://dx.doi.org/10.1787/888933287925

Across the OECD as a whole, the structural fiscal balance was in deficit of -2.9% of GDP in 2007, and this had slightly fallen to -3.0% in 2014 (Figure 1.5). However, this aggregate picture masks both the temporal dimension, as the structural fiscal balance has shifted markedly over the period of the crisis, and the geographical dimension, as different countries have had very different experiences and approaches.

Figure 1.5. **General government structural fiscal balance as a percentage of potential GDP 2007, 2009, 2013 and 2014**

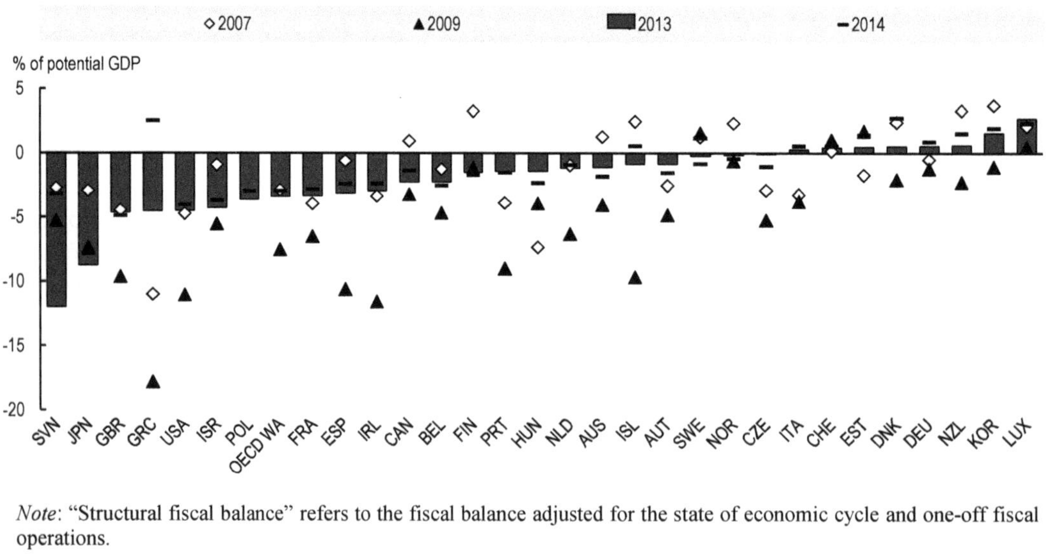

Note: "Structural fiscal balance" refers to the fiscal balance adjusted for the state of economic cycle and one-off fiscal operations.

Source: OECD (2015a), "OECD Economic Outlook No. 97 (Edition 2015/1)", *OECD Economic Outlook: Statistics and Projections* (database), http://dx.doi.org/10.1787/data-00759-en.

StatLink http://dx.doi.org/10.1787/888933287931

In fact, the OECD-wide structural fiscal deficit fell sharply to -7.5% of GDP in 2009 and has been steadily worked back towards its pre-crisis level over the subsequent years, which have been marked by fiscal correction and austerity in many OECD countries. For some individual countries the story has been even more stark: for example, Iceland was running a structural fiscal surplus of 2.4% of GDP in 2007, while Spain was close to structural fiscal balance, but in both countries the impact of the economic collapse (and, in particular, the banking sector fall-out) led to a sudden drop to a structural fiscal deficit of around -10% of GDP in 2009; whereas in the case of Greece, a pre-crisis structural fiscal deficit of -11% of GDP fell further to -17.8% of GDP by 2009. In all three countries, the 2014 position is better than the OECD average, with Greece achieving a structural fiscal surplus of 2.5% of GDP in 2014.

The **primary fiscal balance** (i.e. the balance of expenditures and revenues, omitting debt-interest costs) was in deficit of -1.3% in 2013 across OECD countries, although again the aggregate figure masks important variations. Norway (12.0% of GDP), Korea (3.1%), Iceland (3.0%) and Germany (2.2%) recorded high primary fiscal surpluses, whereas Slovenia (-12.0% of GDP), Greece (-8.3%) and Japan (-6.4%) had high primary fiscal deficits. Reducing a primary fiscal deficit is an essential part of a debt-reduction strategy, and it is notable in this regard that both Slovenia and Greece sharply curtailed their primary fiscal deficits in 2014 to, respectively, -1.6% and a surplus of 0.4%. The United Kingdom, with a high debt level of 96% of GDP in 2014, has seen its primary fiscal balance disimprove slightly from -2.5% to -2.7% of GDP between 2013 and 2014 (Figure 1.6).

Figure 1.6. **General government primary balance and interest spending**

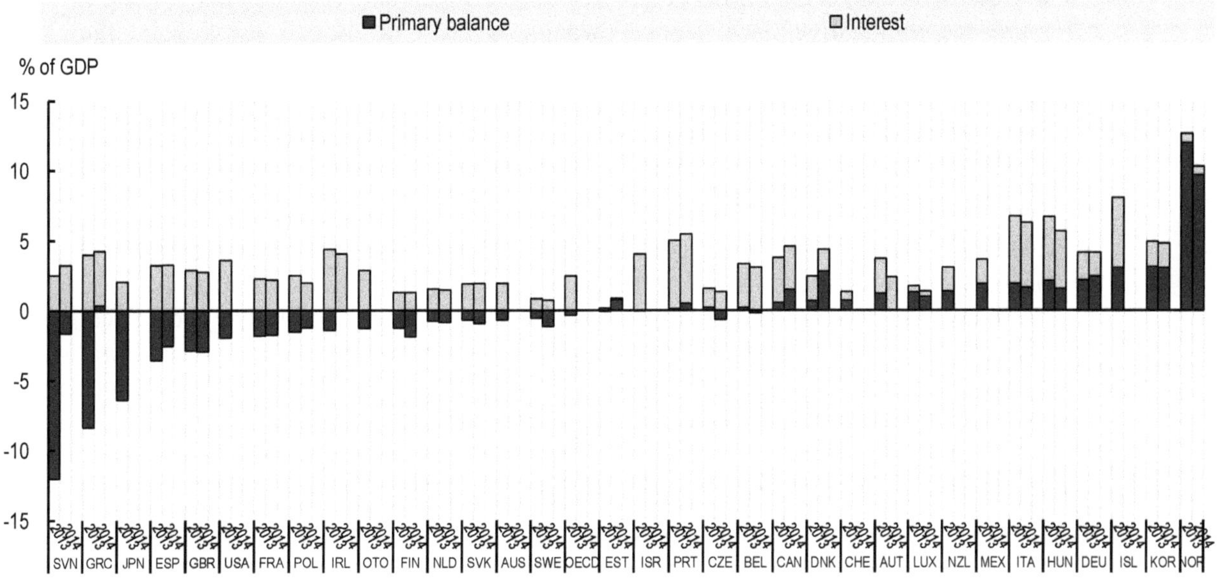

Source: OECD (2015c), *OECD National Accounts Statistics* (database), http://dx.doi.org/10.1787/na-data-en.

StatLink http://dx.doi.org/10.1787/888933287940

Phases of fiscal policy development

While public finances would be expected to suffer an acute cyclical impact from the economic and financial crisis, an analysis of the underlying trends in structural and primary balances over the period of the economic and financial crisis can help to understand how policy responses have evolved over time. Having regard to the trends in the underlying figures (Figure 1.7), and taking account of the country-specific details set out in Chapter 2 of this report, certain distinct phases of policy response can usefully be discerned.

1. **2007-09: Active/accommodative fiscal policy phase**. While OECD countries on average had relatively sound structural and primary fiscal balances in 2007, these balances significantly deteriorated in the wake of the financial crisis. The OECD-wide structural fiscal balance dropped from -2.9% of potential GDP in 2007 to -7.1% in 2009 while the primary fiscal balance dropped from 0.3% of GDP in 2007 to -6.4% in 2009. The swing in the underlying figures reflects a marked counter-cyclical response. The extent to which this counter-cyclical response was deliberate, in the interests of countering the sharp economic downturn, or whether it reflected the play of automatic stabilisers against a more passive fiscal policy background, varied from country to country.
2. **2010-11: Stabilising fiscal policy phase**. With signs of economic stabilisation and concerns about the rapid build-up of public debt, several OECD countries adapted their fiscal policy course to some extent. Again, the precise nature of timing of the fiscal policy response varied among OECD countries. Some countries (e.g. Austria, Belgium and Denmark) began to tighten the fiscal position in 2010 while other countries (e.g. Australia, Canada and Finland) maintained a more accommodative fiscal stance through to 2011 or longer. Looking at the OECD average, structural and primary fiscal balances in 2010 showed only a modest improvement to, respectively, -6.8% and -5.8% of GDP. By 2011, however, most OECD countries had moved decisively towards a path of fiscal correction: in that year, structural and primary fiscal deficits sharply rebounded to -5.9% and -4.3% of GDP, respectively.
3. **2012-14: Progressive fiscal consolidation phase**. Since 2012, structural and primary fiscal balances have continued to improve steadily as fiscal policy has been geared towards progressive consolidation, and as the urgency of fiscal correction has begun to abate in several OECD countries. By 2014, the structural deficit had been almost halved from -5.9% in 2011 to -3.1% and the primary deficit had been curtailed from -4.3% to -1.6% over the same period.

Fiscal consolidation undertaken to date by four categories of countries

The earlier OECD publication on *Restoring Public Finances* and its *2012 Update* (OECD 2011, 2012) categorised OECD countries into four distinct groups. While the criteria which determined those original groupings no longer apply to all of the countries, it is useful to trace the evolution of the public finance position of the original country clusters.

Figure 1.7. **Structural and primary fiscal balances in OECD countries**

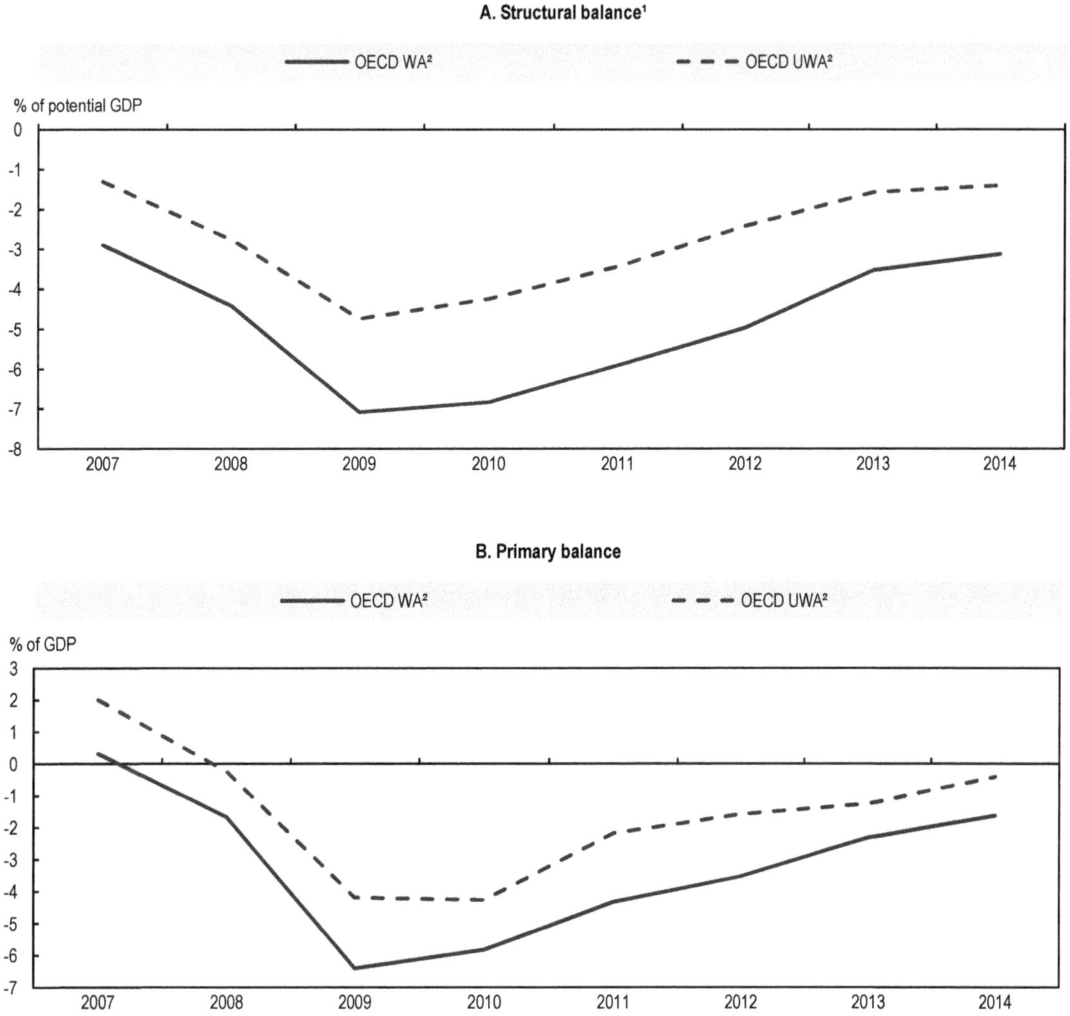

Notes:

1. The structural balance refers to the underlying balance which corresponds to the fiscal balance adjusted for the state of economic cycle and one-off fiscal operations.

2. OECD WA and UWA are weighted and unweighted averages.

Source: OECD (2015a), "OECD Economic Outlook No. 97 (Edition 2015/1)", *OECD Economic Outlook: Statistics and Projections* (database), http://dx.doi.org/10.1787/data-00759-en.

StatLink http://dx.doi.org/10.1787/888933287950

Category A. Countries with IMF/EU/ECB programmes

This category included countries with a formal and ongoing programme with the International Monetary Fund, the European Central Bank, and/or the European Commission. Three OECD countries were in this position: **Greece, Ireland** and **Portugal.**

Both Ireland and Portugal have since exited their financial support programmes and have developed renewed economic momentum, while Greece has continued to work through its acute fiscal difficulties.

Category B. Countries under distinct market pressure

This category included OECD countries with an average fiscal consolidation requirement over the period 2012-30 above 3% of GDP and with an experienced change in long-term interest rates over the period 2006-11 equal to or above zero. This category included **Belgium, Hungary, Italy, Poland, the Slovak Republic, Slovenia** and **Spain.**

Market pressure applying to the various countries has been considerably lessened since 2012, particularly in light of supportive monetary policy in recent years.

Category C. Countries with substantial deficits and/or debt but less market pressure

Category C included OECD countries which met one or more of the following criteria: an average consolidation requirement over the period 2012-30 higher than 3% of GDP, an estimated average general government fiscal deficit of 2011-12 above 3% of GDP, or the 2011 general government gross debt above 60% of GDP.

This category included several OECD countries that are members of the European Union, with deficit levels in excess of the 3%-of-GDP EU limit, and that were the subject of European Commission monitoring in this regard: **Austria, the Czech Republic, Denmark, France, Germany, the Netherlands** and **the United Kingdom.** In addition, the category encompassed other OECD countries that introduced fiscal consolidation plans or fiscal strategies in order to curb the fiscal deficit and/or reduce debt – **Canada, Finland, Iceland, Israel, Mexico** and **New Zealand** – as well as **Japan** and the **United States** which also had large long-term consolidation needs but which had not yet adopted comprehensive consolidation strategies.

Category D. Countries with no or marginal consolidation needs

Finally there were nine countries that did not have significant fiscal consolidation needs: **Australia, Chile, Estonia, Korea, Luxembourg, Norway, Sweden, Switzerland** and **Turkey.** These countries had low long-term consolidation needs (average 1.5% of GDP), their long-term interest rates had reduced over the period 2006-11 and they were characterised by both low deficits/surpluses and low gross debt-to-GDP ratios.

Figure 1.8 shows the fiscal policy course undertaken by each of those four original groupings since 2007. The chart illustrates how *Category A* countries suffered a severe fiscal shock in the period 2007-09, with the deficit level plummeting to -13% of GDP on average, and how a rigorous fiscal correction has seen the deficit levels brought back to -4% of GDP on average in 2014. The 9 percentage point improvement in the fiscal position in fact understates the degree of "fiscal effort" which these countries have had to undertake, as the consolidation was undertaken at a time of stagnant or falling economic growth. Indeed, the countries in *Category A* have now, on average, converged fully with those in the original *Category B*, i.e. with those countries that had weak fiscal positions and were subject to market pressures. Countries in the latter category have improved their fiscal position by 3.2 percentage points on average from their deficit nadir in 2009. The *Category C* countries – i.e. those with poor fiscal positions but less market pressure – have followed a similar adjustment path to their *Category B* counterparts, and indeed have been more successful at correcting their deficits, achieving a 3.6 percentage point improvement on average over the period.

Finally, countries in the original *Category D* have, on the whole, undergone a relatively mild fiscal adjustment, with their sound pre-crisis fiscal surplus enabling them to weather the crisis without imposing a severe pro-cyclical fiscal shock upon their economies.

Figure 1.8. **Fiscal policy responses by four country categories, 2007-14**

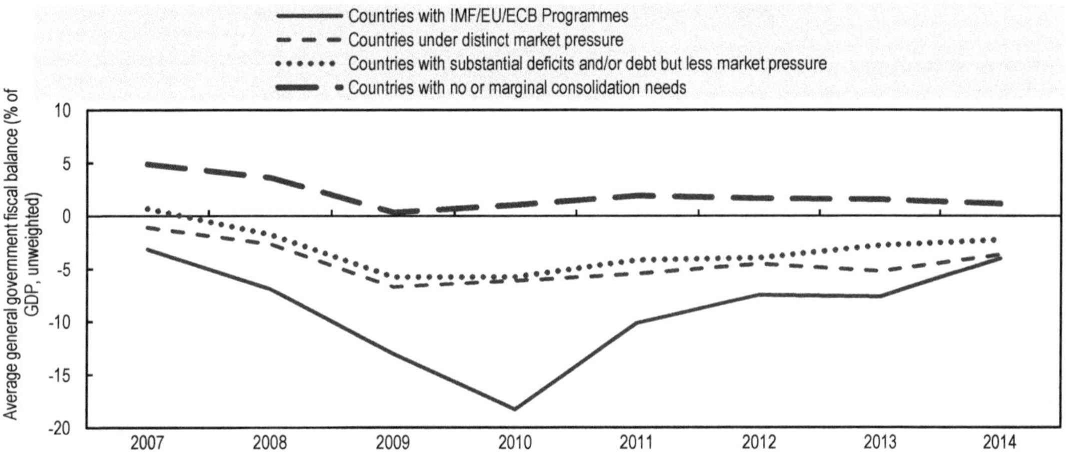

Source: OECD (2015a), "OECD Economic Outlook No. 97 (Edition 2015/1)", *OECD Economic Outlook: Statistics and Projections* (database), http://dx.doi.org/10.1787/data-00759-en.

StatLink http://dx.doi.org/10.1787/888933287966

The impact of banking crises on fiscal balances

The impact of the economic and financial crisis upon the public finances of OECD countries was not uniform, and was in some cases aggravated by the large-scale "bailing-in" of public funds in support of failing banks and other financial institutions. For example, Andrle et al. (2015) categorises banking crises over the period into *systemic* or *borderline* cases, by reference to a range of criteria such as specific signs of financial distress in the banking system and the level and nature of banking policy interventions required to address challenges in the system. On this basis, OECD countries can be grouped into three categories, referring to the experience of a *systemic banking crisis* (Austria, Belgium, Denmark, Germany, Greece, Iceland, Ireland, Luxembourg, the Netherlands, Spain, the United Kingdom and the United States), *borderline systemic banking crisis* (France, Hungary, Italy, Portugal, Slovenia, Sweden and Switzerland) or *no banking crisis*.

The type of shock which countries experienced corresponds with the scale of impact on the public finances, as illustrated in Figure 1.9. The group which suffered from *systemic banking crisis* underwent a sharp deterioration of 8.2 percentage points in their fiscal balance, on average, from 2007 to 2009, as compared with a fall of 6.2 percentage points for the group that experienced no banking crisis. Moreover, Figure 1.9 also illustrates how the *direct* fiscal impacts of a banking crisis are aggravated further by indirect impacts on the real economy, through an attenuated banking sector, increased borrowing costs and depressed growth in economic activity. Countries unaffected by banking crisis experienced a smaller decline of GDP in 2009 and were able to pick up growth in subsequent years without a relapse. At the same time, the group whose members underwent systemic banking crisis also had to contend with significantly lower economic growth; a factor to be borne in mind in assessing the scale of their fiscal effort in bringing the fiscal balance (expressed as a proportion of GDP) back onto a sustainable course.

Figure 1.9. **Fiscal impacts and growth patterns by different levels of banking crisis**

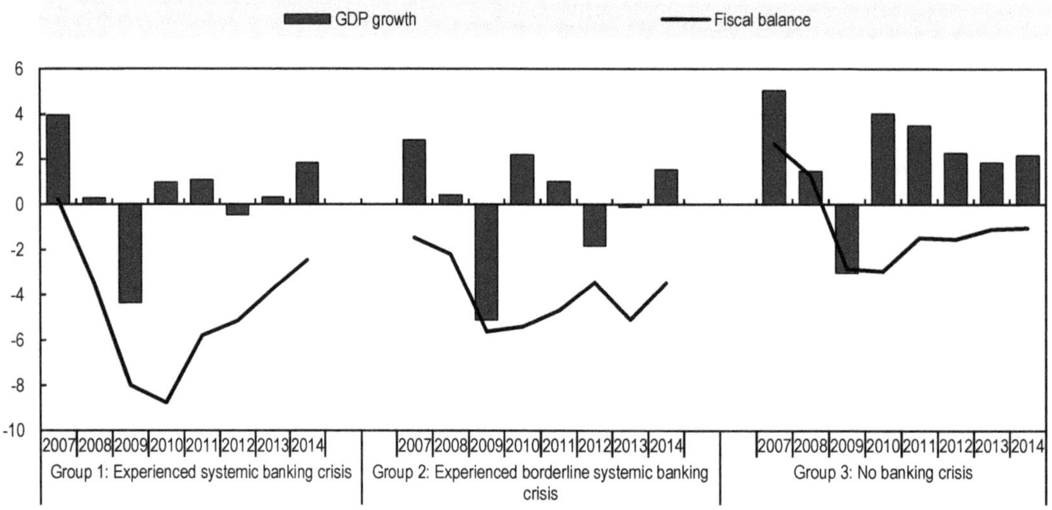

Sources: OECD (2015a), "OECD Economic Outlook No. 97 (Edition 2015/1)", *OECD Economic Outlook: Statistics and Projections* (database), http://dx.doi.org/10.1787/data-00759-en; Laeven, L. et Valencia, F. (2012) "Systemic Banking Crises Database: An Update", IMF Working Paper, WP/12/163 https://www.imf.org/external/pubs/ft/wp/2012/wp12163.pdf

StatLink http://dx.doi.org/10.1787/888933287977

It comes as no surprise that there are significant overlaps between the country categories as presented in both Figures 1.8 and 1.9, since the factors of "distinct market pressure" and "IMF/EU/ECB support" can be expected to correlate strongly with the occurrence of a banking crisis. Indeed, all of the countries in Category A (i.e. those with IMF/EU/ECB programmes) suffered some level of banking crisis, whereas most countries under "distinct market pressure" ended up going through a systemic or borderline banking crisis. A further noteworthy aspect is that countries with substantial deficits (i.e. with 2011 general government gross debt above 60% of GDP), even in the absence of "distinct market pressure", had a 50% chance of ending up with a systemic banking crisis.

Structure, nature and effectiveness of fiscal consolidation

Overview of fiscal consolidation strategies

Table 1.2 illustrates the degree of fiscal consolidation undertaken by OECD countries in the period 2009-14. The table shows that the level of consolidation has been very significant across most countries, with eight countries undergoing consolidation of greater than 4.5% of GDP up to 2014, with a further seven countries consolidating in the range 3-4.5% of GDP.

Table 1.2. **Fiscal consolidation across OECD countries, 2009-14**

	achieved 2009-2014	comment
Australia	▮▮	broad reductions including restrictions on indexation; Temporary Budget Repair Levy on higher earners
Austria	▮▮	broad reductions in subsidies, indexation, health reform; tax agreement with Swizerland / Liechtenstein
Belgium	▮▮	Growing emphasis on expenditure cuts to achieve fiscal consolidation
Canada	▮▮	Strategic Review / Strategic and Operating Review to identify savings; operating budget freeze in effect
Chile		Expenditure restrictions under previous administration to be eased, with focus on structural balance
Czech Republic	▮▮▮	Previous freezes and caps on expenditure being lifted as fiscal consolidation is "paused"
Denmark	▮▮▮	Steady consolidation process underpinned by new legal fiscal framework
Estonia	▮▮	incremental measures, including reforms to unemployment insurance
Finland	0	New, intensive spending review exercise completed in early 2015
France	▮▮▮	Measured fiscal correction in balance with growth-supporting initiatives. Spending ceiling strengthened
Germany	▮▮▮	Fiscal course-correction achieved through disciplined application of rules-based fiscal framework
Greece	▮▮▮▮	broad-based horizontal savings, targeted / sectioral savings and structural (longer-term) savings
Hungary	▮▮	Broad-ranging expenditure reductions, and focused tax measures; measured pace of fiscal correction
Iceland	▮▮▮▮	
Ireland	▮▮▮▮	Comprehensive expenditure reductions, revenue-raising measures and sustained fiscal correction
Italy	▮▮	Move from across-the-board savings to selective measures on basis of major spending review
Japan	▮	Efficiency-focused containment of expenditures, with measured increased in consumption tax
Korea	▮▮	Expenditure growth cap and streamlining of tax exemptions to maintain finances on stable course
Luxembourg	▮	Broad-based expenditure and revenue consolidation since 2011; new expenditure review process
Mexico		Revenue focus to date; "zero-based" public expenditure review planned
Netherlands	▮▮▮	Savings identified using evaluation mechanisms / spending reviews within fixed expenditure framework
New Zealand	▮▮▮	Targeted, efficiency-focused expenditure savings in context of cyclically-sensitive consolidation
Norway	0	No consolidation required; main fiscal policy challenge concerns prudent use of resource endowments
Poland	▮▮▮	Expenditure-focused savings factored into ceilings under MTEF (part of Multiannual State Financial Plan
Portugal	▮▮▮▮	Broad-based fiscal consolidation underway; expenditure ceilings have been strengthened
Slovak Republic	▮▮▮▮	Efficiency-focused spending savings, and streamlining of tax exemptions, in measured consolidation
Slovenia	▮	Broad-based expenditure reductions and revenue-raising measures now underway
Spain	▮▮▮▮	Broad-based expenditure reductions and revenue reforms now underway
Sweden	0	Tax-raising measures to create fiscal space for increased overall expenditure; gradual fiscal correction
Switzerland	0	Spending-based fiscal correction including targeted measures and across-the-board reductions
Turkey		After a counter-cyclical response to the crisis, the fiscal policy focus has shifted to supporting growth
United Kingdom	▮▮▮▮	Intensive expenditure-side consolidation underway, with strong efficiency focus to date
United States	▮▮▮▮	Structural expenditure reforms and revenue-raising measures; measured pace of fiscal correction

LEGEND

0 no significant fiscal consolidation

▮ >0 and ≤1.5% of GDP consolidation (1.5< ▮▮ ≤ 3%, 3< ▮▮▮ ≤ 4.5%, 4.5%< ▮▮▮▮)

Source: OECD (2015d), *State of Public Finances Survey*.

Balance between expenditure and revenue measures

With regard to the broad composition of consolidation, it is notable that the approaches taken have been quite diverse – both across countries, and over time within countries. Figure 1.10 shows the broad balance between expenditure and revenue measures introduced by OECD countries in the consolidation period 2012-14, and illustrates a broadly symmetrical spread of approaches across the OECD, with some countries (Canada, New Zealand, Switzerland and the United Kingdom) focusing strongly upon expenditure-side measures, while others (Finland, Mexico, Spain) have had a strong revenue-raising focus up to now, and a majority of countries showing a broader balance between the two approaches. As illustrated in Panels A and B of Figure 1.10, it is notable that the focus on consolidation can shift over time, reflecting shifts in political preferences as well as economic considerations.

Figure 1.10. **Nature of fiscal consolidation across the OECD in 2012-17**

Share of expenditure reductions and revenue enhancements in fiscal consolidation

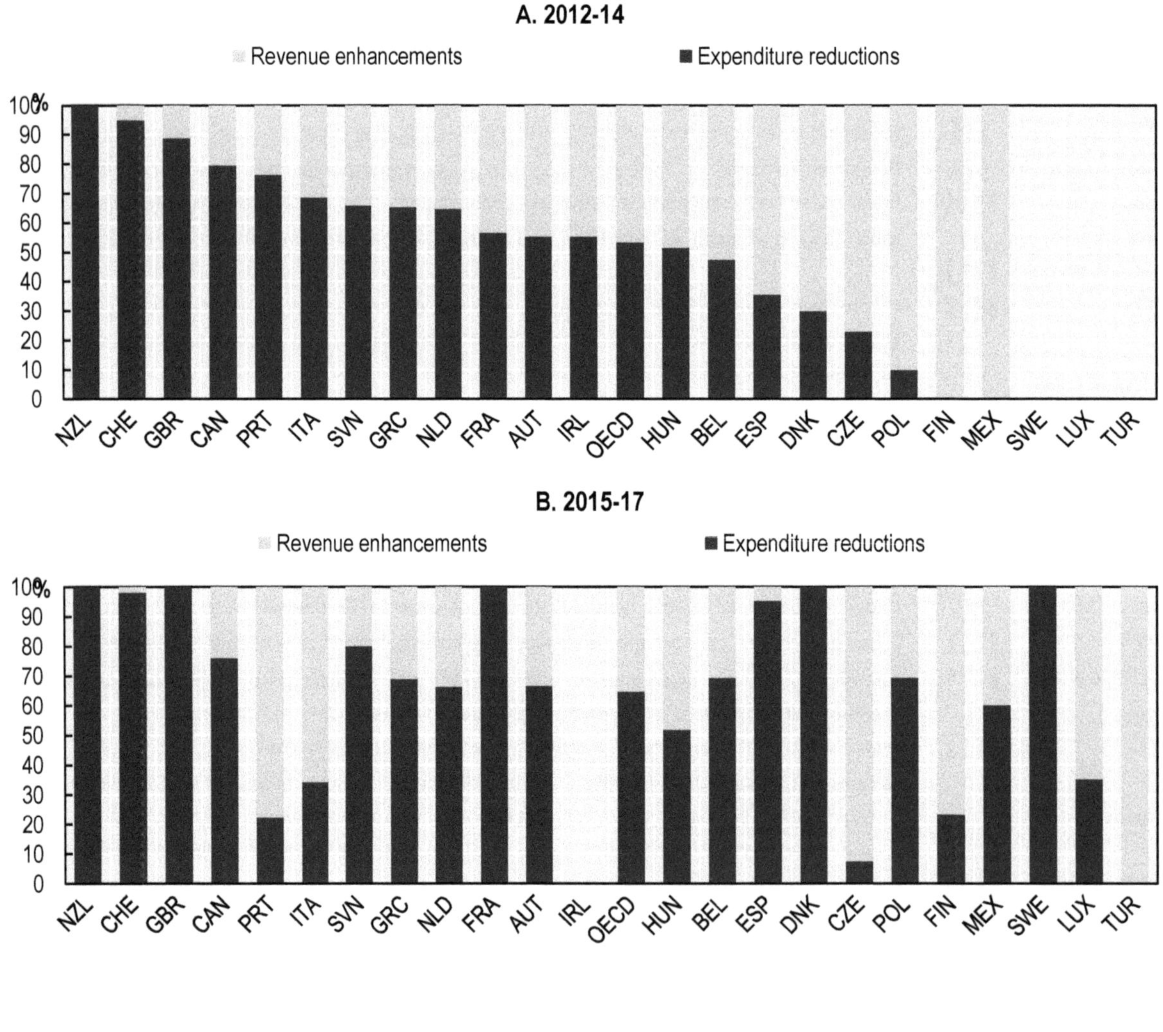

Source: OECD 2015d), *State of Public Finances Survey.*

StatLink http://dx.doi.org/10.1787/888933287987

Spending review as a budgetary tool

The use of a "spending review" mechanism (see Box 1.2) is quite notable among countries that focus upon expenditure-side measures. Over half of OECD member countries report that they have conducted, or are planning to conduct spending reviews: seven OECD countries report the use of spending reviews to help identify specific savings. Other countries, including Mexico and Germany, are considering the introduction of spending reviews as a budget policy tool.

Box 1.2. **Spending review**

Since the crisis, many OECD member countries have been striving to bring deficits and debts back to sustainable levels. This has ignited a renewed interest in spending review as a tool to improve the efficiency and effectiveness of public expenditure. A spending review is the process of identifying and weighing adopting savings options, based on the systematic scrutiny of baseline expenditure, which may take the form of efficiency reviews and/or strategic reviews, and may be either comprehensive in nature or more selectively-focused.

While recent experiences with spending review have been largely driven by the crisis and the need for fiscal consolidation, several OECD country experiences – Australia, Canada, Denmark, the Netherlands and the United Kingdom, for example – show that spending review can be much more than a tool for cutting expenditure. Properly designed, spending review can be an important tool to focus government on improving expenditure prioritisation. Given that the constrained fiscal policy choices are likely to remain a feature of budgeting in OECD countries in the future, there would appear to be value in establishing systematic spending review as a feature, rather than an ad hoc element, of the budget process.

Source: OECD (2015e), Spending Reviews – Background note; Robinson, Marc (2014), "Spending reviews", *OECD Journal on Budgeting*, Vol. 13/2, http://dx.doi.org/10.1787/budget-13-5jz14bz8p2hd.

Case study: Public sector staffing and human resource management

As an illustration of how expenditure consolidation strategy is implemented in practice, the OECD has undertaken an analysis of budgetary impacts on human resource management (HRM) in the public sector, in parallel with the Survey of the State of Public Finances 2015. Compensation of employees accounted for 23.6% of public expenditures on average across OECD countries in 2013, and it is natural that governments will seek to find economies and efficiencies from this significant block of expenditure as part of a broader strategy of fiscal correction.

Across many countries, there has indeed been a renewed efficiency focus within the public sector, coupled in many cases with a broader human resource reform agenda, and balanced with the need to have productive, satisfied, innovative and high-performing employees. The OECD analysis indicates that the various HRM responses to fiscal consolidation can be grouped under seven headings or "bundles" (Figure 1.11), of which two – "employment reforms" and "training system reforms" - are the most commonly-adopted. The full analysis (see Annex A for more details) goes on to trace the impact of austerity-driven HRM reforms on issues of workplace attitude, job satisfaction and recommended policy responses for public sector managers.

Figure 1.11. **Overview of human resource management reforms, 2008-13**

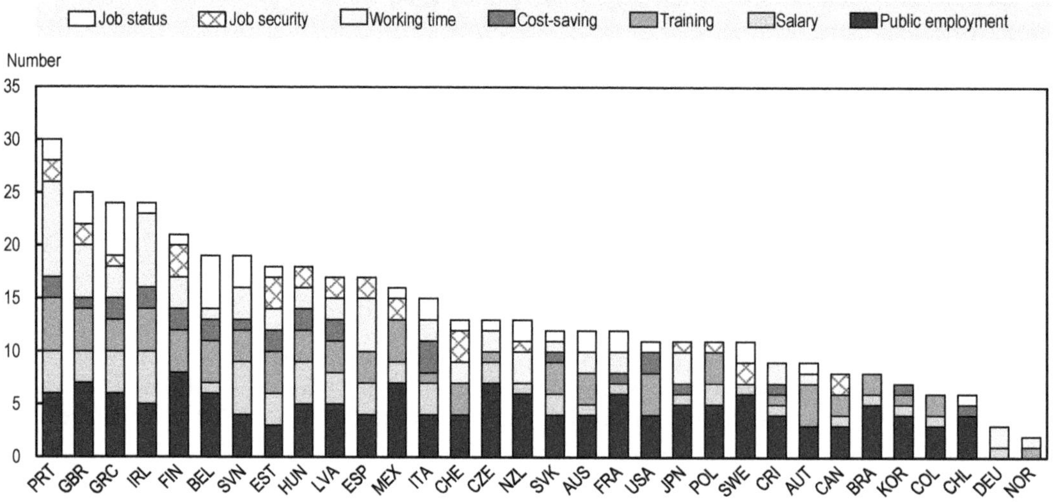

Source: OECD (2014), *Survey on Managing Budgeting Constraints: Implications for HRM and Employment in Central Public Administration*, OECD.

StatLink http://dx.doi.org/10.1787/888933287990

Assessing the effectiveness of fiscal consolidation strategies to date

The effectiveness of fiscal consolidation is a matter of country-specific, political and societal judgement, more than external measurement. Although fiscal consolidation has been underway in many OECD countries since 2009-10, the public debt remains on an upward course in many cases and the public finances remain in a vulnerable position. One indication of external confidence in the state of public finances is long-term bond yields. The crisis demonstrated that even sovereigns could lose access to bond markets as a result of acute fiscal stress. In particular, the long-term bond yields of countries with IMF/EU/ECB Programmes almost tripled from 4.4% in 2007 to 13% in 2012. Since then, bond yields have been decreasing markedly for those countries, and more steadily for OECD countries in general, reflecting both the stabilisation of public finances and the adoption of supportive monetary policy (Figure 1.12).

Future fiscal consolidation needs across OECD countries

Leaving aside the former country classifications and looking afresh at the various different consolidation strategies and outcomes, the patterns among countries based upon the scale of their consolidation – as set out in Table 1.3 – is striking. The table shows outstanding "fiscal consolidation needs", calculated on the basis of the additional consolidation requirements to reduce government debt to a figure of 60% of GDP by 2030. Alongside this, the table shows the public plans announced by OECD countries as of June 2015. The table shows that only five countries (Greece, New Zealand, Portugal, Spain and Sweden) envisage that consolidation of more than 3% of GDP will be implemented in the 2015-16 period. Looking forward, Mexico will be placing a stronger focus on expenditure savings, while the Swedish government envisages raising revenues to generate additional fiscal space.

Figure 1.12. **Long-term bond yields by country groups**

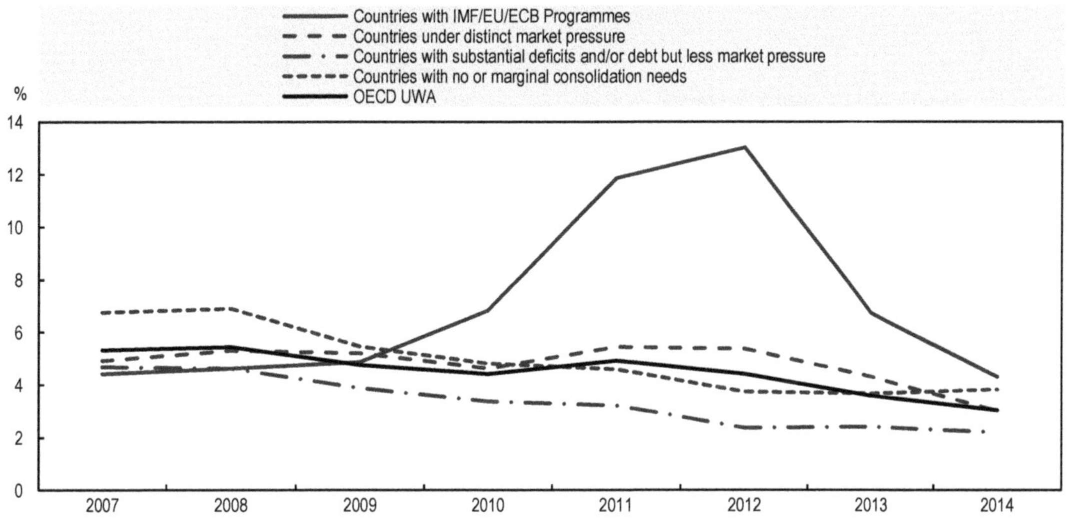

Note: OECD UWA is OECD unweighted average.

Source: OECD (2015a), "OECD Economic Outlook No. 97 (Edition 2015/1)", *OECD Economic Outlook: Statistics and Projections* (database), http://dx.doi.org/10.1787/data-00759-en.

StatLink http://dx.doi.org/10.1787/888933288008

The table also shows that, although OECD countries have achieved a considerable amount of fiscal consolidation from 2009 to 2014, there is still a significant gap left to attain a debt ratio of 60% of GDP by 2030. Therefore, additional fiscal consolidation will be needed beyond 2015-16 consolidation plans, most especially for those countries with very high consolidation needs (Austria, Belgium, Canada, Finland, France, Greece, Hungary, Italy, Japan, Portugal, Slovenia, Spain, the United Kingdom and the United States). While Greece has already made considerable progress in improving its structural fiscal balance, the scale of the debt overhang weighs upon the high consolidation needs that still lie ahead. The position of New Zealand is notable in that it envisages fiscal consolidation above and beyond the technically-calculated "consolidation need", due to the strong priority afforded under domestic policy to restoring the public finances to a very prudent level.

Table 1.3. **Future consolidation needs across OECD countries**

	Fiscal balances			*consolidation needs*	consolidation *planned*
	2007	*2009*	*2014*	*(a)*	*(b)*
(i) Low or no consolidation needs					
Australia	++	– – –	– –	0	
Estonia	++	– –	+	0	
Iceland	++++	– – – –	–	0	
Korea	+++	–	+	0	
Luxembourg	+++	–	+	0	I
New Zealand	+++	– –	+	0	III
Norway	++++	++++	++++	0	0
Switzerland	+	+	+	0	I
Czech Republic	–	– – – –	– –	I	0
Germany	+	– –	+	I	0
Sweden	+++	–	– –	I	III
(ii) Moderate and high consolidation needs					
Ireland	+	– – – –	– – –	II	0
Poland	– –	– – – –	– – –	II	
Slovak Republic	– –	– – – –	– –	II	I
Denmark	++++	– –	+	III	
Israel	–	– – – –	– – –	III	
Netherlands	+	– – – –	– –	III	II
(iii) Very high consolidation needs					
Austria	–	– – – –	– –	IIII	I
Belgium	+	– – – –	– – –	IIII	I
Canada	+	– – –	– –	IIII	0
Finland	++++	– –	– – –	IIII	I
France	– –	– – – –	– – –	IIII	II
Greece	– – – –	– – – –	– – –	IIII	
Hungary	– – – –	– – – –	– –	IIII	
Italy	–	– – – –	– –	IIII	I
Japan	– –	– – – –	– – – –	IIII	
Portugal	– –	– – – –	– – –	IIII	III
Slovenia	–	– – – –	– – – –	IIII	0
Spain	++	– – – –	– – – –	IIII	III
United Kingdom	– –	– – – –	– – – –	IIII	III
United States	– – –	– – – –	– – – –	IIII	II
Chile		– – –			
Mexico	+	–			I
Turkey	–	++++			

LEGEND

+ fiscal position in balance or in surplus (the number of + denotes the strength of surplus)
– fiscal balances in deficit position (the number of - denotes the severity of deficit)
0 no significant fiscal consolidation
I >0 and ≤1.5% of GDP consolidation (1.5< II ≤ 3%, 3< III ≤ 4.5%, 4.5%< IIII)

(a) OECD calculations: consolidation required to meet 60% debt-to-GDP level by 2030
(b) planned consolidation 2015-2016

Source: OECD (2015d), *State of Public Finances Survey*.

Summary of results on fiscal consolidation strategy

Beyond the obvious conclusions relating to countries with extremely positive (e.g. Norway) or extremely difficult (e.g. Greece, Japan) fiscal positions, the following points would appear to arise from the analysis:

- A **strong pre-crisis fiscal position, allied to even modest consolidation,** has generally led to small or no requirements for further consolidation (Korea, Luxembourg, New Zealand and Switzerland being exemplars, along with Germany which had a modest pre-crisis surplus). The notable exceptions are Denmark and Finland, both of which had a significant pre-crisis surplus and currently face high consolidation needs owing to country-specific circumstances.
- A **neutral or weak pre-crisis fiscal position, allied to modest consolidation,** has left countries requiring continued significant or strong consolidation over coming years (e.g. Austria, Belgium, Poland and the Slovak Republic). Indeed, even some countries with apparently strong pre-crisis fiscal positions (e.g. Canada, the Netherlands and Spain) have experienced difficulties in the later years of the crisis, due to the delayed onset of banking difficulties or to a lack of alacrity or urgency in responding to the challenges presented by the crisis.
- A **very weak pre-crisis fiscal position, even allied to strong consolidation,** has still left those countries requiring further significant or strong consolidation (e.g. Hungary, Portugal, the United Kingdom and the United States).

The fiscal policy experiences of the past seven years have underscored the wisdom and indeed the imperative of running a prudent, **counter-cyclical fiscal policy** during a favourable macroeconomic environment. Countries need to have sufficient fiscal room in good times in order to avail of accommodative, countervailing fiscal policy in bad times.

The fact that so few OECD countries – and only two of the OECD's largest seven economies (Canada and Germany) – were, in fact, running a surplus prior to the crisis suggests that the policy tools currently available, or as currently constituted, **do not provide the requisite incentives** for such a policy course to be pursued as the norm. The tools to align political incentives with fiscal policy imperatives, across both the political and economic "cycles", appear to be lacking in many OECD countries.

3. Fiscal rules and associated policy dilemmas

Fiscal rules and objectives

Seventeen OECD countries regard themselves as bound by legal rules that play a determining role in the setting of fiscal policy, as Table 1.4 illustrates. Switzerland's "debt brake" constitutional rule has proven a model for some OECD countries, notably Germany. Most OECD members within the European Union are members of the euro currency zone, which is subject to economic governance rules that have been significantly tightened over the period of the crisis, including under the European Fiscal Compact (to which Denmark, a non-euro zone EU member, has also subscribed). It is notable that some OECD countries within the European Union – Czech Republic, France and Hungary – while formally subject to the EU rules, regard themselves as retaining latitude to temper fiscal objectives by reference to broader pro-growth economic priorities. The Czech Republic and Hungary, which took action during the crisis to bring their deficits below the 3% ceiling that applies under EU treaties, no longer regard their fiscal policies as being primarily guided by any fiscal rules. Norway's fiscal rule guards against excessive reliance on oil revenues within the budget process, and does not direct the course of fiscal policy *per se*.

Nine OECD countries do not have definite fiscal rules in place, although some have legal frameworks requiring clarity about fiscal objectives. The United Kingdom is not, in effect, subject to the EU-wide 3% fiscal deficit ceiling, and is instead governed by domestic budget responsibility legislation which requires the government in office to spell out its medium-term fiscal objectives. This broad model is also applied in Australia, Canada and New Zealand. In Chile, Japan, Korea and Turkey, national medium-term frameworks allow scope for the government to specify its fiscal plans. Fiscal goal-setting in the United States is a more complex affair, as the legislative and executive branches of government negotiate from year to year on the appropriate budgetary course, against the backdrop of statutory limits on appropriations.

Developments in fiscal rules in the wake of the global crisis

The global financial crisis has spurred a re-think of the fiscal framework in many OECD countries, and of the role to be played by fiscal rules and fiscal targets. In particular, the European Union's economic governance framework (as set out in its Treaties, Directives and Regulations) has been subjected to a series of reforms since 2011 (see Box 1.3). Germany adopted a debt brake rule in 2009 which emphasises balanced budgets, replacing the former "golden rule" (Box 1.4). In addition, the United Kingdom recently announced (June 2015) its plan to adopt a budget surplus law which will require the maintenance of a budget surplus when the economy is growing, and which will constrain governments from spending more than they receive in tax revenue in normal times.

Developing a well-designed fiscal framework using fiscal rules and targets that are suitable to country-specific macroeconomic circumstances is a key objective of the reforms introduced in many OECD countries. A recent OECD study (2015f) presents an analytical case for countries to establish fiscal rules which take account of macroeconomic variables such as the business cycle, trade openness and exposure to financial developments. It emphasises that prudent debt targets can serve as a viable "fiscal anchor" to ensure the sustainability of public finances while providing sufficient policy room to cope with adverse shocks. For higher income countries, a debt threshold is in the range of 70-90% of GDP is advocated; for euro area countries that do not have direct access to monetary policy levers, the debt threshold would be lower, ranging from 50-70% of GDP; and for emerging economies which are more exposed to capital flow reversals, the threshold is lower still, at around 30-50% of GDP. Furthermore, it stresses that in most countries it is preferable to combine a budget balance rule with an expenditure rule to achieve two objectives: anchoring fiscal policy expectations around a prudent debt level; and allowing for macroeconomic stabilisation that enhances economic growth, while limiting pro-cyclicality and over-spending. Under this model, the marginal benefit of adding a revenue rule is likely outweighed by its costs in terms of complexity and reduction in fiscal flexibility. Similarly, Andrle et al. (2015) also presents an analytical case for simplification of the overall fiscal governance framework design by introducing a single fiscal anchor (debt ratio) with a single operational rule – whether linked to expenditure growth, revenue growth, an overall balanced budget or a primary balanced budget, would be a matter for each country to decide.

Table 1.4. **Fiscal rules and objectives in OECD countries**

		Comment
Australia	○	Budget Repair Strategy to achieve 1% surplus by 2023-24
Austria	●	Euro-area fiscal rules, with domestic "debt brake"
Belgium	●	Fiscal balance targeted for 2018, in SGP context
Canada	○	Federal debt target of 25% GDP by 2021; balanced budgets by 2015/16
Chile	○	Structural fiscal balance targeted for 2018; previous reliance on expenditure cap now replaced with structural balance
Czech Republic	-	Fiscal targets de-emphasised as government prioritises growth
Denmark	●	European Fiscal Compact measures operational under new law; structural fiscal balance targeted by 2020
Estonia	●	Euro-area fiscal requirements transposed into domestic law
Finland	●	Government aims to bring debt ratio onto downward path by the end of its term; European Fiscal Compact transposed into domestic law
France	◖	SGP fiscal requirements in domestic law; applied as part of, and in balance with, the government's multi-dimensional agenda
Germany	●	Debt brake rule operates as an "anchor" for SGP-related framework
Greece	●	Euro-area fiscal requirements transposed into domestic law
Hungary	◖	Fiscal targets de-emphasised as government prioritises growth; debt brake introduced, will not apply in times of economic contraction
Iceland		
Ireland	●	Euro-area fiscal requirements transposed into domestic law
Italy	◖	Euro-area fiscal requirements transposed into domestic law; applied in balance with requirement to avoid unduly pro-cyclical measures
Japan	○	Halving of primary deficit by 2015; primary surplus targeted by 2020
Korea	○	Fiscal Management Plan sets objectives, with National Assembly input
Luxembourg	●	Euro-area fiscal requirements transposed into domestic law
Mexico		
Netherlands	●	Euro-area fiscal requirements transposed into domestic law, with fixed expenditure framework and revenue-side stabilisation
New Zealand	○	Return to fiscal surplus in 2014/15; reduce expenditure to 30% of GDP; reduce net debt to 20% of GDP by 2020
Norway		Rule insulates fiscal policy from oil-price volatility, and promotes cyclical smoothing
Poland	●	Domestic Stabilising Expenditure Rule; also subject to EU 3% deficit limit
Portugal	●	Euro-area fiscal requirements transposed into domestic law
Slovak Republic	●	Continued steady fiscal correction in line with Euro area rules
Slovenia	●	Urgent fiscal correction now underway in line with Euro area rules
Spain	●	Urgent fiscal correction now underway in line with Euro area rules
Sweden	●	Fiscal policy aligned towards target of fiscal surplus of 1% of GDP
Switzerland	●	Debt brake limits expenditure growth
Turkey	○	Plan to maintain tight fiscal control and achieve surplus in 2017
United Kingdom	○	Government sets out its objectives in Charter for Budget Responsibility; current target is structural balance and falling debt by 2016/17
United States	○	Adventitious budgetary goal-setting between branches of government

Legend

- ● Fiscal rules significantly determine fiscal policy course
- ◖ Fiscal rules significantly influence fiscal policy course but balanced with other objectives
- ○ Fiscal policy objectives are under control of government and/or parliament
- \- Fiscal policy course is not governed by fiscal rules or fiscal policy objectives at present

Source: OECD (2015d), *State of Public Finances Survey*.

Box 1.3. **Changes to the EU Economic Governance Framework**

As a response to the 2010 European sovereign debt crisis, consecutive reforms, including the 2011 Six Pack, the 2012 Fiscal Compact and the 2013 Two Pack have been made. The key elements of the EU fiscal framework applicable to most EU countries (but not all) can be summarised as follows.

Countries must manage their public finances within fixed limits: The debt level and the deficit level must not exceed ceilings of 60% of GDP and 3% of GDP respectively; both expressed in general government terms. The public finances should be maintained close to a balanced position (i.e. a deficit of no more than 0.5% of GDP) in cyclically-adjusted terms, net of one-off factors. The growth in public expenditure must not exceed the underlying medium-term level of economic growth, unless it is financed by additional revenues.

Budgetary correction must proceed at a minimum pace: Any unduly high non-structural budget deficit must be corrected by 0.5% of GDP each year; while any excess above the debt limit of 60% of GDP must be reduced by one-twentieth each year.

Exceptions to these rules are very limited and there are financial penalties for non-compliance. The fiscal limits must be enshrined in national law and the national budget calendar coordinated.

Source: OECD (2015g), "Budget Review: Germany", *OECD Journal on Budgeting*, Vol. 14/2, http://dx.doi.org/10.1787/budget-14-5jrw4sxb32q4.

Box 1.4. **Germany's debt brake rule**

In 2009, the proposal to replace the golden rule with a debt brake rule was approved by the German Parliament and enshrined in the constitution. The objectives were to improve the sustainability of the national finances, with strengthened fiscal coordination among federal and sub-national governments while providing flexibility to deal with cyclical challenges. The core elements of the rule are as follows:

- Balanced Budgets: Federal government must balance revenues with expenditures in their budgets, as a fundamental principle. In normal economic circumstances, "balance" is assumed to be met for federal government when net borrowing does not exceed 0.35% of GDP.
- Symmetrical adjustments over the economic cycle: Automatic stabilisers will operate freely and fully over the cycle. In other words, cyclical deficits may be run in a downturn, and cyclical surpluses must be run in an upturn.
- Limited exceptions: Additional borrowing is allowed to deal with natural disasters and exceptional emergencies beyond state control.

Source: OECD (2015g), "Budget Review: Germany", *OECD Journal on Budgeting*, Vol. 14/2, http://dx.doi.org/10.1787/budget-14-5jrw4sxb32q4.

In summary, there would appear to be a growing analytical case that fiscal rules, which were too complex to be effective in the run-up to the crisis, should in general terms be made **simpler and clearer to enhance compliance, rather than made more complex still.** A simpler approach could, and should, still allow for adaptations to country-specific circumstances.

4. Protecting and promoting economic growth: Country strategies

A sustained fiscal correction, such as has been experienced across the OECD from 2010, carries the risk of impairing economic growth through exacerbating pro-cyclical tendencies and further depressing demand and investment: indeed the question of the correct fiscal stance for governments to adopt, in the face of sustained low growth and fiscal imbalance, has been a highly contentious area of debate among economists and policy makers.

To reconcile fiscal sustainability and growth objectives, some OECD countries have pursued carefully focused and nuanced consolidation strategies, coupling an efficiency dimension with targeted initiatives to spur growth. In addition, the timing, speed and degree of fiscal correction are in some cases carefully planned to minimise negative economic impacts. Moreover, the instruments of monetary policy have increasingly been brought to bear, across many OECD countries and regions, to provide a supportive environment for economic growth and confidence.

Table 1.5 shows, and as summarised below, provides an overview of the range and complexity of approaches adopted in various OECD countries. Some recurring themes are as follows:

1. **Coupling fiscal correction with structural reform**. Some countries have put the primary focus upon structural economic reforms, including labour market improvement, reduction of "red tape" and liberalisation of professions, while maintaining a firm course of fiscal correction. The countries in this category – notably Ireland, Portugal and Spain – are the ones that have had the least room for fiscal manoeuvre, and indeed some governments in this category have justified the rigorous fiscal correction as a necessary means of supporting the confidence necessary for investment and growth to be sustained.
2. **Fiscal relaxation or stimulus**. A second approach has been to undertake growth-supporting fiscal stimulus, either through enhanced prioritisation of capital investment (notably Canada, Chile and Turkey), or through consciously tempering the fiscal correction efforts by adopting a relatively relaxed fiscal stance (Czech Republic).
3. **Fiscal relaxation plus structural reform**. A third approach has been to adopt a relatively relaxed fiscal policy (or at least an attenuation of the fiscal correction), while making a sustained effort to undertake structural economic reforms. France and Hungary have "paused" or re-scheduled fiscal correction while emphasising broad-ranging reforms.
4. **Complex, multi-faceted policy responses**. Some countries are harder to categorise definitively. The United Kingdom is publicly committed to ongoing medium-term fiscal consolidation and it has a strong economic reform agenda (arguing for Category 1 above), yet it has also devoted significant resources towards growth-friendly investment, thus attenuating its fiscal correction course, and indeed it has

re-scheduled the timeline for achieving structural balance (arguing for Category 3). The United States responded to the early phase of the crisis with stimulus measures (2009 Recovery Act, 2010 reduction of payroll taxes) but in later years the 2011 Budget Control Act, with its constraints upon appropriations and sequestration requirements, has formed the starting point for budgetary negotiations. Japan has pursued a broad-based strategy to utilise the various levers of economic policy in support of growth, with a primary focus upon accommodative monetary policy plus intensive structural reform and sound fiscal policy (the "three arrows" of the "Abenomics" strategy), with a heightened focus upon fiscal stabilisation from 2013 in order to remove potential unease concerning the evolution of the public finances.

5. Models of fiscal responsibility: development of fiscal institutions

Role and development of independent fiscal institutions

As set out in the "Recommendation of the Council on Budgetary Governance" (OECD, 2015h), the credibility of fiscal rules and fiscal objectives may be enhanced by the introduction of independent fiscal institutions (IFIs), or other structured institutional arrangements to promote objectivity and professionalism in fiscal forecasting and monitoring. Indeed, Table 1.6 shows that 25 OECD countries now have some such arrangements in place, of which 15 countries now have well-established IFIs. The contrast with the pre-crisis position is very marked: only six IFIs were well-established in 2008, with a further three bodies (the Swedish Fiscal Policy Council, Canadian Parliamentary Budget Office and Hungarian Fiscal Council) very recently in place.

The details shown in Table 1.6 demonstrate the breadth of functions currently carried out by IFIs, which can be grouped as follows:

- **Technical economic functions,** such as preparing or endorsing macroeconomic forecasts, or calculating the structural fiscal balance. The Dutch CPB, the United Kingdom's OBR and Chile's Fiscal Advisory Council exercise such functions.
- **Public transparency and accountability functions,** e.g. building the capacity of parliament to engage with the budgetary process. The "parliamentary budget offices" (PBOs) in Canada, Australia and Italy are examples of this function, along with the National Assembly Budget Office of Korea and the Congressional Budget Office of the United States. The CBO is something of an "outlier" among OECD countries in terms of the scale and significance of its budgetary and policy analysis – reflecting its role in support of the US Congress which itself wields considerable budget-making powers.
- **Policy costings** to inform policy development and debate among politicians and the public. Australia's PBO and the Dutch CPB exercises a distinct function in this regard and Canada has recently moved to promote independent costing capacity within the public service. Again, the US CBO has long-standing functions in this regard.
- A **"fiscal watchdog" role** with regard to the appropriateness – or otherwise – of the government's fiscal policy. Assessment of compliance with fiscal rules is one of the most common roles for fiscal councils that have been established in recent years among the euro currency area, in light of the new economic governance rules for the area. The Irish Fiscal Advisory Council also has a mandate to assess the "prudence" of the government's fiscal policy stance.

Table 1.5. **Strategies to support economic growth during fiscal consolidation**

		Comment
Australia		
Austria	◈	Strengthening of investments in education, universities, R&D and infrastructure to support growth
Belgium	◇	Some measures to reduce cost of labour relative to neighbouring countries
Canada	◈	Maintaining of major infrastructure investments, supported by capital carry-forward facility
Chile	◈	Major increases in capital investment in support of economic activity
Czech Republic	◈	Distinctive approach with fiscal targets displaced in favour of pro-growth fiscal policy stance
Denmark	◆	Maintaining of high public investment levels, and "Growth Plan DK" plan to promote dynamism and reform
Estonia	◇	Estonia 2020' reform plan to increase productivity and employment; education and labour-market focus
Finland	◈	Sale of state assets from 2015 to be used for growth- and job-friendly capital investment
France	◆	Strong focus on reducing red tape and structural economic reform, while attenuating the fiscal correction
Germany	◈	Additional funds allocated for investment in transport infrastructure
Greece	◇	
Hungary	◆	Tax reforms and administrative simplification measures to promote growth; relaxed fiscal policy stance
Iceland		
Ireland	◇	Annual Action Plan for Jobs, structural economic reforms and supportive tax reforms
Israel		
Italy	◆	Pace of fiscal consolidation has been slowed to avoid undue pro-cyclicality; tax-based labour incentives
Japan	‡	High-profile growth strategy of bold monetary policy, flexible fiscal policy and structural economic reform
Korea	◆	Expansionary fiscal policy stance and structural economic reforms
Luxembourg	-	Stimulus measures adopted in 2010-11 but no specific measures in place at present
Mexico	◆	Fiscal stimulus to shield growth; fiscal reform and simplification drive to support economic development
Netherlands	◈	Cyclically-sensitive fiscal policy instruments, with some structural measures to protect potential growth
New Zealand	◆	Automatic stabilisers operated in early part of economic crisis; extra investments via state asset proceeds
Norway	-	No particular growth-related fiscal strategy is in place
Poland	◈	Relaxed pace of fiscal consolidation to avoid undue pro-cyclicality
Portugal	◇	Some targeted growth-friendly tax reforms, in addition to fiscal correction focus
Slovak Republic	◆	Structural economic reforms focused upon labour market; relatively relaxed fiscal adjustment
Slovenia	◈	Investment-oriented budget has been submitted, including measures to attract R&D and FDI
Spain	◇	Structural economic reforms focused upon labour market, financial sector and tax reforms
Sweden	-	New administration will prioritise education, labour market reforms, infrastructure and healthcare
Switzerland	◈	Counter-cyclical fiscal policy tools
Turkey	◈	Major infrastructure investment programme
United Kingdom	‡	Fiscal discipline commitment; intensive structural reform including red-tape reduction; some capital stimulus
United States	‡	Stimulus measures in wake of the crisis; subsequent sequestration measures subject to negotiation

Legend

◆ Fiscal stimulus measures and structural economic reforms

◈ Fiscal stimulus measures (incl. relaxed / counter-cyclical fiscal policy stance and prioritisation of capital investment)

◇ Structural economic reforms and/or reliance on stable position of public finances

‡ Complex, multi-faceted approach to supporting economic growth

Source: OECD (2015d), *State of Public Finances Survey*.

Table 1.6. **Role and status of independent fiscal institutions in OECD countries**

	2008	*2014*	Comment on 2014 position
Australia	-	■	Parliamentary Budget Office (PBO) (2012) provides independent analysis of the budget cycle, fiscal policy, and budget costings. A 10-year forecasting role has been proposed
Austria	■	■	Fiscal Advisory Council (FISK) now endorses fiscal forecasts and provides fiscal policy advice. Austrian Institute of Economic Research (WIFO) provides independent short-term to medium-term macroeconomic forecasts for the Ministry of Finance.
Belgium	■	■	Independent Federal Planning Bureau produces official forecasts. High Council of Finance (HCF) mandate expanded in 2013 to include policy advice and monitoring.
Canada	□	■	Parliamentary Budget Office (2008) provides independent analysis on budgetary issues; also Costing Centre of Expertise being established to promote capacity within civil service
Chile	-	□	Fiscal Advisory Council established in 2013 to provide technical guidance on structural balance calculations and on general fiscal matters
Czech Republic	-	-	No IFI in place, although a new National Fiscal Council is planned under new legislation
Denmark	-	□	Economic Council mandate recently expanded to assesses fiscal forecasts and monitor compliance with fiscal objectives and expenditure ceilings.
Estonia		□	Fiscal council (2014) to assess macro-fiscal forecasts and compliance with fiscal rules
Finland	-	□	Academic Council for Economic Policy Council (2014) assesses forecasts and monitors fiscal policy objectives. National audit office unit monitors fiscal regulations / procedures
France	-	■	High Council of Public Finances (2012), independent unit within national audit office, assesses economic forecasts and whether structural fiscal balance is on course
Germany	-	□	Government's economic forecasts strongly influenced by expert professional inputs. New Independent Advisory Board (Stability Council) assesses compliance with Fiscal Compact
Greece	-	□	Hellenic Parliamentary Budget Office (HPBO) provides fiscal policy analysis and monitoring, including of the budgetary forecasts. Proposal to elevate status to official IFI
Hungary	□	■	Fiscal Council (2008) must sign off on feasibility of State Budget in light of debt rule
Iceland	-	-	No IFI in place
Ireland	-	■	Irish Fiscal Advisory Council (2011) endorses economic forecasts and critiques fiscal stance
Israel	-	-	No IFI in place
Italy	-	□	Parliamentary Budget Office monitors fiscal developments and compliance with rules
Japan	-	-	No IFI in place. Broadly-constituted Fiscal System Council offers advice to Minister.
Korea	■	■	National Assembly Budget Office (2003) facilitates parliamentary engagement on budget figures and objectives
Luxembourg	-	□	*Conseil national des finances publiques* (2014) assesses fiscal forecasts and monitors compliance with rules
Mexico	■	■	Centre for Public Finance Studies analyses the public finances for the Congress
Netherlands	■	■	*De facto* independent CPB (Bureau for Economic Policy Analysis) (1989) produces official economic forecasts; Council of State has assumed monitoring functions re fiscal rules
New Zealand	-	-	No IFI in place
Norway	-	-	No IFI in place
Poland	-	-	No IFI in place
Portugal	-	■	Technical Budget Support Unit (UTAO) facilitates parliamentary scrutiny; Public Finance Council now provides an opinion on official macroeconomic forecasts
Slovak Republic	-	■	Official forecasts approved by advisory Macroeconomic Forecasting Committee. Council for Budget Responsibility independently assesses fiscal performance.
Slovenia	-	□	Institute of Macroeconomic Analysis and Development prepares official forecasts; new IFI under consideration in context of Euro area rules. (2009 Fiscal Council now defunct)
Spain	-	□	Independent Fiscal Responsibility Authority (AIREF) endorses the government's macroeconomic forecasts and may make recommendations in this regard
Sweden	□	■	Fiscal Policy Council (FPC) assesses fiscal policy course and promotes public debate. It may also review and assess the quality of forecasts.
Switzerland	-	-	No IFI in place
Turkey	-	-	No IFI in place
United Kingdom	-	■	Office of Budget Responsibility prepares official macroeconomic forecasts and assesses fiscal policy course by reference to public objectives; also sustainability analysis.
United States	■	■	Congressional Budget Office (1975) provides authoritative independent analysis on fiscal / budgetary measures at both macro and micro levels

Legend

■ IFI has an established role in influencing budget forecasts / fiscal policy

□ IFI very recently established and/or with limited influence in budget forecasts / fiscal policy

\- No IFI role

Source: OECD (2015d), *State of Public Finances Survey*.

- **Broader fiscal policy comment and advice**. Sweden's Fiscal Policy Council exercises such a role, and Japan's broadly constituted Fiscal System Council – while not an "independent fiscal institution" in the strict sense – provides useful policy advice for the consideration of the Minister for Finance.

The relative efficacy and usefulness of IFIs, and other models of channelling professional, independent input to the budgetary process, remain to be definitively established, although there is analytical support for the idea that IFIs tend to support the accuracy of fiscal forecastings (see, e.g. Debrun and Kinda, 2014). In particular, as many OECD countries move from the acute phase of fiscal correction towards a recovery phase, IFIs have a chance to establish their value in promoting an informed public and political discourse about fiscal policy options and risks.

6. Involving parliaments and citizens

As a response to rising unemployment and public debt, the level of public trust in government has declined by 3 percentage points in OECD countries over the course of the economic crisis (see OECD, 2015g). As part of the OECD's broader trust strategy, increased attention is being paid to enhanced transparency, engagement and participation throughout public governance. New information and communication technologies (ICTs) allow for the disclosure of a wide range of budgetary information, facilitating access for various stakeholders, including civil society organizations (CSOs), parliaments and citizens. In order to foster better policies and understand how economic decision making affects them, people face the challenging task of accessing the often opaque, technical processes of budgeting.

The "Recommendation of the Council on Budgetary Governance" (OECD, 2015f) calls for "an inclusive, participative and realistic debate on budgetary choices" by offering opportunities for the parliament and its committees to engage with the budget process "at all key stages of the budget cycle, both *ex ante* and *ex post* as appropriate", and by "facilitating the engagement of parliaments, citizens and civil society organisations in a realistic debate about key priorities, trade-offs, opportunity costs and value for money."

Given the sensitivities that come with budgetary decision making in a time of consolidation, it is informative to see how OECD member countries have sought to involve parliaments and citizens throughout the recent period, as illustrated in Table 1.7.

Most OECD countries have a strong tradition of formal parliamentary authorisation of the budget, extending in several cases to the ability to propose modifications to draft budget proposals from the executive. However, the United States is an "outlier" among OECD countries in that the parliament, as a co-equal branch of government, has strong budgeting prerogatives. Beyond the United States, it is notable that no OECD country has yet moved to engage either parliament or the public in a substantive manner with the processes of budgetary formulation, oversight and accountability, to the full extent envisaged in the Budgetary Governance Recommendation.

However, there is a more general pattern of enhanced transparency and steadily enhanced engagement across many OECD countries over recent years. A small number of countries (Canada, France and Korea) have taken initiatives to enhance parliamentary scrutiny and involvement, while a larger number (notably Czech Republic, Finland, Germany, Ireland, Luxembourg, Slovak Republic, Spain and the United States) have introduced web- or tablet-related initiatives to promote public accessibility and "budget literacy". The Czech Republic and Portugal have introduced a "citizen's budget" while New Zealand has sought to promote civic engagement in budgeting matters.

Table 1.7. **Engagement of parliament and citizens in budgeting issues**

		Comment
Australia	▷	PBO has enhanced parliament engagement capacity; some civic engagement in performance audit
Austria	-	
Belgium	-	
Canada	▷	Streamlined estimates, online searchable InfoBase of financial reporting documents
Chile	-	
Czech Republic	▷	Open data portal (data.mfcr.cz) and "Citizen's Budget" providing accessible budget data
Denmark	-	
Estonia	-	
Finland	▷	Budget data available in open formats and budget overview available in tablet-friendly version
France	▷	View of parliament to be obtained on outcome of annual spending reviews
Germany	▷	Online information portal for citizens. Parliament has long-standing engagement in budget process
Greece	-	
Hungary	-	
Iceland		
Ireland	▷	Online information on expenditure allocations and performance metrics (irelandstat.gov.ie)
Italy	▷	Open data portals for central/regional government expenditure and for the State budget
Japan	▷	Accessible budget fact-sheets available to public. Diet receives summary of draft budget
Korea	▷	Extra time for parliamentary scrutiny of budget; each ministry to maintain budget status on internet
Luxembourg	▷	Budget documents and data available to the public on user-friendly website (budget.public.lu)
Mexico	▷	Extensive budget transparency portal (www.transparenciapresupuestaria.gob.mx)
Netherlands	-	
New Zealand	▷	Initiatives under way to promote civic engagement with budgetary policy-making
Norway	-	
Poland	-	
Portugal	▷	"Citizen's Budget" introduced in 2013; "To Know the Budget" online initiative in 2015
Slovak Republic	▷	Web portal provides information for citizens on budget structure and processes
Slovenia	-	
Spain	▷	General measures to promote transparency and access, incl. new transaprency website
Sweden	-	
Switzerland	-	
Turkey	-	
United Kingdom	-	
United States	▶	Congress is co-equal in budgeting; website (performance.gov) provides data on public goals

Legend

▶ Strong engagement of parliament and/or citizens in budgeting policy incl. policy formulation and accountability

▷ Accessibility and transparency of budgetary information for parliament and/or citizens

- No particular initiatives to promote engagement / accessibility for parliament and/or citizens in budgeting

Source: OECD (2015d), *State of Public Finances Survey.*

7. Sub-national budgetary governance: Key themes

Chapter 3 provides a detailed analysis of the role and impact of sub-national government finances on overall budgetary management. However there are some core elements of this analysis that should be highlighted as part of the broader narrative on *The State of Public Finances* in the wake of the economic crisis.

The debt of sub-national governments (SNGs) represented only 13% of GDP on average in OECD countries in 2013 (unweight average across individual countries: the weighted average across the OECD area as a whole is 23.8% of GDP), and 17% of overall public debt (see Figure 1.13). The figures for SNG debt are considerably higher in Canada (61.2%) and Japan (37.3%), while the figures for Germany, Spain and the United States are all around 29% of GDP.

Figure 1.13. **Government gross debts across levels of government as percentage of GDP, 2013 and 2014**

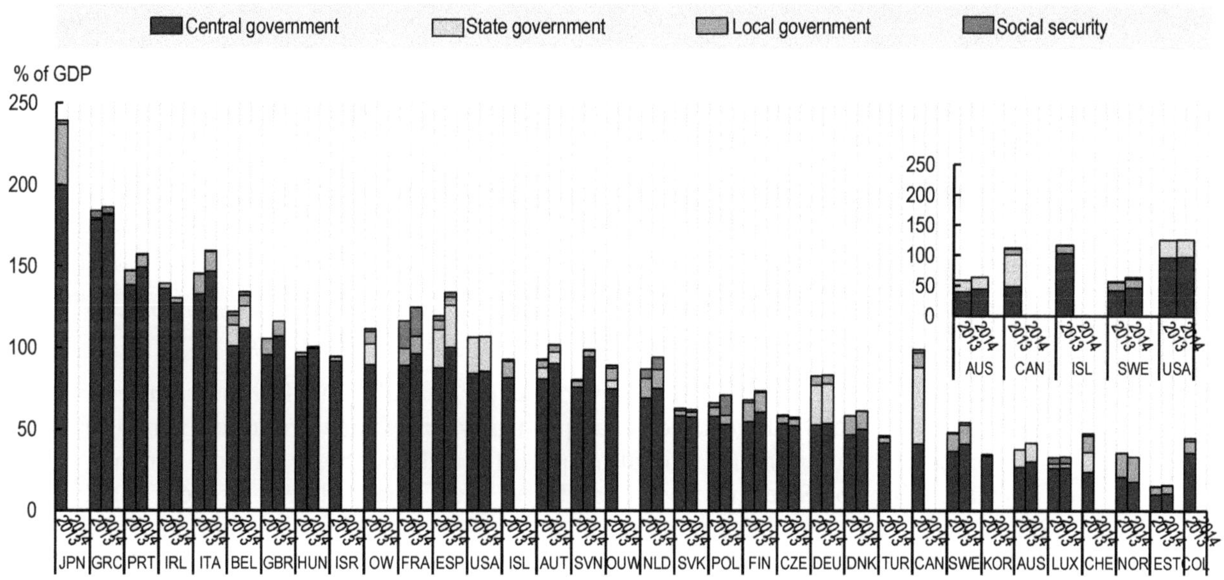

Sources: OECD (2015c), *OECD National Accounts Statistics* (database), http://dx.doi.org/10.1787/na-data-en; European Commission (2015), *Government Finance Statistics* (database), Eurostat, http://ec.europa.eu/Eurostat/web/government-finance-statistics/data/database.

StatLink http://dx.doi.org/10.1787/888933288014

The distribution of overall debt across levels of government has seen an increase in the SNG share of debt by 4.2 percentage points on average over the period 2007-13. However, a considerable decline in the SNG share of debt has taken place in some OECD countries, e.g. Estonia (11.8 percentage points), Denmark (8.9 percentage points) and the United Kingdom (8.3 percentage points). In all of these cases, overall government debt has in general been on the increase, and the relative decline in SNG debt can be attributed to its lower rate of growth as compared with central-level debt.

There are a number of reasons why the public finances at SNG level demand special attention:

- In general, SNGs enjoy less autonomy for improving their fiscal situation than central government (CG) (Vammalle and Hulbert, 2013), owing to their smaller revenue base, limited autonomy to increase revenues and higher reliance on transfers.
- In addition, the expenditures for which SNGs are responsible are, in many cases, either mandatory or difficult to cut owing to high political and social costs. On average, SNGs spend 50% of their budgets on education, health and social protection. Some of these areas are vulnerable to demographic pressures, and in other cases the rules and standards of expenditure delivery are dictated by central government.
- Fiscal rules often allow SNGs comparatively little room for manoeuvre in response to cyclical fluctuations, with restricted access to debt financing, leading to direct impacts on expenditures when revenues fall. For example, almost all states in the United States have a balanced budget rule in their constitution, and wide-ranging expenditure cuts were implemented in 2008-09 during the early stages of the global financial crisis.
- SNGs sometimes have power to establish autonomous agencies whose finances do not appear on the national accounts, potentially giving rise to contingent liabilities that are difficult to monitor.

OECD countries and SNGs have adopted a range of tools and mechanisms to keep SNG finances in check and to address some of the challenges outlined above:

- A range of tools are used by governments to help in the medium-term management of SNG budgets. For example **rainy day funds** are used to smooth out cyclical revenue in many federal or quasi-federal countries: Canada, Finland, Germany, Mexico, Sweden, Switzerland and the United States. In the United States, nearly all states have introduced some form of stabilisation fund over the past two decades, and many US cities benefit from a type of rainy day fund known as "ending balances", estimated to represent 12.7% of cities' revenues in 2012 (down from 25% prior to the crisis) (Box 1.5).
- **Fiscal rules**: In the context of managing SNG finances, the types of fiscal rules fall under three categories:
  - balanced budget rules, including golden rules
  - borrowing constraints
  - expenditure limits.

Box 1.5. **Rainy day funds to address cyclical shocks**

Several countries have introduced “rainy day” funds for sub-national governments. These are stabilisation funds which accumulate reserves in periods of growth and disburse them in times of fiscal stress, to compensate for declines in SNG revenues. The creation of rainy day funds is an alternative to the optimisation of SNG revenues sources in order to reduce the volatility of sub-national revenues. For instance, as of January 2013 county councils in Sweden are allowed to build such funds to transfers budget surpluses from one year to another.

The most well documented use of rainy day funds is that of US states. During the last two decades, nearly all states have introduced some form of stabilisation fund – although the amounts saved in those funds vary widely from one state to another. Tight rules regulate the accumulation of funds in these entities. In most states, total funds accumulated must be under 5% of a state's budget; in others, the limit is at 10%, and a few states have no limit on the amount they can save in stabilisation funds. Research tends to find that rainy day funds reduce the volatility of SNG revenues and expenditures, but they have not proven sufficient to balance such a deep crisis as that of 2009-10.

US cities also benefit from a type of rainy day fund, called “ending balances”. Ending balances are reserves used by cities to smooth fluctuations of revenues. In contrast to states' rainy day funds, there are no trigger mechanisms to force the release of the funds. In 2012, a report estimated that ending balances represented roughly 12.7 % of cities' expenditures (down from 25% prior to the recession).

Rainy day funds may be created by SNGs themselves, or introduced by central governments. This is the case for instance in Mexico, where the federal government manages the *Fondo de Estabilization de Ingresos de las Etidades Federativas* (FEIEF). This fund is used to provide additional revenues to federated entities when grants from the CG are reduced in times of fiscal stress.

Source: Vammalle, C., R. Ahrend and C. Hulbert (2014), “A sub-national perspective on financing investment for growth II - Creating fiscal space for public investment: The role of institutions", *OECD Regional Development Working Papers*, No. 2014/06, OECD Publishing, http://dx.doi.org/10.1787/5jz3zvxc53bt-en.

Chapter 3 provides a detailed assessment of the effectiveness of these rules and examples of initiatives and refinements that have been introduced over recent years:

- **Inter-governmental co-ordination bodies and procedures:** Many federal and quasi-federal countries recognise that all levels of government must act in a co-ordinated manner, while respecting legal and constitutional prerogatives, to ensure the national finances are managed responsibly. Examples of national co-ordination bodies to facilitate such an arrangement are the Australian Loan Council, Belgium's High Council on Finance, Germany's Stability Council and Spain's Fiscal and Financial Policy Council. Austria has in recent years adopted an Internal Stability Pact to promote co-ordinated action and Italy has introduced a similar Domestic Stability Pact.

- **Expenditure efficiency initiatives:** For example, several OECD countries have introduced reforms to improve efficiency and to minimise the fiscal risks associated with health sector spending at both central government and SNG level.

8. Other specific reforms in budgetary governance

The "Recommendation of the Council on Budgetary Governance" (OECD, 2015f) presents a multi-dimensional framework comprised of ten principles of good practice (see Box 1.6) and qualitative/contextual guidance on their application. In general terms, the Recommendation – based on analysis and consideration by the OECD Senior Budget Officials – envisages a coherent, inter-connected and mutually supportive set of practices that underpin sound, responsive budgeting.

Box 1.6. **OECD's ten principles of budgetary governance**

1. Manage budgets within clear, credible and predictable limits for fiscal policy.
2. Closely align budgets with the medium-term strategic priorities of government.
3. Design the capital budgeting framework in order to meet national development needs in a cost-effective and coherent manner.
4. Ensure that budget documents and data are open, transparent and accessible.
5. Provide for an inclusive, participative and realistic debate on budgetary choices.
6. Present a comprehensive, accurate and reliable account of the public finance.
7. Actively plan, manage and monitor budget execution.
8. Ensure that performance, evaluation and value for money are integral to the budget process.
9. Identify, assess and manage prudently longer-term sustainability and other fiscal risks.
10. Promote the integrity and quality of budgetary forecasts, fiscal plans and budgetary implementation through rigorous quality assurance including independent audit.

Source: OECD (2015f), "Recommendation of the Council on Budgetary Governance", 18 February, www.oecd.org/gov/budgeting/Recommendation-of-the-Council-on-Budgetary-Governance.pdf.

Table 1.8 outlines the degree to which OECD countries have prioritised the application of these principles to date within their national frameworks, in the context of the budgetary consolidation agenda. While 3 countries (Austria, Canada and Ireland) have implemented broad-based budgetary reforms, a further 13 OECD countries have taken some level of action to progress budgetary reform. While diverse aspects of budgeting are touched upon, the most popular reform themes are **performance management** (11 countries), strengthening of **medium-term frameworks** for budgeting (9 countries) and development of **spending review** procedures (4 countries) (see also the spending review section above in this regard). However, there is a large minority of OECD countries that report little or no significant progress in these areas over recent years.

Table 1.8. **Intensity of budgetary reform during fiscal consolidation**

	Budget reform intensity	Comment
Australia		
Austria	▲	MTEF, performance budgeting, gender budgeting; similar reforms implemented in some Länder
Belgium	-	
Canada	▲	Streamlined spending review, focus on performance objectives, effective MTEF, accrual information
Chile	△	Strong evaluation focus, performance budgeting
Czech Republic	-	
Denmark	△	New guidelines on perfomance management; strengthened multi-year spending ceilings
Estonia	-	
Finland	-	
France	△	Ongoing spending review integrated into budget calendar, and streamlining of performance budget
Germany	△	Top-down multi-year fiscal management; some additional performance narrative with budget
Greece		
Hungary	-	
Iceland		
Ireland	▲	MTEF, performance budgeting, periodic spending review and ongoing evaluation focus
Italy		
Japan	△	Strong evaluation focus, and greater use of performance-related information in budget cycle
Korea	△	Performance budgeting and MTEF
Luxembourg	-	
Mexico		
Netherlands	△	Streamlining of performance budget; strengthening of MTEF
New Zealand	△	Performance focus; inter-generational equity principle established in law
Norway	-	No particularly marked budgetary reform initiatives
Poland	-	No particularly marked budgetary reform initiatives
Portugal	△	Strengthened MTEF
Slovak Republic	-	
Slovenia	-	
Spain	△	Enhanced budget accuracy, transparency and surveillance in context of 2011 constitutional reform
Sweden	-	
Switzerland	-	
Turkey	△	Some developments on MTEF and programme budgeting
United Kingdom	△	Ongoing refinement of performance budgeting, multi-year budgeting; welfare spending cap
United States	△	Distinctive performance approach with organisational HR focus; strategic spending reviews underway

Legend

▲ Reform activity intensive and/or broadly-based across various aspects of budgetary governance

△ Reform activity moderate and/or focused on specific aspects of budgetary governance

- No significant focus on budgetary reform

Source: OECD (2015d), *State of Public Finances Survey.*

References

Andrle, M. et al. (2015) "Reforming Fiscal Governance in the European Union", *Staff Discussion Notes*, No. 15/9, International Money Fund, Washington DC, www.imf.org/external/pubs/cat/longres.aspx?sk=42932.

Debrun, X. and T. Kinda (2014), "Strengthening Post-Crisis Fiscal Credibility – Fiscal Councils on the Rise: A New Dataset", *IMF Working Paper*, WP/14/58, www.imf.org/external/pubs/ft/wp/2014/wp1458.pdf.

European Commission (2015), *Government Finance Statistics* (database), Eurostat, http://ec.europa.eu/Eurostat/web/government-finance-statistics/data/database.

OECD (2015a), "OECD Economic Outlook No. 97 (Edition 2015/1)", *OECD Economic Outlook: Statistics and Projections* (database), http://dx.doi.org/10.1787/data-00759-en.

OECD (2015b), OECD Economic Outlook, Interim Report September 2015, OECD Publishing, Paris, http://dx.doi.org/10.1787/eco_outlook-v2015-sup1-en.

OECD (2015c), *OECD National Accounts Statistics* (database), http://dx.doi.org/10.1787/na-data-en.

OECD (2015d), *State of Public Finances Survey,* Unpublished internal document.

OECD (2015e) Spending Reviews – Background note, Unpublished internal document

OECD (2015f), "Achieving prudent debt targets using fiscal rules", *OECD Economics Department Policy Brief,* No. 28, July 2015, www.oecd.org/eco/achieving-prudent-debt-targets-using-fiscal-rules.htm

OECD (2015g), "Budget review: Germany", *OECD Journal on Budgeting*, Vol. 14/2, http://dx.doi.org/10.1787/budget-14-5jrw4sxb32q4.

OECD (2015h), "Recommendation of the Council on Budgetary Governance", 18 February, www.oecd.org/gov/budgeting/Recommendation-of-the-Council-on-Budgetary-Governance.pdf.

OECD (2014), *Survey on Managing Budgeting Constraints: Implications for HRM and Employment in Central Public Administration*, OECD.

OECD (2012), *Restoring Public Finances, 2012 Update*, OECD Publishing, Paris, http://dx.doi.org/10.1787/9789264179455-en.

OECD (2011), *Restoring Public Finances,* www.oecd.org/gov/budgeting/47558957.pdf.

Robinson, Marc (2014), "Spending reviews", *OECD Journal on Budgeting*, Vol. 13/2, http://dx.doi.org/10.1787/budget-13-5jz14bz8p2hd.

Vammalle, C., R. Ahrend and C. Hulbert (2014), "A sub-national perspective on financing investment for growth II - Creating fiscal space for public investment: The role of institutions", *OECD Regional Development Working Papers*, No. 2014/06, OECD Publishing, http://dx.doi.org/10.1787/5jz3zvxc53bt-en.

Chapter 2

Public finances in context: Country notes

This chapter presents profiles of OECD countries with regard to their economic situation, their broad strategy for managing the public finances, and related themes and developments in budgetary governance.

Within each country note, Section 1 gives a brief overview of the main economic developments including real GDP, fiscal balance, structural balance and gross debt figures.

Section 2 provides an overview of each country's fiscal objectives, policy priorities, the broad approach to fiscal consolidation, as well as other related elements of budgetary governance such as the quality of the economic forecasting and engagement of parliament and citizens.

Note that the position for each country note generally reflects the position as of June 2015, and has not been updated to reflect political, economic and budgetary developments since that time.

Australia

1. Economic situation

Growth is projected to dip to 2.25% in 2015 but pick up to nearly 3.0% in 2016. Gathering momentum in consumption, non-resource investment and exports help the economy adjust and recover from the fall in commodity prices and unwinding resource-sector investment. Consumer price inflation has been dented by lower oil prices and will remain moderate due to economic slack.

Monetary policy firepower should be held in reserve given uncertainties about the outlook and the downside aspects of rate cuts on the booming housing and credit markets. Given Australia's comparatively healthy public finances, fiscal policy should continue to provide support if needed through the operation of automatic stabilisers. Structural reform should facilitate post-resource-boom adjustment, and in particular a further shift towards indirect taxes.

The unwinding of resource-sector investment reflects large-scale projects reaching completion and easing up of investment plans given commodity-price falls. Plans to boost investment in public infrastructure are welcome, but project selection requires rigorous cost-benefit analysis.

Key economic indicators: Australia

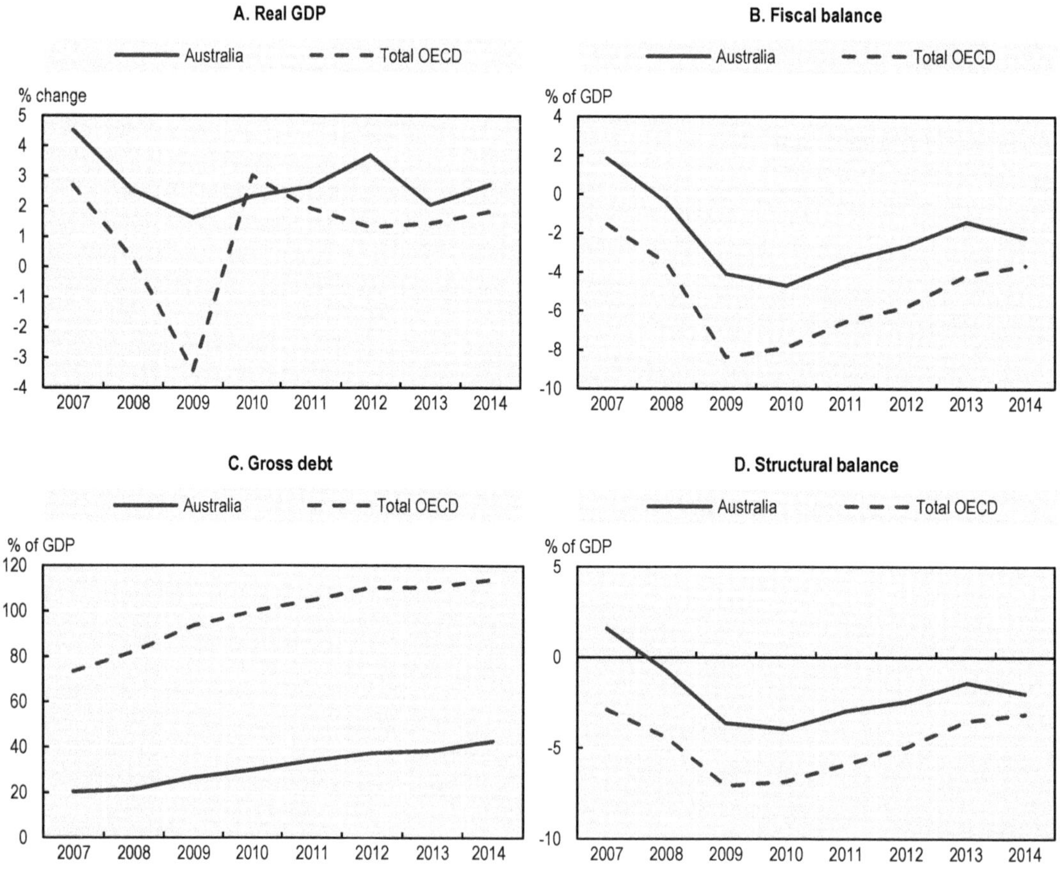

Source: OECD (2015a), "OECD Economic Outlook No. 97 (Edition 2015/1)", *OECD Economic Outlook: Statistics and Projections* (database), http://dx.doi.org/10.1787/data-00759-en.

StatLink http://dx.doi.org/ 10.1787/888933288027

2. Fiscal policy and budgetary governance

Australia's general government fiscal deficit was as low as 4.7% of GDP (gross domestic product) in 2010, but has slowly declined, reaching 1.4% of GDP in 2013. A large fall in Australia's terms of trade commencing 2011 and the transition away from growth led by mining investment has constrained the pace of fiscal consolidation. Therefore, the Government's fiscal consolidation measures aim to build savings over time. In late 2013 the new government committed to restoring public finances by returning the budget to sustainable surpluses that build to at least 1% of GDP by 2023-24. As at December 2014, the budget was not expected to return to surplus until 2019-20. The Public Governance, Performance and Accountability Act 2013 now forms the legal basis for budgeting in Australia, replacing the 1997 legislation.

Fiscal objectives

The Government's fiscal strategy comprises two parts: the Medium-Term Fiscal Strategy and the Budget Repair Strategy.

- The Medium-Term Fiscal Strategy is to achieve budget surpluses, on average, over the course of the economic cycle. The main change since 2011 is the move from a cap on real spending growth in favour of a focus on reducing the payments-to-GDP ratio ("payments" referring in this context to cash expenditures).
- The Budget Repair Strategy, introduced in the 2014-15 budget, is designed to deliver budget surpluses building to at least 1% of GDP by 2023-24.

While legal limits on the total face value of public debt issued (Commonwealth Government Securities, CGS) have been removed, the Treasurer must still stipulate the maximum face value (currently AUD 500 billion or around 31% of GDP).

Spending-side measures

The main savings measures on the expense side of the 2014-15 budget include:

- indexing the age pension and equivalent payments to the consumer price index (CPI) rather than wages from September 2017, and indexing the Parenting Payment Single by the CPI from 1 July 2014;
- better targeting of family tax benefits;
- continuing the move by the previous Government to increase the age pension eligibility age to 67 years by 1 July 2023, by further increasing it to 70 years by 1 July 2035;
- pausing temporarily indexation of many payments and programmes including: eligibility thresholds for family tax benefit, unemployment benefits; thresholds for the Medicare Levy Surcharge, Private Health Insurance Rebate and most Medicare Benefits Schedule fees; and indexation of Local Government Financial Assistance Grants, Official Development Assistance (ODA) and 112 government administered programmes;
- reducing the footprint of government by streamlining the public sector to focus on areas where Commonwealth Government involvement is necessary; and

- reforming agreements with the States and Territories to reduce growth in Commonwealth funding for schools over the medium term, generating momentum for longer term reforms to be considered in the White Paper on Reform of the Federation and the White Paper on the Reform of Australia's Tax System.

Tax-side measures

The main revenue measure in the 2014-15 budget for improving the bottom line was an income tax surcharge (the Temporary Budget Repair Levy) of 2% for individuals with annual taxable incomes above AUD 180 000. Levied from 1 July 2014 to 30 June 2017, this measure aims to increase revenue by AUD 3.1 billion over three financial years to 2016-17.

Budget costings and execution

The new Australian Government appointed a National Commission of Audit in late 2013 to make recommendations for the 2014-15 budget. The Commission had a broad remit to examine the scope for efficiency and productivity improvements across all areas of Australian Government expenditure, and to make recommendations to achieve savings sufficient to deliver a surplus of 1% of GDP prior to 2023-24. The Government also commissioned a range of reviews in particular sectors, for example higher education and welfare reform.

A new resource management framework under the Public Management Reform Agenda aims to support a productive, innovative and adaptable public sector while retaining robust systems of management and accountability. The framework embodies the principles that performance is more than financial, and that engaging with risk is a necessary step in improving performance. The Auditor-General has new powers to review the appropriateness of performance indicators and how they are reported by public bodies.

Protecting economic growth

To help drive the productivity required to generate longer term economic growth, spending has been refocused on infrastructure, reforms to higher education, and measures to improve incentives to seek employment and training. The 2014-15 budget outlined a major structural reform agenda designed to drive economic growth and create jobs. This included deregulation of higher education institutions, negotiation of free trade agreements with China, Japan and South Korea; measures to increase incentives for all age groups to increase workforce participation; measures to redirect spending from government consumption to capital spending and future medical research; and reductions in industry assistance. In addition, the fiscal strategy provides necessary flexibility for the budget position to vary in line with economic conditions.

Policy priorities

The main priorities in the fiscal plan are: deficit reduction, returning the budget to surplus and reducing the Government's borrowing requirement; re-prioritising spending from government consumption to infrastructure spending; and structural reforms to boost productivity growth in the longer term.

Long-term sustainability and fiscal risks

The fiscal consolidation strategy in the 2014-15 budget is partly designed on the need to ensure the budget is sustainable and avoids leaving Australia vulnerable to external shocks, ill-equipped to cope with population ageing, and increasingly reliant on future generations to pay off debt. Restraining growth in fast-growing programmes such as health and social security and welfare is necessary in part to better prepare for the ageing population. Planned savings from some budget measures remain subject to passage through Parliament; for example, the change in indexation arrangements for age and disability pensions and related payments from 2017-18, and measures to help rebalance health expenditures from the Government to individuals and families.

More generally, the Government publishes regular ten-year projections of major fiscal aggregates, including baselines of cash revenues and expenditures, as well as ten-year structural balance charts. Forty-year intergenerational reports are published every five years to highlight demographic and other pressures to long-term sustainability. From 2014-15, the budget paper "Statement on Risks" includes additional details on loans over AUD 200 million.

Sub-national budgeting

There has been no change to the role of sub-national levels of government in Australia. Contributions to budget repair are expected from all levels of government. There are two major reviews underway – on reform of the Australian taxation system and the reform of the Australian Federation – which may have repercussions for the roles and responsibilities of different levels of government.

Budgetary forecasts and independent oversight

The Parliamentary Budget Office was established in 2012 to prepare policy costings for parliamentarians, to conduct research and analysis on budget and fiscal policy issues, among other tasks.

Engagement of parliament and citizens

The Parliamentary Budget Office has significantly enhanced the capacity of the national parliament to engage in budgetary and fiscal issues, and has improved the transparency and accountability of budget and fiscal frameworks.

The Australian National Audit Office has been piloting and developing citizen input, via its website, to the evidence-collection phase of their performance audits.

Austria

1. Economic situation

Economic growth will remain subdued in 2015, but will strengthen and reach 1.7% in 2016. Going forward, geopolitical and euro-wide developments should support export growth and recovery in investment. The income-tax reform will boost private consumption.

Close monitoring and supervision of banks is essential to revive confidence. Structural reforms in the service sector would boost competition. Further increasing the labour participation of the elderly, and in particular of women, would help make growth more inclusive. Preparations for the planned alignment of women's retirement age with those of men should be brought forward.

Key economic indicators: Austria

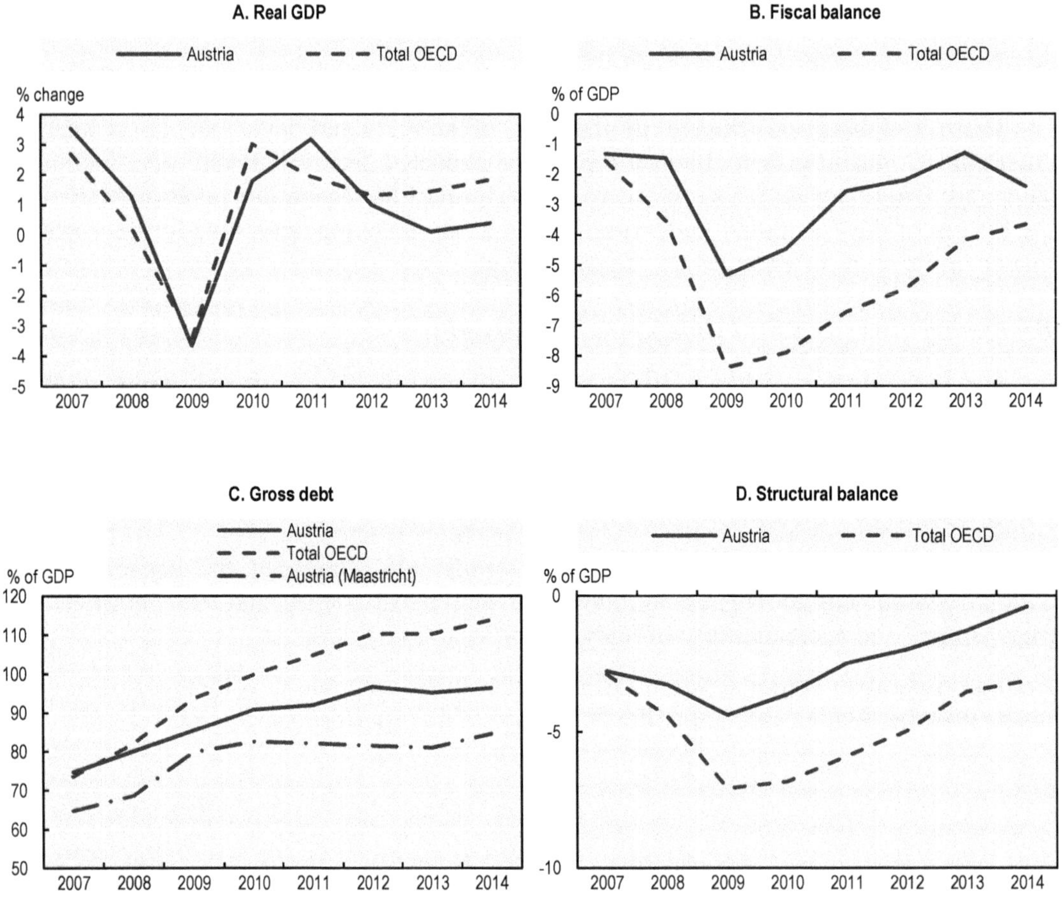

Source: OECD (2015a), "OECD Economic Outlook No. 97 (Edition 2015/1)", *OECD Economic Outlook: Statistics and Projections* (database), http://dx.doi.org/10.1787/data-00759-en.

StatLink http://dx.doi.org/10.1787/888933288031

Investment rates, although declining recently, remain considerably higher than in other European countries, partly because of a higher share of residential construction and transport infrastructure investment. The share of intellectual property investment has risen markedly after the crisis and has partly offset declines in the share of business investments in buildings, structures and information and communication technologies (ICT) equipment. Government initiatives towards the support of venture capital and crowd-funding as well as intense engagement within the European Fund for Strategic Investment have the potential to boost entrepreneurship and business investment.

2. Fiscal policy and budgetary governance

The Austrian Government is pursuing a strategy of growth friendly, fiscal consolidation with a mix of measures on the expenditure and revenue side. It has been subject to the preventive arm of the Stability and Growth Pact since 2014. The European Council recommended that Austria significantly strengthen the budgetary strategy in 2015 to reach and maintain thereafter the medium-term objective, and ensure that the debt rule is met in order to keep the general government debt ratio on a sustained downward path. The fiscal deficit was 5.3% of GDP in 2009 but fell to 1.5% of GDP in 2013. The general government deficit is forecasted to increase in 2014, mainly due to the effect of the establishment of a Liquidation Entity (*Abbaueinheit*) to wind down the impaired assets of the Hypo group Alpe Adria bank (Hypo). The decline in the headline deficit thereafter reflects in large part the diminishing impact of the one-off support to Hypo.

Fiscal objectives

Austria is adhering to a system of multiple fiscal rules comprising the fiscal rules of the strengthened European Stability and Growth Pact (Austria has been subject to the preventative arm of the pact since 2014) and the debt brake rule in the Austrian Stability Pact 2012. As part of this, a balanced general government budget must be achieved by 2016 and a structurally balanced budget by 2017 onwards. The debt brake rule agreed by the Austrian Parliament states that the structural balance of the central government will not be less than -0.35% of GDP. The structural deficit of the public sector amounted to 0.3% of GDP in 2014. In addition, expenditure growth is limited to the growth rate of potential output, with any expenditure above this to be financed by tax-side measures. Debt above the threshold of 60% of GDP has to be reduced by 1/20 annually on a three-year average. In 2014, the general government debt ratio was 84.5% of GDP and fell two percentage points short of expectations (86.5%).

Spending-side measures

The Austrian Government is exercising spending restraint through implementing measures such as:

- a freeze on public sector hiring and moderate wage increases
- reform of administrative bodies
- below inflation increases in pensions and tightened requirements for early old-age pension
- a health reform package
- cutting subsidies to enterprises such as Austria Railway Company.

Tax-side measures

Tax-side measures include taxes agreements with Switzerland and Liechtenstein. The agreement with Switzerland was expected to bring about EUR 1 billion in one-off revenues in 2013. In 2014, the agreement with Liechtenstein was expected to result in one-off revenues of EUR 500 million.

Budget costings and execution

The independent Fiscal Advisory Council, set up in 2013, has a key role in monitoring public budgets in order to strengthen fiscal discipline at the federal level as well as in states and municipalities.

Protecting economic growth

The Austrian Government is strengthening investments in the areas of education, universities, R&D (research and development) and infrastructure to support growth and employment. For example, the Government plans to spend a so-called additional "university-billion" on R&D during 2013-2015. Additional funds are also planned for an extension of all-day care in schools and new secondary schools (*Neue Mittelschule*), research, thermal renovation of housing as well as the care fund.

Policy priorities

The Austrian Government is pursuing a fiscal and economic policy with the objective of attaining sustainable economic growth and a high level of employment. Four key areas have been identified:

- comprehensive tax reform
- consistently proceeding with the successful structural fiscal consolidation
- maintaining structural reforms in the field of public administration, subsidies, pensions and labour market
- strengthening investments in the areas of education, universities, R&D and infrastructure to support growth and employment.

Long-term sustainability and fiscal risks

In June 2015, the Austrian Parliament adopted the Special Pension Scheme Limitation Act. This restricts the maximum level of special pensions and levies existing pensions with pension security contributions. There have also been recent reforms where measures were introduced to increase the retirement age and the participation rate for older employees. The Healthcare Reform Act 2013 also introduced measures to improve the cost effectiveness and sustainability of healthcare and long-term care services.

Sub-national budgeting

The Austrian Stability Pact 2012 regulates the national budgetary co-ordination between the federal government, states and municipalities. The debt brake rule, implemented as part of the Austrian Internal Stability Pact 2012, obliges state and local governments to keep their structural deficit below -0.1% of GDP. States are also implementing budget reform projects. For example, Styria has implemented a budget reform based on the Federal Budget Reform in 2015; Salzburg, Burgenland and Carinthia have decided to join the reform as well. In 2013, the Federal Government, *Länder* and local government associations agreed to explicitly avoid excessive risk in their respective treasuries and to adhere strictly to a risk-averse financial policy. In addition, all *Länder* governments autonomously implemented a ban on speculation of public entities.

Economic forecasting

Regulation (EU) No. 473/2013 requires the draft budget to be based on independently endorsed or produced macroeconomic forecasts. The macroeconomic forecast underlying the Draft Budgetary Plan has been produced by the Austrian Institute of Economic Research (WIFO). It has been a long-standing practice in Austria that the Ministry of Finance bases its fiscal plans on the macroeconomic forecast produced by the Institute. WIFO is a non-profit association and its governing board is composed of representatives of non-governmental organisations (NGOs), financial institutions, the Austrian National Bank, business associations, academia as well as representatives of the central and regional government.

Engagement of parliament and citizens

Austria has no particular initiatives in place to enhance the inclusiveness or participative nature of the budget process.

The government's planned fiscal consolidation: Austria

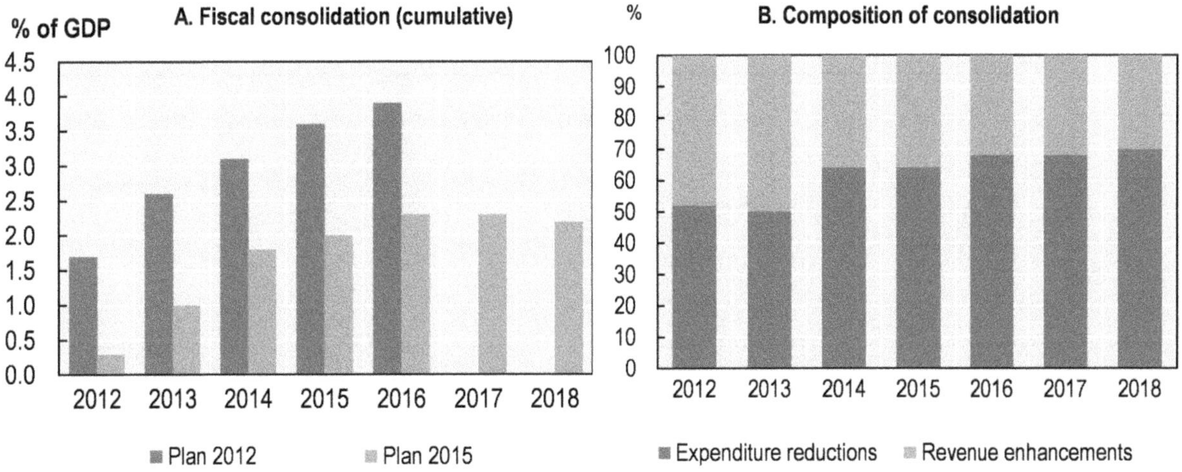

Source: OECD (2015b), *State of Public Finances Survey 2015*; OECD (2011), *Restoring Public Finances*, www.oecd.org/gov/budgeting/47558957.pdf.

StatLink http://dx.doi.org/10.1787/888933288362

Belgium

1. Economic situation

The recovery is projected to gradually strengthen. Economic growth is expected to broaden with rising exports and business investment owing to supportive financial conditions and improving external demand. Household consumption growth will be held back by fiscal consolidation and wage restraint. Inflation will pick up somewhat in 2016 as the effects of falling oil prices wear off.

Fiscal consolidation is set to resume, mainly on the spending side. Further structural reforms to secure fiscal sustainability and promote employment and competitiveness should be pursued, such as increasing the effective retirement age, reforming wage setting and shifting the tax burden from labour to less growth distortive taxes, such as consumption and environmental taxes.

Investment in the aftermath of the crises has been stronger than in other euro area countries. While recovery in business investments is set to continue, public investment remains subdued and low in international comparison, reflecting needed fiscal consolidation. However, further cuts to infrastructure spending may undermine future growth.

Key economic indicators: Belgium

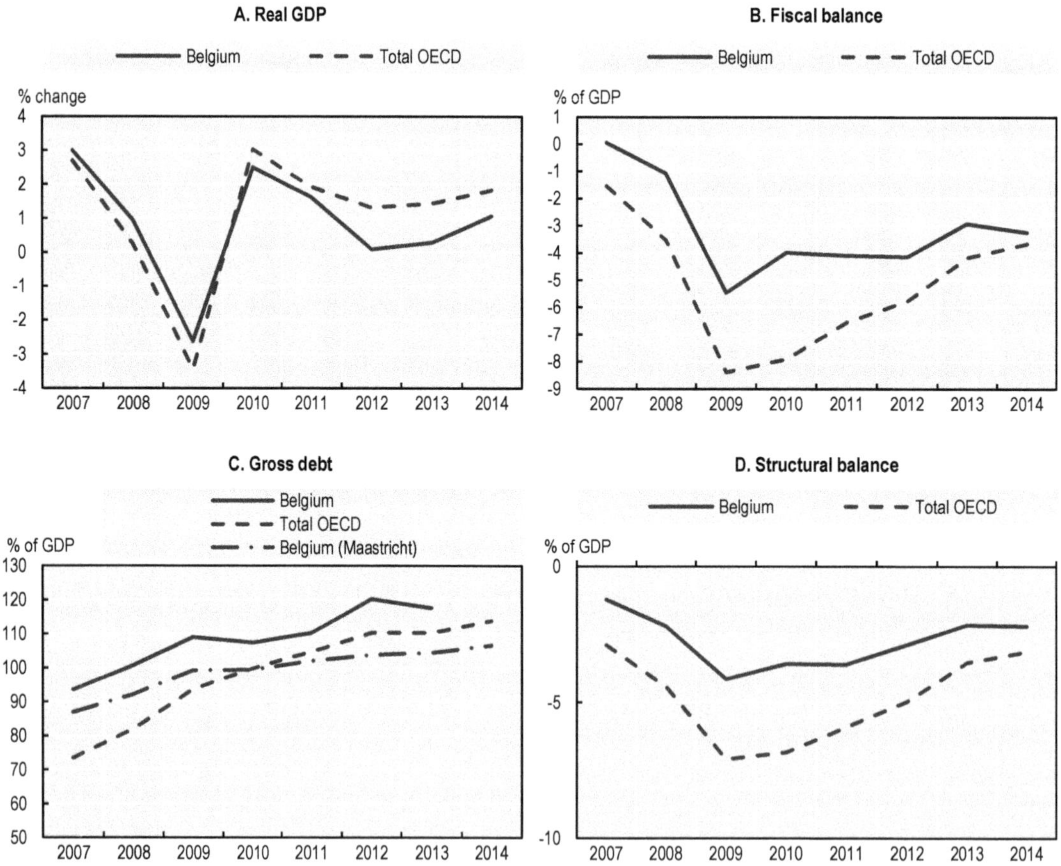

Source: OECD (2015a), "OECD Economic Outlook No. 97 (Edition 2015/1)", *OECD Economic Outlook: Statistics and Projections* (database), http://dx.doi.org/10.1787/data-00759-en.

StatLink http://dx.doi.org/10.1787/888933288042

2. Fiscal policy and budgetary governance

The Belgian Government adopted a new fiscal plan in October 2014, covering the five year period to 2018. The fiscal deficit reached -5.5% of GDP in 2009 but has since been reduced (to -2.9% of GDP in 2013) and the plan outlines measures to achieve fiscal balance by 2018. To safeguard economic growth, expenditure reductions are being carried out cautiously and are focused on non-distorting areas.

Fiscal objectives

It is the objective of the Belgian Government to achieve fiscal balance (0% of GDP) by 2018. The ratio for fiscal consolidation for the period 2015-18 is 70% expenditure reductions, 30% revenue enhancements. This represents a growing emphasis on expenditure reductions relative to fiscal consolidation in recent years.

Spending-side measures

Fiscal consolidation is largely to be achieved through expenditure reductions. The federal government is reducing public expenditure, both in public service departments and in social security. Specific measures include:

- linear cuts to central government expenditure and a limited replacement rate of civil servants
- closer monitoring of expenses
- downward revision to health expenditure growth
- stricter conditions for some social benefits and reform of the pension system.

In addition, the regions and communities have announced a series of expenditure cuts.

Tax-side measures

Measures that will reduce revenues include suspension of the wage indexation mechanism and transformation of welfare adjustments of social benefits into a tax credit. Measures that will increase revenues are some indirect tax hikes and an advanced taxation of pension savings. There is a broader aim to simplify the tax system by reducing exemptions. Additionally, the Government is planning a tax shift away from labour to other sources of income.

Budget accounting and execution

Following the European legislation, a monthly reporting has been put in place.

Protecting economic growth

The fiscal consolidation plan has been adapted in response to lower than expected economic growth, with drastic fiscal consolidation measures being avoided. In addition, the Government has taken several measures to lower the cost of labour relative to neighbouring countries and promote economic growth. This includes suspending the wage indexation mechanism and reducing the employer contribution to social security from 33% to 25%. Wage moderation is key in the government policy. To this end, the federal government is pursuing a wage policy that does not hamper growth and increases the competitiveness of Belgian companies.

Policy priorities

Five priorities stand out in the coalition agreement:

1. sustaining the economy through lowering the cost of labour
2. reforming the pension system
3. making the labour force more flexible
4. fighting social and fiscal fraud
5. reducing public expenditure, both in service departments and in social security.

Long-term sustainability and fiscal risks

The new government is reforming the pensions system to reduce spending associated with an ageing population. This includes increasing the pensionable age and tightening conditions for full pension allowances. Through the fiscal consolidation path, the high level of the debt ratio is to be reduced. The low interest rates have been a windfall in the past few years. There is a risk of increasing interest rates in the medium-term future, but if the debt ratio can be reduced as planned, this risk can be contained.

Sub-national budgeting

New mechanisms to co-ordinate fiscal policy across different levels of government have been introduced. A co-operation agreement has been concluded between the federal government and the different regional governments to co-ordinate the fiscal consolidation process. The High Council of Finance (an independent institution) proposes a fiscal consolidation path for both central and regional governments. There is also a consultation procedure in place to ensure that regional governments are involved in formulating the general fiscal consolidation path. As a result of the recent sixth state reform, regions and communities are responsible for a higher budget as competences have been transferred from the central to the regional level. As such, the sub-national levels can pursue their own policies in the newly acquired fields.

Economic forecasting

The independent Federal Planning Bureau produces macroeconomic forecasts. Both the federal government and the communities and regions base their budget forecasts on these figures. Recent history shows that the macroeconomic forecasts are not significantly skewed in one way or another.

Engagement of parliament and citizens

Belgium has no particular initiatives in place to enhance the inclusiveness or participative nature of the budget process.

The government's planned fiscal consolidation: Belgium

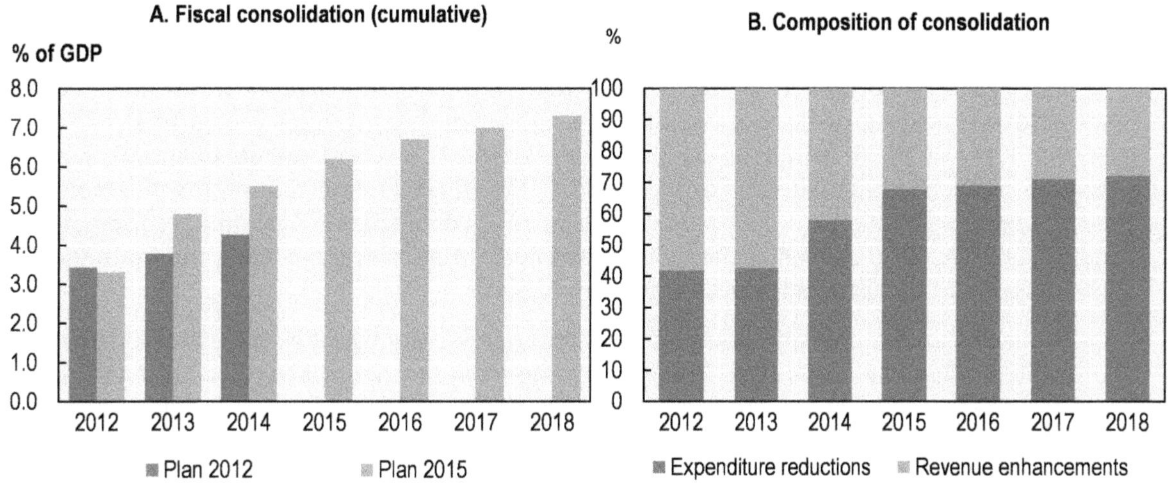

Source: OECD (2015b), *State of Public Finances Survey*; OECD (2011), *Restoring Public Finances,* www.oecd.org/gov/budgeting/47558957.pdf.

StatLink http://dx.doi.org/10.1787/888933288374

Canada

1. Economic situation

Since the acute economic shock of 2009, Canada's economy has proven resilient and has enjoyed steady growth over recent years. However, growth is projected to slow to around 1.1% in 2015 before rising slightly in 2016. The recent fall in oil prices has resulted in declines in related investment and GDP. However, substitution towards non-energy exports is underway, supported by the currency depreciation and stronger foreign-market growth. With economic slack fully absorbed, inflation is projected to return to the 2% midpoint of the inflation target range by mid-2016.

Monetary accommodation is assumed to be progressively withdrawn from early 2016 to counter inflationary pressures. High household debt and house prices pose financial-stability risks, and further macro-prudential measures may be required should these risks increase. Fiscal consolidation will need to continue as planned. Barriers to foreign direct investment should be reduced.

Key economic indicators: Canada

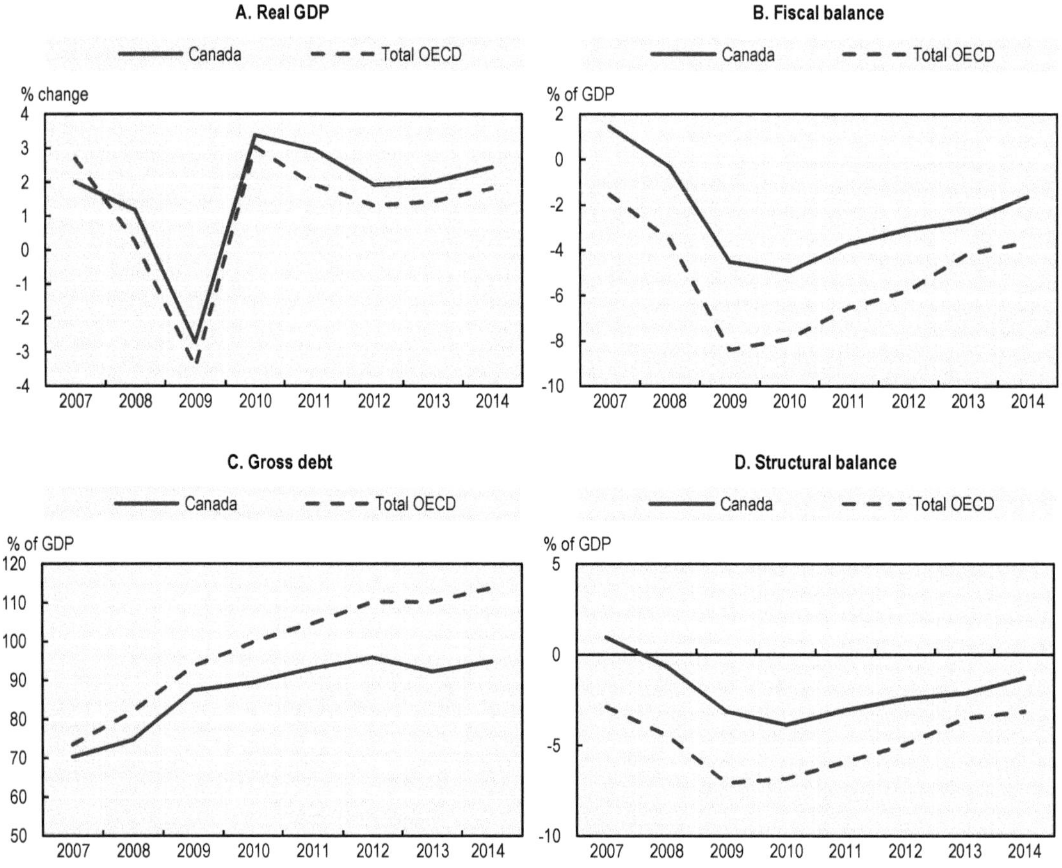

Source: OECD (2015a), "OECD Economic Outlook No. 97 (Edition 2015/1)", *OECD Economic Outlook: Statistics and Projections* (database), http://dx.doi.org/10.1787/data-00759-en.

StatLink http://dx.doi.org/10.1787/888933288051

2. Fiscal policy and budgetary governance

The Canadian Government has pursued a three-fold approach to restoring public finances since its 2010 budget, centred on:

- gradual withdrawal of the exceptional fiscal stimulus measures, which were introduced to deal with the global economic crisis
- targeted programme spending cuts
- comprehensive efficiency review of public administration.

On this basis, the deficit has been scaled back from its peak level of CAD 55.6 billion (in 2009-10) to CAD 5.2 billion in 2013-14. It is notable that this broad approach has been maintained, re-stated and refined over recent years.

Fiscal objectives

In the overall context of the above three-pronged strategy, new, clear fiscal objectives have been laid down. In October 2013, the Government set itself the target of a federal debt level of 25% of GDP by 2021; and in February 2014, it confirmed the objective of eliminating the federal deficit and returning to balanced budgets in fiscal year 2015-16.

Spending-side measures

In achieving targeted spending reductions, Canada's approach to comprehensive review is of particular note.

- Under the **Strategic Review** process (introduced in 2007 as part of Canada's Expenditure Management System), public bodies were required to propose reallocations of 5% of their expenditure from lowest priority, lowest performing areas to other areas. The Strategic Reviews in the years up to 2010 yielded annual savings of CAD 2.8 billion.
- This process was elaborated into a one-year **Strategic and Operating Review,** introduced in 2011, to place a greater focus upon administrative and efficiency savings. The results of this exercise, announced in Budget 2012, are credited with annual savings of CAD 5.2 billion by 2014-15, representing 6.9% of an aggregate review base of CAD 75.3 billion.
- An **operating budget freeze** was introduced in 2011-12 for two years, then again in 2014-15 for another two years, alongside close monitoring of compensation costs. This measure will require departments and Crown corporations to place a greater focus on achieving internal efficiencies.

Taken as a whole, the Government credits the expenditure-restraint measures with cumulative savings of over CAD 104 billion in the period 2010-11 to 2019-20.

Tax-side measures

Spending measures have been complemented with measures aimed at promoting the fairness, integrity and neutrality of the tax system, notably through addressing "international aggressive tax avoidance"; ensuring fair treatment as between personal and business income; strengthening tax compliance and removing tax breaks from certain trusts and estates.

Budget costings and execution

The Government has established a Costing Centre of Expertise to strengthen the ability to contain costs and increase its ability to challenge costings. In addition, it has improved the quality of costing information produced by departments through prescribing more stringent Chief Financial Officer attestations.

Protecting economic growth

Fiscal consolidation has been focused upon reducing the cost of government operations without reducing programmes that support services or economic capacity. Accordingly, the Government has been able to continue to launch major investments in infrastructure to stimulate growth. Moreover, the capital budgeting framework has been enhanced through a new "capital carry-forward" facility, which gives departments and agencies more predictability and flexibility in budgeting and project schedules.

Policy priorities

The Government's over-arching priority is to return to balanced budgets by 2015, as a basis for supporting jobs and growth. Other key sectoral priorities are identified by the Government as follows:

- creating and protecting jobs and economic growth
- training a highly skilled workforce
- supporting advanced research and innovation in support of a vibrant entrepreneurial culture
- reducing red tape and the regulatory burden faced by businesses
- conserving Canada's natural heritage and developing natural resources in a responsible way
- encouraging trade and foreign investment in Canada's manufacturing sector
- investing in public infrastructure including under the New Building Canada Plan – the largest long-term federal investment in infrastructure in Canada's history – and a new Public Transit Fund
- additional support for families through tax reductions and benefit increases
- managing public sector compensation costs, including through modernising the government's disability and sick-leave systems, and transitioning to equal cost-sharing for retired employees in public healthcare.

Long-term sustainability and fiscal risks

Since 2012, the annual Update of Economic and Fiscal Projections includes an annex of long-term fiscal projections to illustrate the sustainability of public finances over time. In Budget 2012, the Government announced an increase in the age of eligibility for state pensions from 65 to 67 years. The latest assessment of risks to the fiscal projections is also provided in each annual update.

Sub-national budgeting

Canada's Provincial and Territorial governments are largely autonomous. The federal government provides significant fiscal support through large-scale transfers such as Equalization, the Canada Health Transfer and Canada Social Transfer, and the Gas Tax Fund, in accordance with federal/provincial and territorial agreements.

Economic forecasting

Since 1994, the economic forecast underlying Canada's fiscal projections is based on an average of private-sector economic forecasts. For the 2015 Economic Action Plan, the Government maintained a downward adjustment for risk to the private sector forecast of nominal GDP over the 2015-16 to 2019-20 period to account for continued uncertainty in the global economic outlook. This adjustment results in a set-aside for contingencies of CAD 1.0 billion per annum over the period 2015-16 to 2017-18, CAD 2.0 billion in 2018-19 and CAD 3.0 billion in 2019-20. If this prudent set-aside is not required for such contingencies, the Government has committed to using these funds to lower the federal debt.

As regards to an independent assessment of the fiscal position, in 2006 legislation was passed to establish the position of Parliamentary Budget Officer (PBO). The mandate of the PBO, under establishing legislation, is to provide independent analysis to the Senate and the House of Commons on the state of the nation's finances, the Government's estimates and trends in the Canadian economy; and upon request from a committee or parliamentarian, to estimate the financial cost of any proposal for matters over which Parliament has jurisdiction.

Engagement of parliament and citizens

To promote the quality of scrutiny and debate by parliament, and accessibility to the public, the Government of Canada has adopted the following measures:

- The Estimates (Budget) documents have been streamlined, with detailed supporting information moved to electronic annexes.
- Introduction of a new "departmental highlights" section in the Main Estimates, to assist in focusing the debate.
- Introduction of a standardised format for the *Reports on Plans and Priorities* and the *Departmental Performance Reports,* and reporting on programme performance to the lowest level of programmes.
- Publication of departmental accrual-based future-oriented financial statements.
- The Government has also released an online searchable database (InfoBase) that allows public access to summary financial information and integrates key elements of financial reporting documents in a single location.

The government's planned fiscal consolidation: Canada

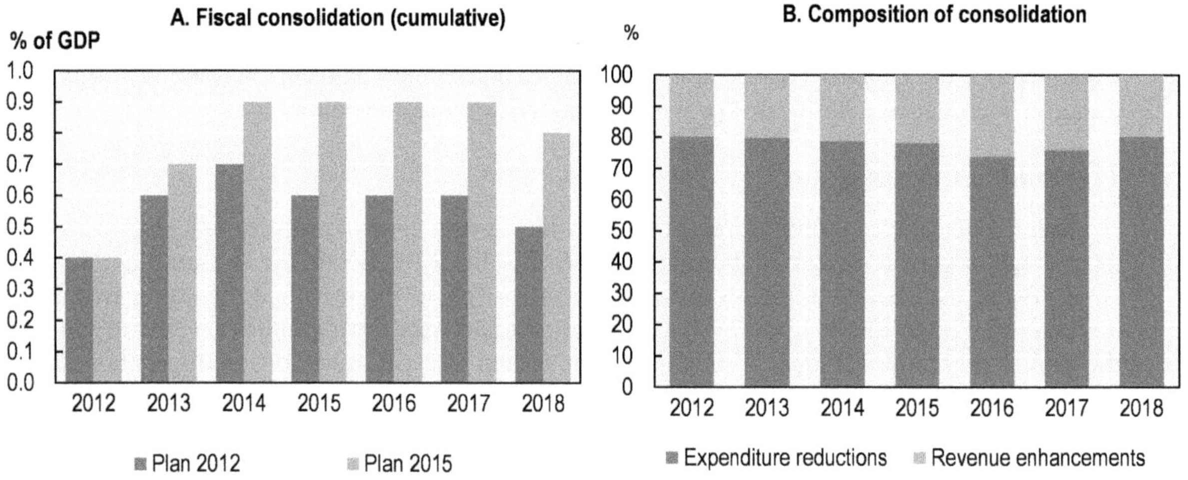

Source: Government of Canada (2015), *Economic Action Plan 2015*, http://actionplan.gc.ca/en; OECD (2015b), *OECD State of Public Finances Survey*; OECD (2011), *Restoring Public Finances*, www.oecd.org/gov/budgeting/47558957.pdf.

StatLink http://dx.doi.org/10.1787/888933288385

Chile

1. Economic situation

After a sharp slowdown in 2014, the economy is projected to recover gradually in 2015 and 2016. The pick-up in activity will initially be driven by higher public spending, but will increasingly be supported by stronger external demand for industrial goods from the United States and Europe.

As the exchange rate has stabilised, inflation is moderating, although it remains above the central bank's target band. Since inflation expectations remain well anchored, monetary policy can continue to support growth in the near term, before moving to a more neutral stance as growth strengthens. The underlying stance of fiscal policy is expected to be expansionary in 2015, but then to become neutral in 2016 as the government remains committed to achieve a zero structural balance by 2018.

The large decline in copper prices in the aftermath of the commodity super-cycle has affected the investment plans of mining companies, which have significantly reduced investment since 2012. Therefore, advancing the Productivity Agenda, which is meant to broaden the base of the economy, is essential. Structural reforms to open markets further to competition will be particularly important to boost investment outside the mining sectors, increasing and making growth more inclusive.

Key economic indicators: Chile

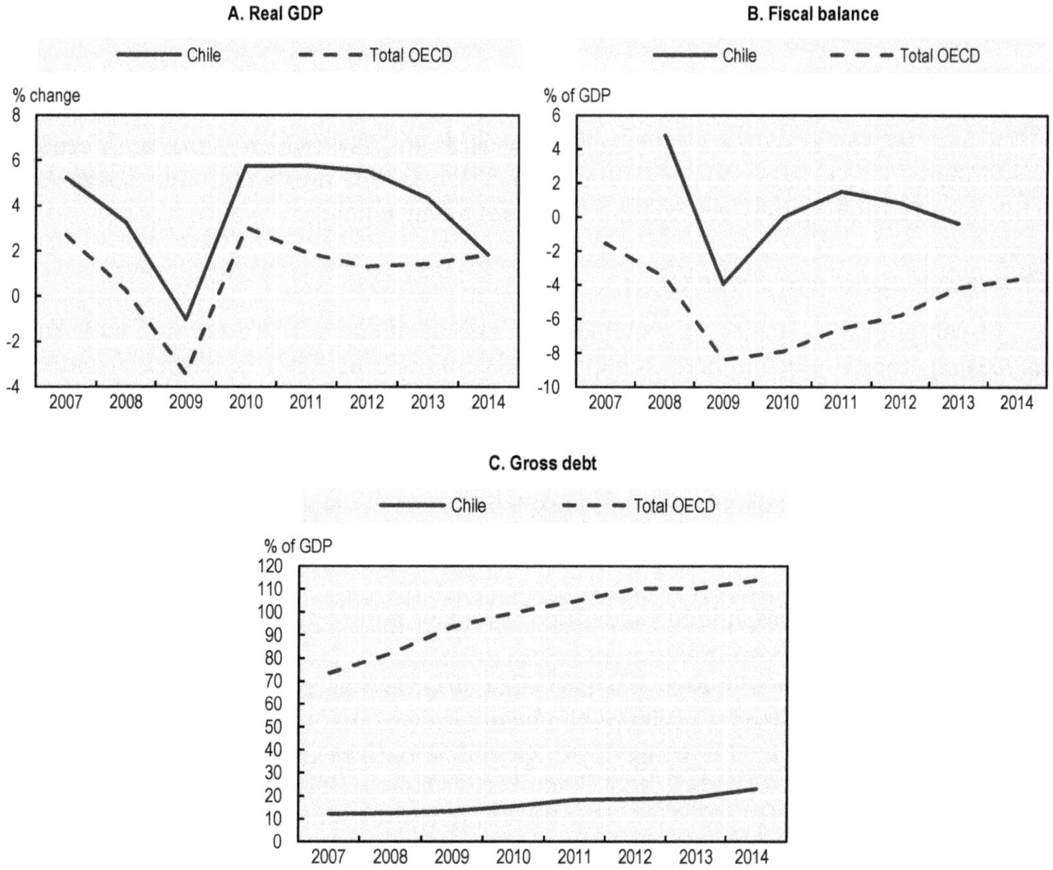

Sources: OECD (2015a), "OECD Economic Outlook No. 97 (Edition 2015/1)", *OECD Economic Outlook: Statistics and Projections* (database), http://dx.doi.org/10.1787/data-00759-en, OECD (2015c), *Government at a Glance 2015*, OECD Publishing, Paris. DOI: http://dx.doi.org/10.1787/gov_glance-2015-en. StatLink http://dx.doi.org/10.1787/888933288065

2. Fiscal policy and budgetary governance

Against the background of the Fiscal Responsibility Law (2006), Chile has a tradition of a strong "fiscal anchor" in its budgetary management. However this tradition was tested as Chile's public finances swung from a high fiscal surplus of almost 5% of GDP in 2008 to a deficit of almost 4% of GDP in 2009 – an example of a strong surplus, accumulated during a period of cyclical strength, being retained for use in a counter-cyclical manner in the face of a severe downturn. Since then the fiscal balance has been brought under control and the Government of Chile has reiterated fiscal sustainability as a key element of overall policy.

Fiscal objectives

In its Fiscal Policy Decree No. 892 of 2014, the Government of Chile has laid down a clear policy objective of achieving a structural fiscal balance (0% of GDP) by 2018. This, in addition to the Structural Balance Rule limiting annual expenditure according to long-term growth projected, shapes the path of expenditure until 2018.

Spending-side measures

While the previous administration had in place an expenditure growth rule (capping expenditure growth by reference to GDP growth), the current government is focusing instead on the structural balance rule, the fiscal discipline framework committed and the structural balance goal for 2018.

Tax-side measures

A tax reform measure was brought forward in 2014 which aims to incentivise expenditures in education (there is draft legislation in this area) and other social areas, while also facilitating the over-arching structural balance goal.

Protecting economic growth

Fiscal policy in Chile has included a strong focus on preserving, and indeed increasing, capital expenditures in support of economic activity, in particular since the weak GDP growth, most marked from 2012. From 2014, the execution of investment programmes has been accelerated in line with the Government's "Productivity, Innovation and Growth Agenda". The 2015 budget provides for a 27.5% increase in capital investment, compared with 6.4% growth in current expenditures.

Policy priorities

The Government of Chile has identified, as a key policy priority, the need to address inequalities in society and promote inclusive growth. The policy agenda to address this challenge has been broad-based, but particular priority has been afforded to education reform and the strengthening of the public health system. Existing budgetary reallocation tools have been used in this context; no special initiatives and procedural innovations have been introduced.

Long-term sustainability and fiscal risks

Since the introduction of the Fiscal Responsibility Law in 2006, Chile produces an annual analysis of long-term sustainability challenges, in particular those arising in the expenditure areas of education, health and pensions, where demographic factors are projected to play a significant role over coming decades.

Sub-national budgeting

The Government of Chile is currently preparing a law to improve the budgetary management of its regions, and ensure compatibility of their fiscal policies with broad national requirements.

Economic forecasting

A Fiscal Advisory Council (the CFA) was established in 2013 to provide technical advice to the Government about structural balance calculations (including on any proposed changes to the calculation methodology), as well as to provide advice more generally to the Minister of Finance on fiscal matters.

Engagement of parliament and citizens

Chile has no particular initiatives in place to enhance the inclusiveness or participative nature of the budget process.

Czech Republic

1. Economic situation

The economic expansion has gained momentum, driven by domestic demand. Renewed consumer confidence and income growth are supporting consumer spending, while public spending and an improving outlook are raising investment. Stronger growth in trading partners will drive further growth in exports. Global commodity price falls have temporarily reduced inflation but rising domestic cost pressures will push it towards the target during 2016.

Monetary policy is expected to remain very expansionary to ensure that inflation moves towards the 2% target. The exchange rate should be allowed to float freely again when deflationary risks have largely receded. Fiscal policy is expected to tighten slightly in 2016. Structural reforms to promote competition and reduce skill mismatches in the labour market would raise incomes and make growth more inclusive.

Business investment began recovering in 2014. This upswing is being spurred by accommodative financial conditions. Public investment is currently boosted by efforts to use expiring EU funds. Given the infrastructure gap, effective use of these funds could raise productivity and incomes.

Key economic indicators: Czech Republic

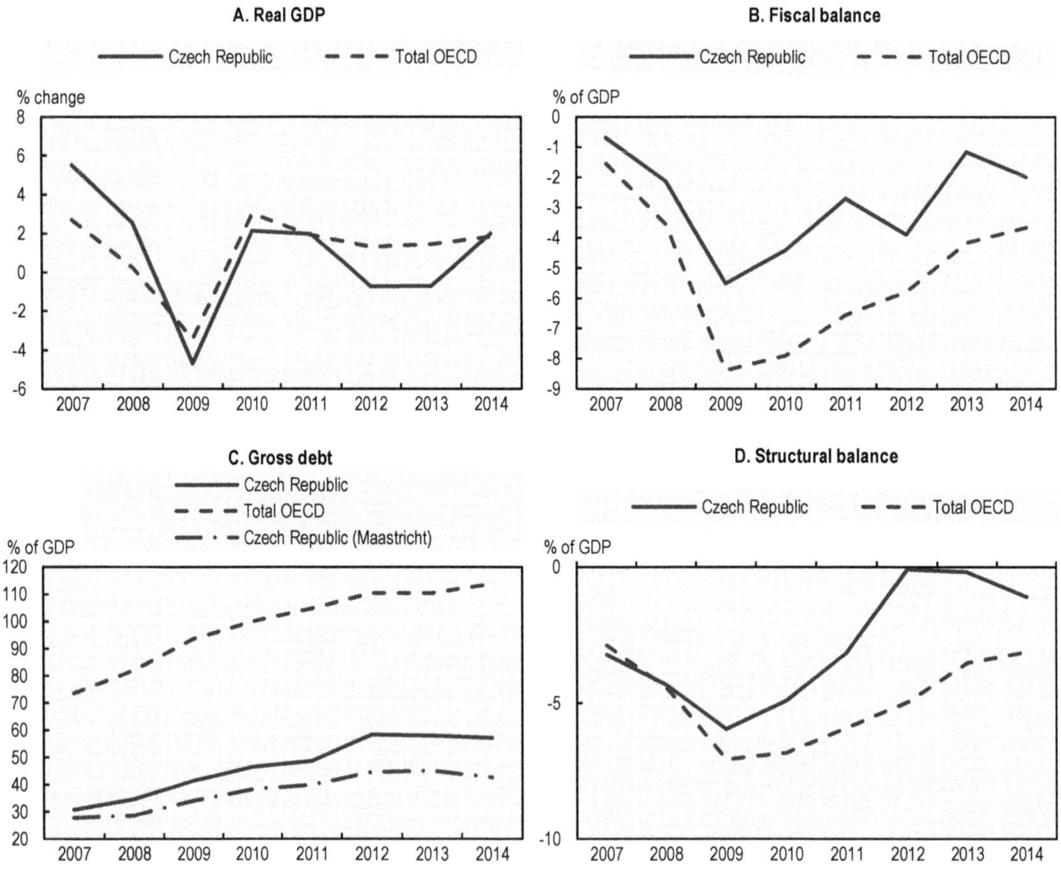

Source: OECD (2015a), "OECD Economic Outlook No. 97 (Edition 2015/1)", *OECD Economic Outlook: Statistics and Projections* (database), http://dx.doi.org/10.1787/data-00759-en.

StatLink http://dx.doi.org/10.1787/888933288071

2. Fiscal policy and budgetary governance

The Czech Government succeeded in bringing its "excessive deficit" below the European Union's key 3%-of-GDP threshold in 2013, from a high of 5.5%-of-GDP in 2009. However, the fiscal consolidation measures were seen domestically as harmful to economic growth, resulting in a deeper negative output gap. The new Czech Government has adopted a "pause" in fiscal consolidation in order to support economic recovery, mainly by increasing the volume of expenditures in "pro-growth" areas.

Fiscal objectives

In line with its policy of paused fiscal consolidation, the Czech Government is prepared to see the government deficit rise once again from 1.2% of GDP in 2013 to 1.9% by 2015. However, the Government's forecasts envisage a steady tapering of the deficit back to 0.6% of GDP by 2018. The decrease implies a decline in the deficit adjusted for the business cycle and one-off and temporary measures from 1.5% of GDP in 2016 to 1.1% of GDP in 2018, which virtually corresponds to the medium-term budgetary objective. Instead of a numerical fiscal target *per se,* the government is prioritising fiscal policy principles including the effectiveness of tax collection and tackling of tax evasion. The intention is that this approach will boost growth and at the same time contribute to positive fiscal effort.

Spending-side measures

The focus of the Government's macro-fiscal policy action lies in the expenditure sphere. The key adjustments in public expenditure fall mainly in the following areas:

- the ending of a wage bill freeze
- the ending from 2015 of a restriction on indexation of pensions
- additional funding for public investment
- offsetting the above spending increases with operational efficiencies including reduced spending on external IT and other consulting services
- the inclusion of liquidity from the treasury system in financing the state budget deficit
- the state central purchasing system.

Tax-side measures

The Czech Government has no plans to alter personal income tax (PIT) or social security contributions, which will thus develop in line with the growth of the wage bill in the economy (or above it, if combating tax evasion is effective in boosting the revenues from PIT, CIT and social contributions). However, some proactive tax policies have been announced:

- a strong focus on measures to combat tax evasion
- introduction of a second reduced value-added tax (VAT) rate of 10% (in addition to the existing rates of 21% and 15%)
- cancellation of previously announced reforms to direct taxes and payments

- termination of the recently introduced "pension savings pillar", for reasons of principle as well as low take-up.

Protecting economic growth

The Czech Government's approach is distinctive in that the achievement of fiscal policy objectives has explicitly been displaced as a policy goal, in favour of the adoption of a fiscal policy stance that more directly supports economic activity and growth.

Policy priorities

With the pause in expenditure consolidation, no measures have been put in place in the Czech Republic to reallocate funds from low-priority to higher-priority areas. The fight against tax evasion is the main priority of the current coalition government and it is the basis from which the whole tax administration concept will in principle develop. The main measures should include electronic VAT reporting and fiscalisation of cash payments (electronic evidence of sales). At the same time, other systematic steps are being taken to increase the effectiveness of the activities of financial administration, both in its organisation and in the proposal of legislative measures on tax regulation. On the expenditure side, according to Resolution of the Government No. 924/2014, the purchase of specific commodities, starting from 2016, should be carried out through the state central purchasing system. Participation in this system will be obligatory (respecting certain limitations) for central bodies of state administration and their subordinate organisations.

Long-term sustainability and fiscal risks

Reforms to the pension system were approved with effect from 30 September 2011. These include modifying the reduction thresholds when calculating pensions (in a budgetary neutral manner), shifting the statutory retirement age without a fixed upper limit and, at the same time, removing benefits for women with children (i.e. a uniform retirement age will be applied to all people born in a certain year).

Sub-national budgeting

Up to now, sub-national levels of government have enjoyed constitutional autonomy over fiscal policy. However, those prerogatives will be circumscribed in the near future with the adoption of a Constitutional Act on Fiscal Responsibility and the Act on Rules of Fiscal Responsibility, which will implement the EU Council Directive 2011/85/EU.

Economic forecasting

The Czech Republic does not have any institutionalised mechanisms for independent input into economic policy forecasting, assessment or advice. A non-political National Economic Council was established in 2009 to channel advice to the Government, but it is inactive. A National Fiscal Council will be provided for under the fiscal responsibility legislation outlined above. To ensure that fiscal planning is founded on realistic macroeconomic and budgetary forecasts based on the most probable or more prudent scenario, the draft Act on the Rules of Fiscal Responsibility proposes to establish a Committee for Fiscal Forecasts.

Engagement of parliament and citizens

The Czech Government has an open data portal (http://data.mfcr.cz) and a website which provides accessibility of budget data and documents to the public. Government strategic documents (e.g. Convergence Programme) are discussed in Parliament during the commentary procedure. Since 2014 the Ministry of Finance has issued a "Citizens Budget" brochure, presenting the budget in a manner that is understandable and accessible to the public. It is divided into two parts: the glossary of key terms of budget is introduced in the first part, followed by the simplified version of the state budget for each year.

The government's planned fiscal consolidation: Czech Republic

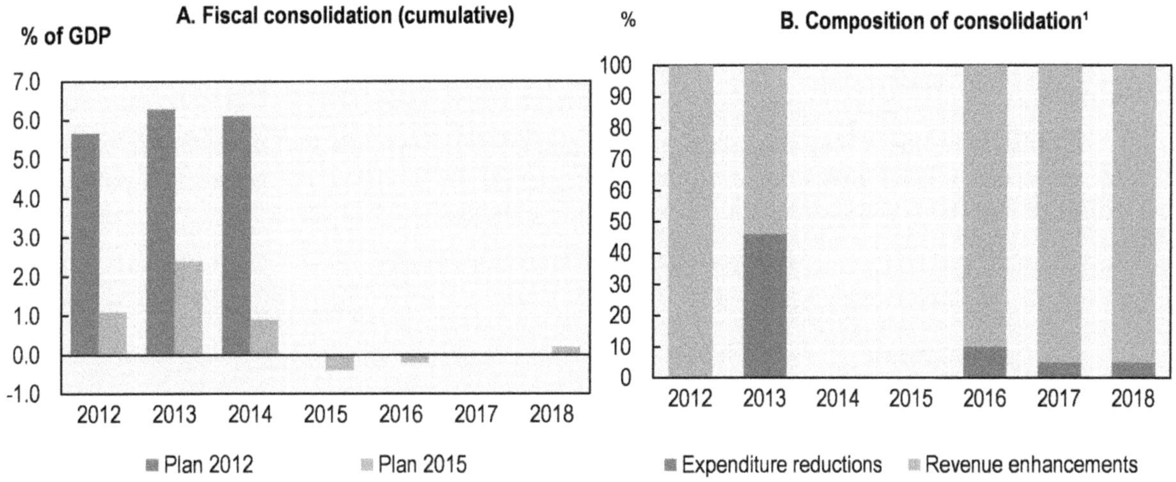

Note[1]: No composition of consolidation data for 2014 and 2015

Source: OECD (2015b), *OECD State of Public Finances Survey 2015*; OECD (2011), *Restoring Public Finances*, www.oecd.org/gov/budgeting/47558957.pdf.

StatLink http://dx.doi.org/10.1787/888933288399

Denmark

1. Economic situation

Economic growth is projected to rise to 1.9% this year and 2.3% in 2016, thanks to improved trade prospects, a weaker effective exchange rate, lower energy prices and easing financial conditions. Improved confidence, recovering house prices and a savings surplus in the private sector will underpin gathering momentum in business investment and private consumption.

Very accommodative monetary policy continues to ease access to credit, but it could also result in house prices that exceed fundamentals. To maintain macroeconomic stability, the authorities should bring forward the planned restoration of the link between property value and taxation, currently scheduled for 2020. As planned, the current supportive fiscal policy needs to move to a neutral stance with the recovery of the economy.

Public investment that supported growth during the downturn will decline gradually to pre-crisis levels. Investment opportunities could be boosted by further structural reforms, such as policies enhancing competition in domestic services.

Key economic indicators: Denmark

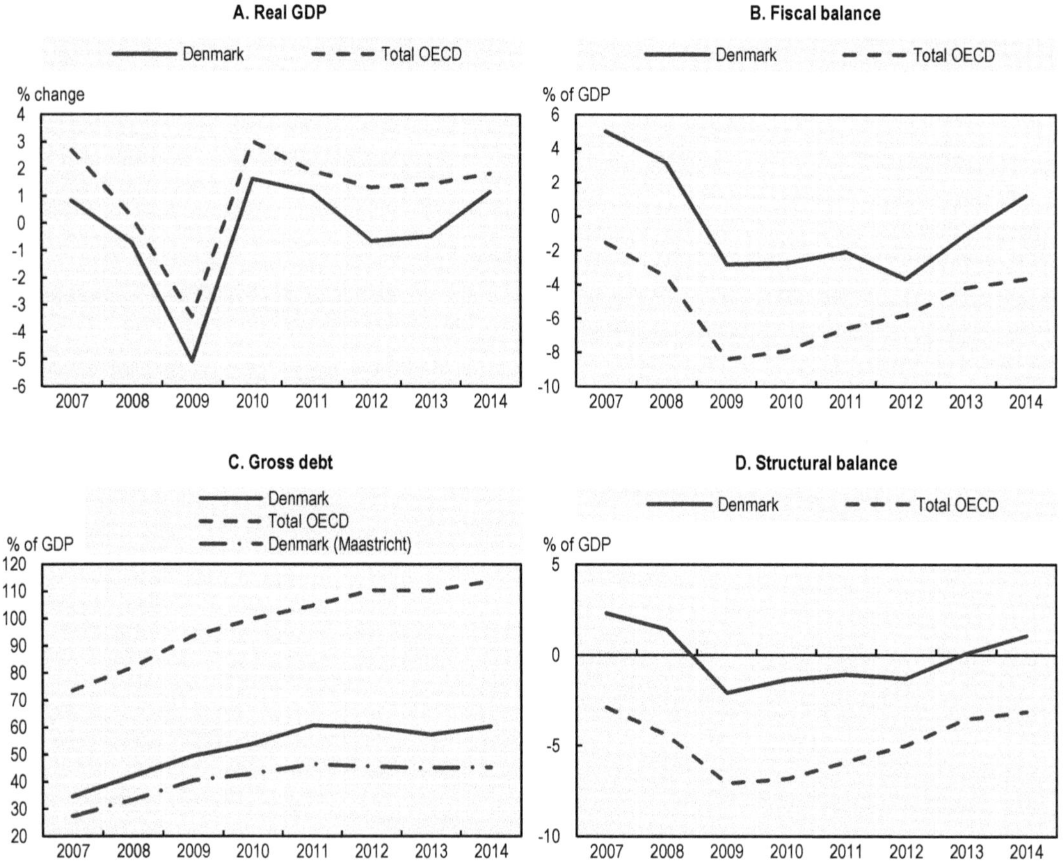

Source: OECD (2015a), "OECD Economic Outlook No. 97 (Edition 2015/1)", *OECD Economic Outlook: Statistics and Projections* (database), http://dx.doi.org/10.1787/data-00759-en.

StatLink http://dx.doi.org/10.1787/888933288089

2. Fiscal policy and budgetary governance

The Danish Government's "2020-plan", coupled with the 2012 Budget Law, is based upon three elements:

- positive indicator of fiscal sustainability
- annual structural deficits of no more than 0.5% of GDP
- a target for structural budgetary balance by 2020.

While not a member of the eurozone, Denmark is subject to the EU Treaty deficit limit of 3% of GDP. Denmark's budget balance swung from a surplus of over 3% of GDP in 2008 to a deficit of almost the same magnitude in 2009 as a result of the financial crisis. Over the period 2011-13, fiscal policy was conducted in accordance with the EU Recommendation under the Excessive Deficit Procedure, which included a primary requirement to bring the general government budget deficit below 3% of GDP by 2013 and furthermore to improve public finances in structural terms by 1.5% of GDP in total. Subsequently these requirements were judged to have been met and the Excessive Deficit Procedure was abrogated by June 2014. In response to the fiscal and economic crisis, the Danish parliament passed a Budget Law in 2012 which enshrines the new fiscal framework.

Fiscal objectives

As outlined above, the Government's fiscal policy is heavily accented towards clear fiscal rules, as the Budget Law embodies the key elements of the European Fiscal Compact Treaty, including: a budget balance requirement (i.e. annual structural budget deficit of no more than 0.5% of GDP); and an automatic correction mechanism in case of a "significant deviation" (i.e. a deviation of at least 0.5% of GDP) from this objective. Since 2014, the Budget law has begun to play a determining role in the shaping of medium-term fiscal policy. In this overall context, the Danish Government has adopted a target of gradual achievement of a structural balanced budget by 2020.

Spending-side measures

The Budget Law introduced binding multi-annual expenditure ceilings for each level of government. For the period 2014-18, the ceilings have been set to allow for moderate growth, consistent with the achievement of a balanced budget by 2020.

Tax-side measures

Tax measures were an integral part of fiscal consolidation over the period 2011-13. For instance personal income tax thresholds were not indexed. Subsequently, specific taxes and duties have been reduced in a fully financed manner, e.g. the corporate tax rate is being gradually reduced from 25 % in 2013 to 22 % in 2016.

Protecting economic growth

Public investment in Denmark has been maintained at relatively high levels by historical standards. This is credited by the Government as helping to sustain levels of economic activity during the acute phase of the downturn. More broadly, policy initiatives in sectoral areas such as social housing and energy are seen by the Government as supportive of the overall economic investment climate. In addition, a number of structural reforms – e.g. the Retirement Reform 2011 and Tax Reform 2012 – have been adopted, which should contribute positively to potential growth and economic activity in the medium and long term.

Policy priorities

In May 2012, the Danish government introduced a medium-term fiscal strategy ("Denmark employed – challenges to the economy towards 2020") which – in addition to identifying fiscal policy objectives – created a framework for the challenges faced by the Danish economy. These challenges related to weak competitiveness, demographic trends, and the need for economy in the public sector. This plan has been updated by the Danish Government's overall economic plan of February 2013 – "Growth Plan DK" – which contains a reform track aimed at improving economic dynamism thereby increasing structural GDP by DKK 40 billion towards 2020 and modernising the public sector, with the aim of freeing up a large volume of resources (DKK 12 billion) in the period to 2020 for reallocation to other priority areas.

Long-term sustainability and fiscal risks

The Retirement Reform measures, adopted in 2011, remain the foundation of recent fiscal sustainability reform in Denmark. Under these measures, the increase in formal retirement ages has been brought forward, and other eligibility restrictions have been introduced.

Sub-national budgeting

With the introduction of the 2012 Budget Law, the annual financial agreement between the Government and the Danish regions and municipalities must comply with the expenditure ceilings for sub-national levels of government. Within these limits, these levels of government maintain their autonomy in determining levels of service. The expenditure ceilings are supported with sanction mechanisms.

Performance budgeting

New non-binding guidelines for performance management were issued by the Danish Ministry of Finance in September 2014.

Resource flexibility

The Budget Circular 2014 introduces some additional constraints on access by line ministries to carryover appropriations from the previous year.

Economic forecasting

Medium-term fiscal plans continue to be prepared by the Danish Ministry of Finance, but the Budget Law introduces a "precautionary principle" whereby the medium-term projections can only take account of the effect of structural reforms and other budget-improving initiatives that have the support of a majority in Parliament – and which therefore have a realistic chance of being effected. As a separate part of the Budget Law the independent Economic Council (established in 1962) was given a new role as a "Fiscal Watch Dog". The Economic Council is obliged by law to make an annual assessment of public finances, including assessing whether fiscal policy is on a long-term sustainable path or not and monitoring compliance with the expenditure ceilings.

Engagement of parliament and citizens

Denmark has no particular initiatives in place to enhance the inclusiveness or participative nature of the budget process.

The government's planned fiscal consolidation: Denmark

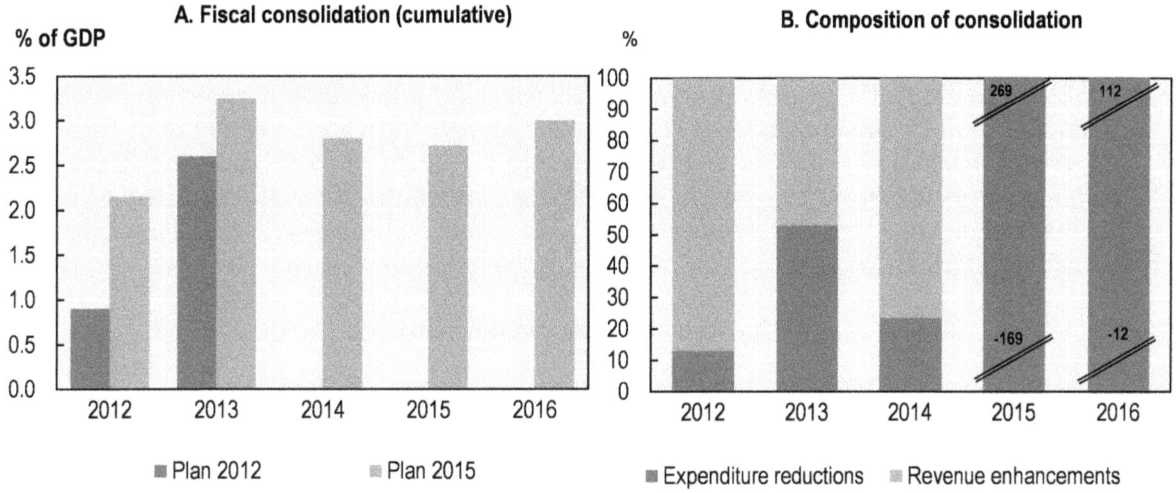

Source: OECD (2015b), *OECD State of Public Finances Survey 2015*; OECD (2011), *Restoring Public Finances*, www.oecd.org/gov/budgeting/47558957.pdf.

StatLink http://dx.doi.org/10.1787/888933288408

Estonia

1. Economic situation

Economic growth is projected to strengthen gradually. Strong wage growth will fuel private consumption and investment will recover somewhat. Export growth will pick up only slowly, however, hampered by weak economic growth in some of Estonia's main trading partners.

The Government's fiscal stance is expansionary, but public debt remains very low. Reducing the high structural surplus would be appropriate to finance medium-term fiscal priorities, including education and infrastructure spending. Lower taxes on labour earnings, in particular on low earnings, would raise growth by stimulating employment. To raise productivity, structural reforms need to focus on improving skills and knowledge transfer to Estonian firms.

Key economic indicators: Estonia

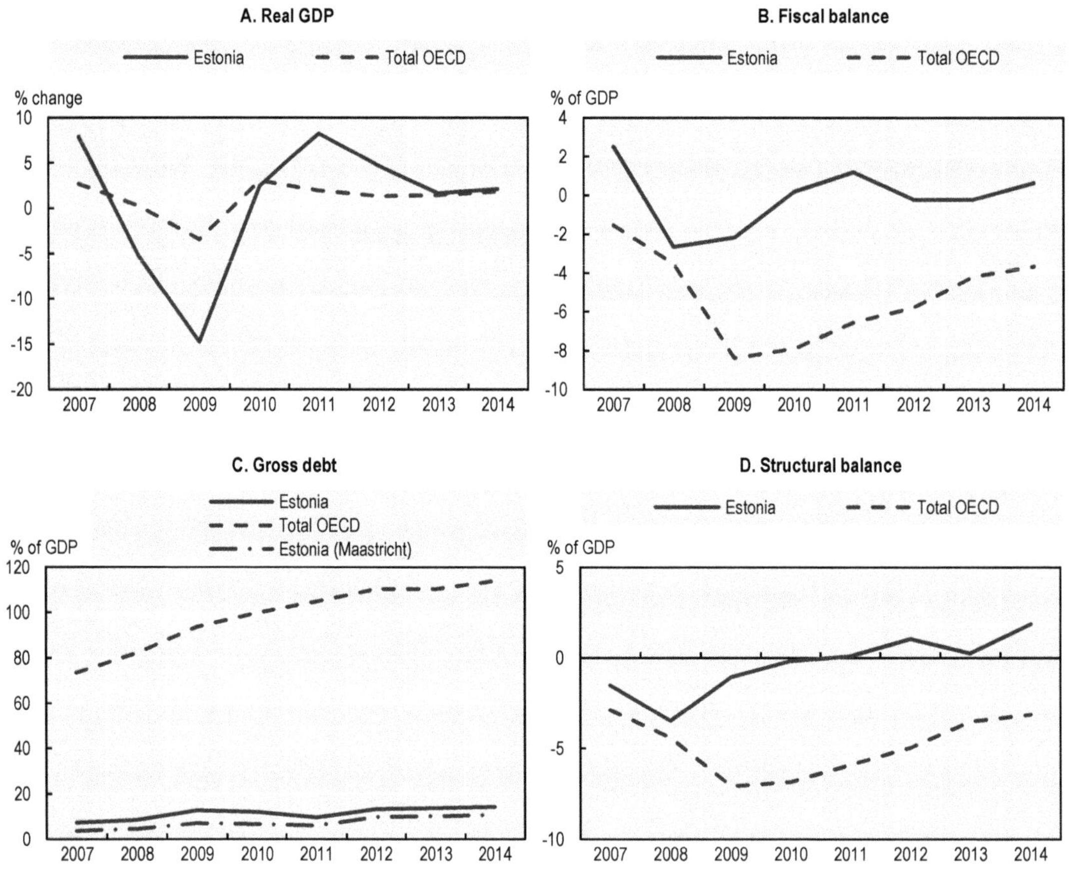

Source: OECD (2015a), "OECD Economic Outlook No. 97 (Edition 2015/1)", *OECD Economic Outlook: Statistics and Projections* (database), http://dx.doi.org/10.1787/data-00759-en.

StatLink http://dx.doi.org/10.1787/888933288098

The investment-to-GDP ratio declined in recent years, despite robust GDP growth. Uncertainty, in part due to heightened geopolitical tensions, is holding back business investment. Public investment has also weakened as transfers from the European Union have fallen temporarily and projects funded via earlier sales of Kyoto permits are being phased out. More investment to expand access to European transport networks and energy supply would improve medium-term growth prospects.

2. Fiscal policy and budgetary governance

Estonia had a general government fiscal deficit of 3.6% of GDP in 2008. The general government balance returned to a surplus in 2010 and 2011 before becoming a deficit again in 2012 and 2013. However, the structurally adjusted budgetary position of general government has been in surplus since 2009 and is projected to be 0.8% of GDP in 2015. Debt levels are comparatively low with general government gross financial liabilities standing at 13.5% of GDP in 2013. Because of this fiscal position, the Estonian Government does not have a fiscal consolidation plan. However, the Government aims to exercise a conservative fiscal policy to maintain the structural balance as this is deemed necessary for the future growth and competitiveness of the economy.

Fiscal objectives

Estonia is subject to the preventive arm of the Stability and Growth Pact and should ensure sufficient progress towards its medium-term budgetary objective (MTO). The MTO set in 2007 is to have a general government structural surplus. Since 2009, after the global economic crisis the budgetary position of general government has been in structural surplus, and thus this rule has been met. The strengthening of the binding nature of expenditure ceilings in the medium-term budgetary framework and/or the introduction of multi-annual expenditure rules has not yet been achieved. A new state budget law was adopted in 2014 to improve fiscal planning and introduce the requirements of the EU's improved fiscal governance framework.

Spending-side measures

On the expenditure side, the total incremental deficit-increasing effect of discretionary measures decided in the context of the Estonian Draft Budgetary Plan 2015 is 0.2% of GDP in 2015. Measures mostly focus on the expenditure side. These include reform of the ability to work programme (Unemployment Insurance Fund) and the growth of state defence expenditures.

Tax-side measures

The Estonian Draft Budgetary Plan 2015 included two measures which have an impact on revenues; the raising of state duties (which is anticipated to have a positive budgetary impact) and rescheduling of dividend distribution from state-owned enterprises from 2014 to 2015 (which is anticipated to have a negative impact on the budget in 2014, but a positive impact in 2015).

Budget costings and execution

The 2014 new state budget law introduced provisions for an independent fiscal council and improved budget processes.

Protecting economic growth

The National Reform Programme "Estonia 2020" was approved in 2011 and it describes the objectives for 2015 and 2020 established to improve competitiveness. The two central objectives of the programme are increasing the productivity and employment in Estonia. The main focus in the coming years is on education and employment, with an emphasis on integration of long-term and young unemployed people in the labour market and on the development of their skills.

Policy priorities

Estonia 2020 sets out that the Government aims to have a sustainable and adaptive public sector. Priorities of Government policy are:

- reaching a government sector budget surplus by 2014 and maintaining this position in the long term
- improving the sustainability of social expenditure in the public sector in the face of decreasing working-age population and ageing population, ensuring effective healthcare and well-oriented and effective social policy (including the necessary support services)
- continuing a budgetary policy that supports competitiveness (high level of productive expenses, increased flexibility, controlling public sector wage costs, planning the local government revenue base in state budget strategy)
- continuing the gradual reduction of taxes on labour and profits and to increase taxes on consumption and use of natural resources
- avoiding macroeconomic imbalances.

Long-term sustainability and fiscal risks

In Estonia as in other developed countries, one challenge is ensuring long-term financial capability for public social spending. In order to develop continuous financing of the social insurance system, it will be analysed further how to develop possible changes in health insurance, pension insurance and unemployment insurance, including in the context of developing a new scheme for capacity for work. To keep otherwise capable and well-trained people active in the labour market and aim resources at providing other social services, it would be expedient to review the special pensions system and to reduce or abolish the old-age pensions under favourable conditions. Likewise, the general pension age reform decided in late 2009 is being implemented.

Economic forecasting

The Ministry of Finance prepares the macroeconomic forecast but the 2014 new state budget law introduced provisions requiring the officials preparing the forecasts to operate independently. The Government states that the objectivity and independence of the forecast is assured through the transparency of the forecast process, involvement of different outdoor economists and through continuous comparison of forecasting results. For example, the preliminary version of forecast is discussed with the forecasting team of Bank of Estonia. The main assumptions and results are also discussed in joint seminar with different forecasters of Estonia, who belong to the central bank, commercial banks and other institutions dealing with economic analysis. There are approximately ten institutions taking part in this seminar. In addition, the Fiscal Council provides its opinion on the macroeconomic forecast within two weeks of its publication.

Engagement of parliament and citizens

Estonia has no particular initiatives in place to enhance the inclusiveness or participative nature of the budget process.

Finland

1. Economic situation

Economic growth is projected to resume in 2015 after three years of contraction. Nevertheless, sluggish incomes and high unemployment will continue to weigh on private consumption and remaining spare capacity will delay investments. A pick-up in exports on the back of the global economic recovery and the weaker euro should progressively spill over to the domestic economy.

The fiscal deficit exceeded 3% of GDP in 2014 for the first time since the mid-1990s and is expected to fall only slowly. The new government will need to restore fiscal sustainability without prejudice to the recovery. Structural reforms to raise employment and public-service efficiency will be essential.

Business investment is expected to recover slowly, as demand picks up and capacity utilisation rises. Slow income growth, high unemployment and uncertainty hold back residential investment despite low borrowing costs. Public investment has been steadily growing since 2010 and will rise further in 2015, but is then set to weaken as fiscal constraints tighten.

Key economic indicators: Finland

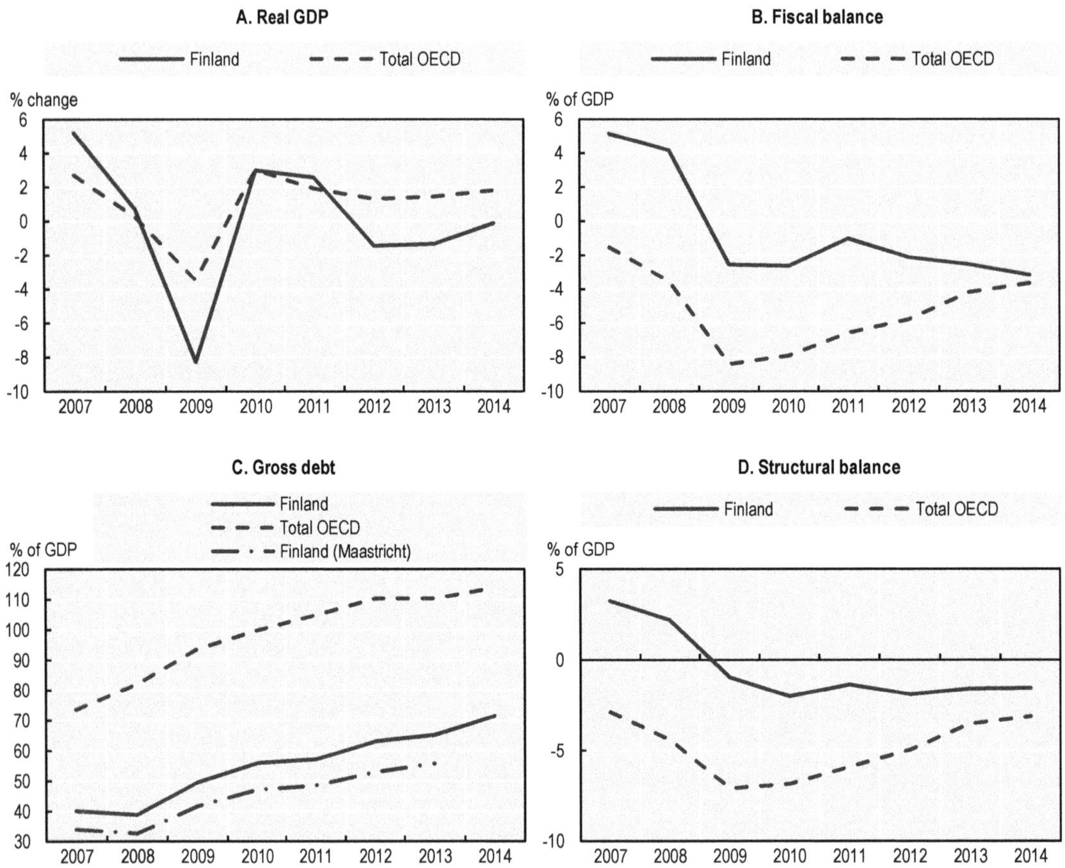

Source: OECD (2015a), "OECD Economic Outlook No. 97 (Edition 2015/1)", *OECD Economic Outlook: Statistics and Projections* (database), http://dx.doi.org/10.1787/data-00759-en.

StatLink http://dx.doi.org/10.1787/888933288105

2. Fiscal policy and budgetary governance

As in the case of several other OECD countries, Finland's fiscal balance swung from an apparently strong surplus (over 4% of GDP) in 2008 to a large deficit (around 2.5% of GDP) in 2009. The government that assumed office in late 2011 focused fiscal policy upon achieving a downward trajectory of the debt ratio, but progress has been difficult to achieve and the fiscal position remains challenging. Following the leadership re-shuffle in 2014, the newly constituted government maintained the Fiscal Plan 2015-18 that had been adopted in April 2014. A notable feature of Finland's approach to fiscal consolidation has been the political co-ordination within the coalition government via the *sekstetti*, i.e. the conciliar "sextet" of government party leaders.

Fiscal objectives

The Finnish Government aimed to bring the central government debt-to-GDP ratio onto a downward path by the end of its term. That objective has proven difficult, in the face of contracting economic growth. As a signatory to the European Fiscal Compact, Finland adopted domestic legislation which requires the setting of a medium-term fiscal objective close to balance (the target has been set at 0.5% of GDP) and the maintenance of a tightening fiscal stance until this objective is achieved. This legislation (the FIPO Act) took effect from the start of 2013.

Balance of spending-side and tax-side measures

After assuming office in 2011, the Finnish Government focused upon "spending limits decisions" (originally introduced in 2003) each spring to govern medium-term expenditure policy for central government (a four-year future horizon). These decisions were re-visited each year, as consolidation efforts have been intensified and to reflect policy reprioritisations in favour of supporting growth (see below). The Fiscal Plan (adopted in April 2014) adopts a general government perspective, in line with the requirements of EU rules. A spending review was conducted in spring 2011 but during the government's term (2011-15), decision making has not relied upon specific spending reviews. A new, more comprehensive spending review was finished in spring 2015 and is being used to inform government negotiations.

For most of the Government's mandate (2011-14) the intention was to share the burden of fiscal adjustment in central government finances 50:50 between tax increases and expenditure reductions; however, in practice revenue measures have had the dominant effect during these early years, with expenditure measures coming on stream from 2015 onwards. For general government, tax increases have formed the majority of fiscal adjustment, largely due to increases in social security contributions and local government taxes.

Protecting economic growth

Recognising the need to offset the pro-cyclical tendencies of a contractionary fiscal policy, the general government Fiscal Plan of April 2014 – which replaced the previous annual "spending limits decision" – included a "growth package". The centrepiece of this package was the generation of one-off revenues of EUR 1.9 billion (from sale of state assets/equity holdings) and the allocation of one-off extra expenditure of EUR 750 million in 2014-15. The extra expenditure includes investments in future growth industries, export activities and universities, as well as traditional "job-friendly" investments in transport infrastructure.

Policy priorities

The high-level government priorities adopted at the outset of the Government's mandate in 2011 have remained broadly stable. The priorities identified by the newly configured government in 2014 were as follows:

- reducing poverty, inequality and social exclusion
- consolidating public finances
- promoting sustainable economic growth, employment and competitiveness
- implementing the Structural Policy Programme to bridge the sustainability gap in public finances.

Long-term sustainability and fiscal risks

The Finnish Ministry of Finance has calculated that a "sustainability gap" of 5% of GDP exists by reference to projections for 2019 – i.e. that government finances must be adjusted by this amount to bring them into balance. The bulk of this sustainability gap is attributable to age-related expenditure, and it is notable that the old-age dependency ratio is projected to increase to 45% in 2030, from 25% in 2008. Pension reform is scheduled for implementation from the beginning of 2017 that will reduce the sustainability gap in public finances by around one percentage point. It is projected that the reform will both increase the employment rate and reduce pension expenditure.

To bridge the remaining sustainability gap, the Finnish Government 2013 introduced a structural policy programme aimed at "bridging the sustainability gap" in the public finances. Key elements of this broad-based programme are:

- efficiencies in local government sector and improvement in financial management, including a requirement to balance local government finances
- productivity growth in the provision of public services, including through healthcare and social welfare reform
- extending the length of working careers and thus the supply of work
- work incentives and other active labour-market policies aimed at reducing structural unemployment
- structural economic reform (competition, reduction of regulation, etc.) to enhance the output potential of the economy.

Sub-national budgeting

As indicated above, the Finnish Government has aimed to implement measures which will lead to balancing of local government finances. These measures involve a scaling back in the functions of municipalities, expenditure reductions and efficiencies, and a new steering system for local government finances (to take effect from 2015). In light of these reforms, the incoming Finnish Government will be in a position to set budgetary targets for general government as a whole, as well as setting targets for each level of government. In this context, the central government is going to set a maximum limit for changes in local government finances arising from central government measures. However, the budgetary objectives set in this way apply to the local government sector as a whole and are not binding on individual municipalities.

Economic forecasting

An independent Economic Policy Council was set up in 2014 with the task of assessing economic policy and the extent to which the fiscal policy objectives are being met. In addition, the national audit office has been given the new task of monitoring overall compliance with the procedural and regulatory requirements of the FIPO Act.

Engagement of parliament and citizens

Finland's budget information is now available in open data format (.csv and .xls) and the budget overview is available to citizens in a tablet-friendly version.

The government's planned fiscal consolidation: Finland

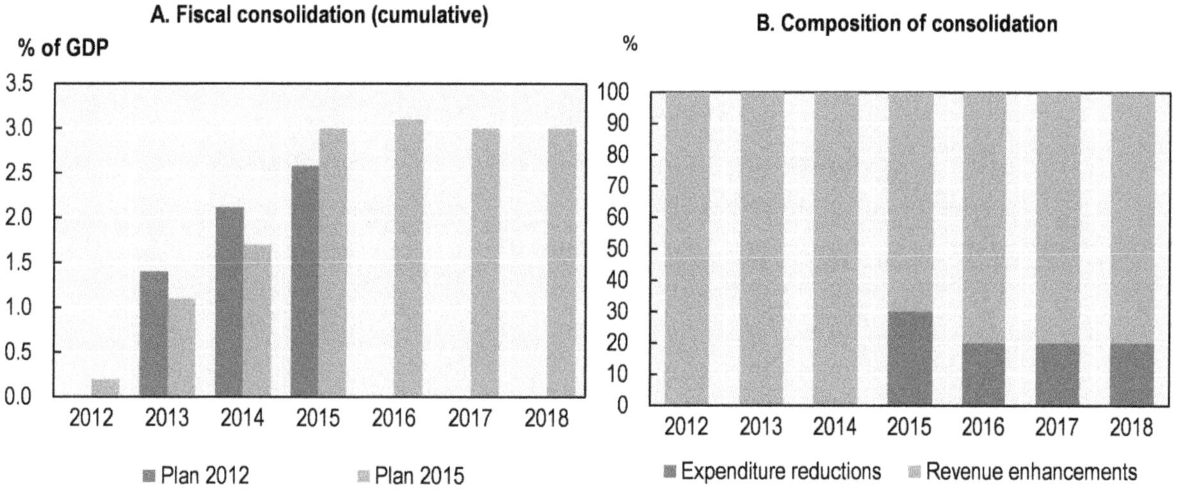

Source: OECD (2015b), *OECD State of Public Finances Survey 2015*; OECD (2011), *Restoring Public Finances*, www.oecd.org/gov/budgeting/47558957.pdf.

StatLink http://dx.doi.org/ 10.1787/888933288411

France

1. Economic situation

Economic growth is projected to gain momentum in 2015 and 2016. Lower energy prices, improving financial conditions, slowing fiscal consolidation, strengthening external demand and a pro-competitive reform agenda should underpin an increase in consumption and export volumes. Weak business confidence entails a delayed pick-up in hiring and only marginal decline in unemployment.

Budget deficit reduction over 2015-16 will be based on spending restraint, while revenues are set to decline. The resulting structural consolidation, amounting to 1% of GDP over the two years, needs to be strictly adhered to if France is to achieve its deficit objectives, the automatic stabilisers should be allowed to play freely to avoid endangering the recovery.

The low pace of investment puts France's competitiveness at risk, though business managers foresee a moderate expansion of capital formation in 2015-16, partly boosted by ongoing structural reforms. Public investment will remain weak due to lower transfers to local authorities.

Key economic indicators: France

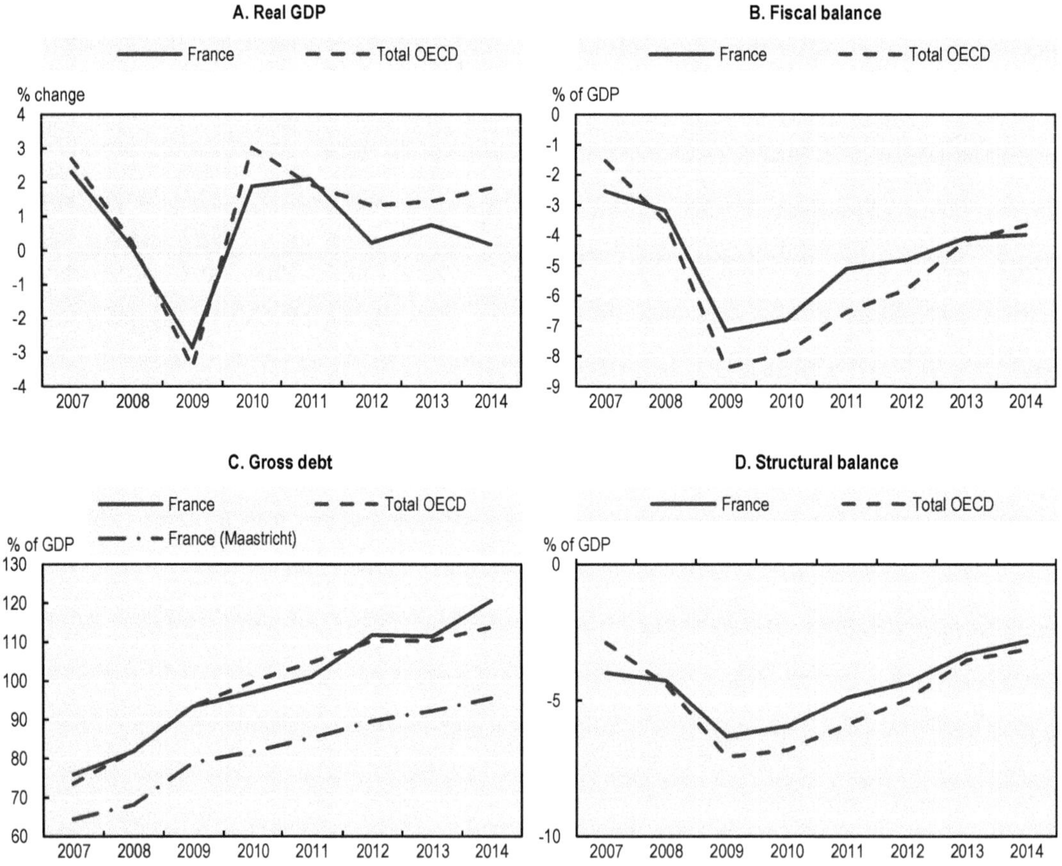

Source: OECD (2015a), "OECD Economic Outlook No. 97 (Edition 2015/1)", *OECD Economic Outlook: Statistics and Projections* (database), http://dx.doi.org/10.1787/data-00759-en.

StatLink http://dx.doi.org/10.1787/888933288118

2. Fiscal policy and budgetary governance

France was running a large fiscal deficit of around 2.5% of GDP in 2007, before the global financial and economic crisis, and its fiscal position worsened over subsequent years, with the deficit reaching around 7% of GDP in 2009-10. Since then, the headline deficit has been reined in towards 4% of GDP by 2014; with economic growth remaining moribund and inflation low, the underlying structural fiscal effort has been greater still. The French Government has recently sought to couple gradual fiscal consolidation with structural economic reforms to promote dynamism and competitiveness. A notable institutional feature of France's fiscal consolidation is the Government Expenditure Strategy Council *(Conseil stratégique de la dépense publique),* a top-level government committee instituted in January 2014 and headed by the president to identify comprehensive government-wide savings. A notable structural feature is the reliance upon medium-term expenditure caps and ceilings.

Fiscal objectives

The 2012 Institutional Act on Public Finance Governance applies the core EU fiscal governance requirements in French domestic law, notably the requirement to set down a medium-term fiscal target in the Multiannual Public Finance Planning (MPFP) Bill covering at least three years. While the French Government is committed to bringing public finances into structural balance in the medium term, in practice the Government has pursued a multi-dimensional economic strategy, which seeks to balance steady fiscal consolidation, shielding of domestic consumption, and structural economic reform. France is currently under the EU "excessive deficit procedure" under which it must commit to bringing its headline deficit below the 3%-of-GDP EU ceiling by a certain date; although in practice the EU institutions have acknowledged the French Government's multi-dimensional agenda by affording it extensions of the correction deadline. As of 2014, France was committed to correct the excessive deficit (i.e. to bring it below 3% of GDP) by 2015; however that deadline has since (April 2015) been extended further to 2017.

As regards the fiscal discipline elements of the economic strategy, France has put in place a strengthened complex of fiscal rules since 2011, with a strong focus on expenditure limits:

- The expenditure ceiling for central government (the *norme de dépenses),* originally introduced in 2004, has been significantly strengthened in its application; the annual budgetary bills lay down this ceiling which may not be exceeded without supplementary legislation.
- In determining the *norme de dépenses,* the MPFP Act 2014-19 hardens the "zero nominal growth rule": Government expenditures stemming from pension, debt service and transfers to local authorities will decrease, in real terms, by EUR 0.8 billion by 2017. In addition, aggregate government spending (including pensions and debt service) must not exceed the growth rate of inflation ("zero real growth rule"). Taken together, these rules impose a tight limit on spending growth, and require that any additional savings from debt-servicing costs, etc. must go towards deficit reduction rather than towards increased expenditure.

- For each policy area within the *norme de dépenses,* the ceiling cap applies over a three-year period. These sectoral cappings may change during the period but only if a new bill modifies them.
- For social security and healthcare expenditures, "ceilings" (or rather targeted upper bounds) are in place. The healthcare ceiling *(objectif nationale d'évolution des dépenses d'assurance maladie* or ONDAM) is subject to close monitoring to maintain expenditure within its bounds. A committee is specifically in charge of this monitoring, and, in the event of a forecast of important deviation (superior to 0.75% of the initial target), measures are to be implemented to maintain health expenditure under their ceiling. Thanks to this procedure, the ONDAM target has been met since 2010, even if it is not legally binding and can be overshot without any supplementary legislation.
- This target specifically pinpoints operating expenditure to encourage their reduction in order to maintain the level of local administration investments. This ceiling is regarded as a governance and good practice measure, and is therefore not legally binding.

Spending-side measures

Over the period 2010-13, public expenditure was protected in real terms and did not contribute to France's "fiscal effort". For 2014, the balance of fiscal effort was moved towards the expenditure side, with EUR 15 billion of broad-based reductions in operating expenditures and in subsidies/benefits, and additional measures amounting to EUR 5 billion implemented via three supplementary bills.

Based upon the deliberations of the top-level Government Expenditure Strategy Council, substantial consolidation measures of EUR 50 billion are laid down for the period 2015-17 in the Multiannual Public Finances Act 2014-19 – of these savings, 40% are front-loaded to the 2015 budget. However, it is notable that these substantial savings are not all allocated to deficit reduction, but a large element is reallocated towards a growth-enhancing package of measures (see below). In achieving the overall EUR 50 billion savings, a general government approach is adopted as follows:

- EUR 19.3 billion from central government and agencies: notably through pay restraint, efficiency gains, shared services and across-the-board reductions.
- EUR 10.7 billion from local government, with central government transfers reduced by this amount to reflect anticipated savings from a range of structural reforms in this sector.
- EUR 10 billion in savings from health insurance through implementation of a national healthcare strategy, involving streamlining of healthcare operations, increased use of outpatient services and use of generic medicines; as a result of these measures, national healthcare expenditure growth is anticipated to be contained to an average of 2% per annum.
- EUR 10 billion savings in other social protection expenditure, including through reforms to pensions, family benefits and unemployment insurance.

These consolidations measures are to be strengthened, as detailed in the Stability Programme published in mid-April 2015 and transmitted to the European Commission: another EUR 9 billion of savings are to be implemented (EUR 4 billion in 2015 and

EUR 5 billion in 2016), relying on a central government spending reduction, further curbing of health expenditure, increased association of local government to the fiscal consolidation and some additional incomes.

Tax-side measures

As indicated above, fiscal consolidation in the period 2010-13 was focused on revenue enhancement measures (notably through introducing steeper progressivity into the income tax and corporate tax system); these discretionary measures are credited with yielding additional revenues of EUR 29 billion over the period. In recent years the focus has switched to expenditure reductions. Indeed, some of the expenditure savings will help to finance tax credits aimed at promoting competitiveness and employment (see below).

Protecting economic growth

As indicated above, the French Government has introduced broad-based measures to stimulate private-sector job creation, investment in innovation and overall economic activity, as a counterweight to the fiscal consolidation strategy. Key elements are:

- A Responsibility and Solidarity Pact, announced by the French Government announced in early 2014, laying down an over-arching strategy for streamlining and reducing the tax burden on employers and businesses; cutting red tape; securing commitments from employers in relation to hiring and training of staff, and in particular to offering quality jobs to young people; and introducing solidarity measures for the least well-off households.
- A Competitiveness and Jobs Tax Credit that effectively reduces the cost of labour to employers.
- A Growth and Economic Activity Bill (popularly dubbed *la Loi Macron*) which liberalises economic markets and professions and promotes employment and social dialogue.
- Radical administrative streamlining and regulatory reform (the "simplification shock") that implements business-friendly, citizen-friendly guiding principles for public administration: "tell us once"; "trust is assumed"; "silence means acceptance". In addition, an Administrative Streamlining Board, established in January 2014 and co-chaired by a member of parliament and a business executive, is tasked with developing further proposals to progress this agenda.

Performance, evaluation and value-for-money

The MPFP Act 2014-19 provides for a spending review *(revue de dépenses)* to identify further savings. From 2016 onwards the review will be integrated into the annual budgetary calendar to be completed by the end of February each year. With the involvement of Parliament, the outcome of the review will feed directly into the annual budget.

Budget accounting and execution

In addition to providing quarterly data to the European Commission on public finances, France adheres to the International Monetary Fund's Special Data Dissemination Standard Plus (SDDS Plus), whereby a broader range of budget execution data for central government is made available monthly. As regards budget accounting, a decree of 2012 revamped the whole public accounting system to ensure consistency across public institutions and agencies.

Policy priorities

France's expenditure-containing fiscal rules (the "zero nominal growth rule" and "zero real growth rule"), coupled with the multi-year spending caps, effectively require the government and its agencies to prioritise within overall allocations. A Circular of the Prime Minister from January 2013, which lays down rules for responsible management of government expenditure, underlines that all new priorities must be financed by savings on other expenditure.

At a more aggregate level, the MPFP 2012-19 commits the government to stabilising public sector numbers overall, with job creation in priority sectors (education and justice) offset by reductions in non-priority areas.

Long-term sustainability and fiscal risks

The Government introduced major pension reforms in 2013, building on earlier initiatives, with the aim of restoring the financial balance of the pension system by 2020. The reforms include increased contributions, a longer contribution period, and a new Pension Steering Committee to report annually upon financial sustainability. As regards private-sector supplementary pensions, the national multi-sector (labour-employer) agreement of March 2013 provides for below-inflation pension adjustments (resulting in an effective pension benefit freeze in 2014) and an increase in the revenue contribution rate.

Regarding fiscal risks more generally, the MPFP 2014-19 introduces a new procedure for monitoring public-private partnerships (PPPs), with a view to enhancing the understanding of these contracts and to control more tightly the fiscal risks that may be entailed. Hospitals and public agencies are now precluded from signing PPPs in their own right; while local authorities will be subject to tighter control in this regard from 2016 onwards, with every major project submitted to government evaluation.

Sub-national budgeting

As outlined above, transfers to sub-national levels of government (regions, *départments* and municipalities) will be reduced by EUR 10.7 billion over 2015-17 as part of the French Government's overall EUR 50 billion reduction plan. The French Government envisages that this reduction will incentivise local governments to improve efficiency including through rationalising their operations. Moreover, the MPFP 2014-19 sets a spending cap for the local government sector as a whole. From 2016 onwards, this target will be specified for each level of sub-national government. Against this background, plans for a reform of local government financing are underway, and will be considered by the 2016 budget; and a major restructuring of local government structures, including a reduction in the number of mainland regions from 22 to 13 (already adopted), and a project proposed by the Government of re-drawing of boundaries, and re-thinking the competencies at each level of government is currently discussed in the Parliament.

Economic forecasting

The 2012 Institutional Act on Public Finance Governance established the High Council of Public Finances (HCFP), an independent institution attached to the *Cour des comptes* (supreme audit institution). The HCFP is required to assess the realism of macroeconomic forecasts presented by the Government, in the context of its annual stability programme and budget bill, and to check whether the structural fiscal balance is on course with the French commitment to reach structural balance over the medium term.

The Institutional Act also requires the assumptions underlying the Government's medium-term economic forecasts to be outlined clearly. The forecast must be submitted in advance to the HCFP, which delivers an opinion as to their quality. This opinion may be taken into account by France's Constitutional Council (supreme court on constitutional matters) if budget bills are referred to it for review.

Engagement of parliament and citizens

Parliamentary capacity to scrutinise the budget bill has been enhanced through the creation of the HCFP, and through the new legal requirement upon the Government to produce a detailed annex of fiscal assumptions. As indicated above, the view of Parliament is also to be sought in future upon the outcome of annual spending reviews as part of the annual budget policy formulation process. The MPFP also provides for the publication of many reports, in order to give to the Parliament all the strategic information and analysis needed to ensure the utmost transparency (report on the agencies, on the remuneration spending of healthcare institutions, on financial forecast of the unemployment insurance, on tax expenditure, on the underlying hypothesis for the calculation of the structural balance, etc.).

The government's planned fiscal consolidation: France

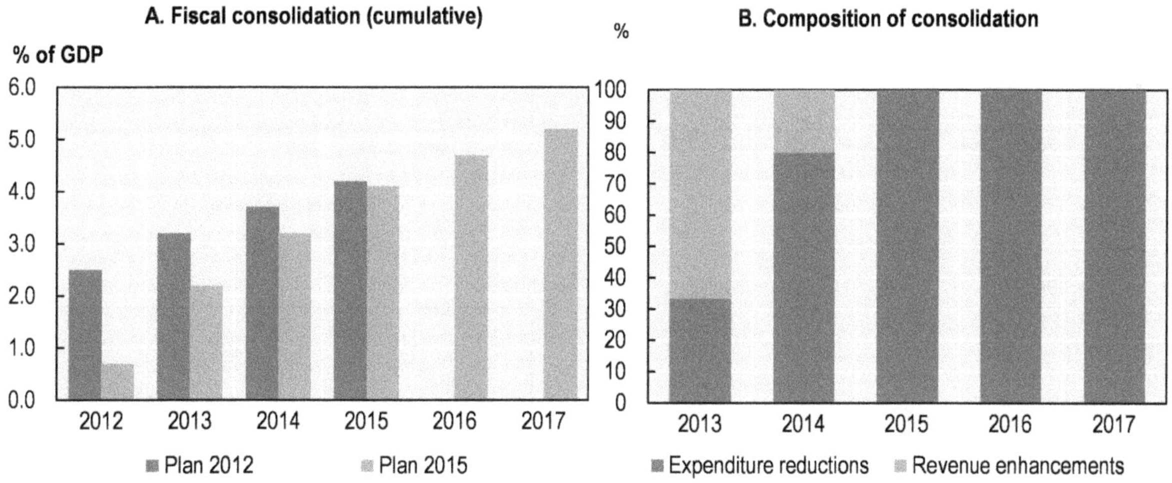

Source: OECD (2015b), *OECD State of Public Finances Survey 2015*; OECD (2011), *Restoring Public Finances,* www.oecd.org/gov/budgeting/47558957.pdf.

StatLink http://dx.doi.org/10.1787/888933288427

Germany

1. Economic situation

Economic growth is projected to strengthen, driven by both domestic and external demand. A robust labour market, low interest rates and low oil prices will underpin household spending, while the recovery of the euro area and the depreciation of the euro will boost exports. Business investment is expected to recover as capacity utilisation rises. The already low unemployment rate will fall further, while consumer price inflation is projected to rise in 2016.

In the near term, the structural budget surplus could be reduced to increase long-term growth-enhancing government spending, in particular to improve childcare services and provide more support in the education system for youth from low socio-economic backgrounds.

Key economic indicators: Germany

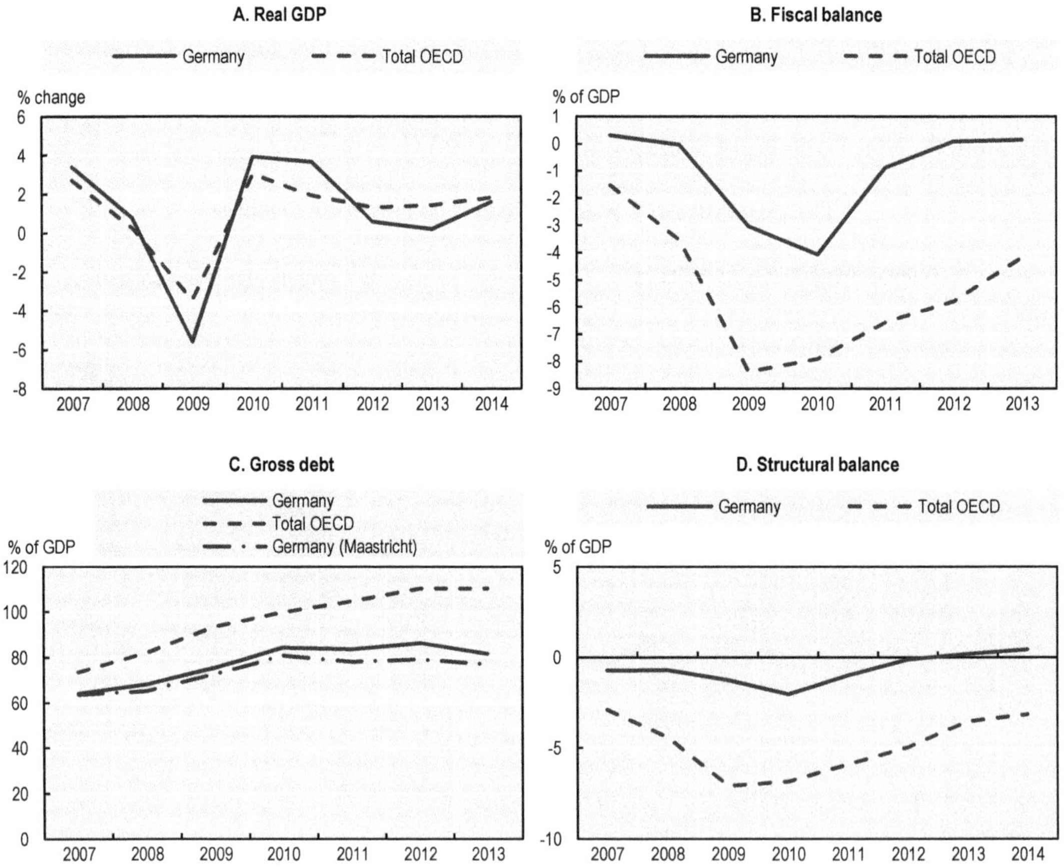

Source: OECD (2015a), "OECD Economic Outlook No. 97 (Edition 2015/1)", *OECD Economic Outlook: Statistics and Projections* (database), http://dx.doi.org/10.1787/data-00759-en.

StatLink http://dx.doi.org/10.1787/888933288122

While residential investment has expanded robustly since the outbreak of the global financial crisis, non-residential fixed investment and spending on knowledge-based capital has remained subdued, despite unusually favourable financing conditions. Structural reforms to strengthen competition in services sectors would raise potential growth and investment. Public investment has fallen short of depreciation over the past ten years. Investment in transport infrastructure needs to be raised.

2. Fiscal policy and budgetary governance

In 2010 the German general government fiscal deficit stood at -4.1% of GDP and the federal government adopted a budget consolidation package signalling its intent to pursue growth-friendly fiscal consolidation policies. The budget consolidation package has achieved its effect and Germany anticipates being able to comply with national debt rules and the *Maastricht* deficit criteria and the fiscal compact in the medium term. In 2014, the general government budget surplus was 0.4% of GDP. From the 2015 federal budget onwards, just as in 2014, the Federation will not require any new borrowing. Even though Germany's successful consolidation efforts have reversed the debt ratio trend, the negative effects of the financial and economic crisis are still being felt with the debt-to-GDP ratio about 12 percentage points higher in 2013 than it had been in 2008, before the crisis.

Fiscal objectives

Germany is subject to the preventive arm of the Stability and Growth Pact and must preserve a sound fiscal position, which ensures compliance with the medium-term objective. The upper limit for the general government structural deficit is 0.5% of nominal GDP. Germany has been complying with this medium-term budgetary objective since 2012 and is expected to continue to comply with it in 2014 and 2015. The Government also aims to further reduce the *Maastricht* debt-to-GDP ratio from 80.3% in 2010, to 74% in 2014 and 64% in 2018. It aims to reduce this ratio to less than 60% by 2023. The debt-to-GDP ratio stood at 76.9% in 2013.

Spending-side measures

Most of the leeway achieved so far through consolidation is being used to increase public investment in infrastructure, education and research, as recommended by the Council.

Tax-side measures

The German Government is currently pursuing initiatives to fight tax evasion. In addition, there has been a reduction in the VAT rate, an increase in the basic personal allowance to limit the burden of tax and social security contributions, especially for low earners and further development of the heavy goods vehicle toll.

Budget costings and execution

Since the end of 2013, an independent body of experts (the advisory board) has supported the Stability Council in monitoring compliance with the general government structural deficit limit.

Protecting economic growth

The fiscal policy focus of the general government budget can be described as broadly neutral, tending towards slightly expansionary. Under the coalition agreement, an additional EUR 5 billion is being made available for investment in transport infrastructure over the 2014–17 period and this is having a positive impact on growth and employment. In accordance with the advice given by several international organisations the Federal government decided on an increase of additional investment expenditure of EUR 10 billion over the period 2016-18.

Policy priorities

Overall, the fiscal policy focus of the general government budget can be described as broadly neutral, tending towards slightly expansionary.

Long-term sustainability and fiscal risks

New pension measures were introduced on 1 July 2014. These allow eligible workers to retire at 63 and increase pension payments for older mothers and those with reduced earning capacity. Critics argue that the new package will be too great a burden for public finances and the economy to bear. However, there are measures being undertaken to enhance cost-effectiveness in the areas of healthcare and long-term care. For example, adjustments are being made to the health insurance system so that it can cope with demographic change and rising expenditure levels.

Sub-national budgeting

The Federation and *Länder* are continuing their efforts to achieve fiscal consolidation and reduce their deficits while local authorities are maintaining their surpluses. The debt brake for the Federation and *Länder* that was enshrined in the Basic Law (constitution) in 2009, together with existing fiscal rules for the social security funds and local authorities, aim to ensure compliance with Germany's medium-term objectives. A review of fiscal relations between the different layers of government (Federation, *Länder* and local authorities) is ongoing.

Economic forecasting

The federal budget and fiscal projections at the level of general government are based on the federal government's own macroeconomic forecast, which is not formally endorsed by an independent body as defined in Regulation (EU) No 473/2013. The federal government is currently reviewing options to address this shortcoming as well as suitable changes. Notwithstanding this, Germany has a distinctive system of objective and professional independent input to the budgeting process, including economic forecasts, as noted in the recent OECD Budget Review. Spring and autumn forecasts are produced by the Inter-departmental Macroeconomic Forecasting Group under the direction of the Federal Ministry for Economic Affairs and Energy, involving specialists from the federal ministries, the Deutsche Bundesbank, the Institute for Employment Research and the Federal Statistical Office. The preparation of the Government's projections involves the independent Joint Economic Forecast which is issued twice a year by leading research institutes shortly before the Government's spring and autumn projections. The Government considers the Joint Economic Forecast as a benchmark for its own forecasts and customarily explains deviations.

Engagement of parliament and citizens

In 2013, the presentation of the federal budget and options for obtaining detailed information on line were significantly improved and expanded. As a result, citizens can access information and participate in the budget dialogue. For example, citizens can now undertake topic-based searches and compare figures for various years, for the 2012 budget and onwards.

The government's planned fiscal consolidation: Germany

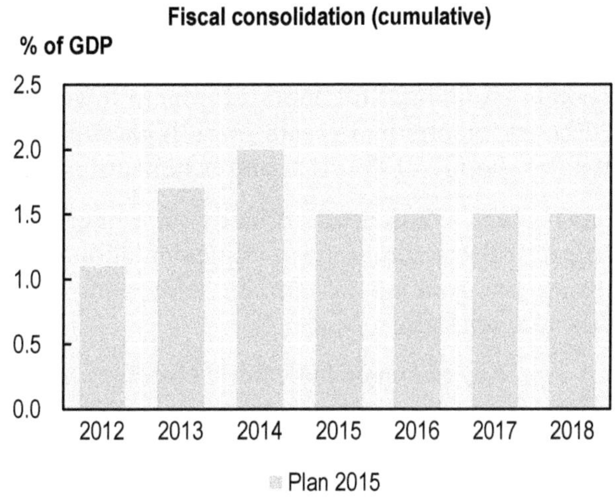

Source: OECD (2015b), *OECD State of Public Finances Survey 2015.*

StatLink http://dx.doi.org/10.1787/888933288433

Greece

1. Economic situation

Economic growth in 2015 remains weak, as uncertainty related to the reform programme and deteriorating liquidity conditions have undermined business confidence and investment. In 2016, growth will gain momentum and unemployment will decline somewhat as exports and investment recover while reform momentum is renewed.

The debt burden will remain very high, and fiscal sustainability requires continued restraint for some time. Fiscal policy should aim at a small primary surplus. Reforms of the tax system and tax collection are essential to raise revenues, while further pension reforms would help contain spending. Structural reforms to lower barriers to competition and investment would boost exports and create more higher-quality jobs. Social policy reforms should aim at a fair sharing of the costs and benefits of adjustment.

The recovery of investment will depend critically on a return of business confidence and on stepping up the pace of structural reform implementation. Better access to credit is also essential. Stabilising the banking system by addressing the high level of non-performing loans is therefore critical.

Key economic indicators: Greece

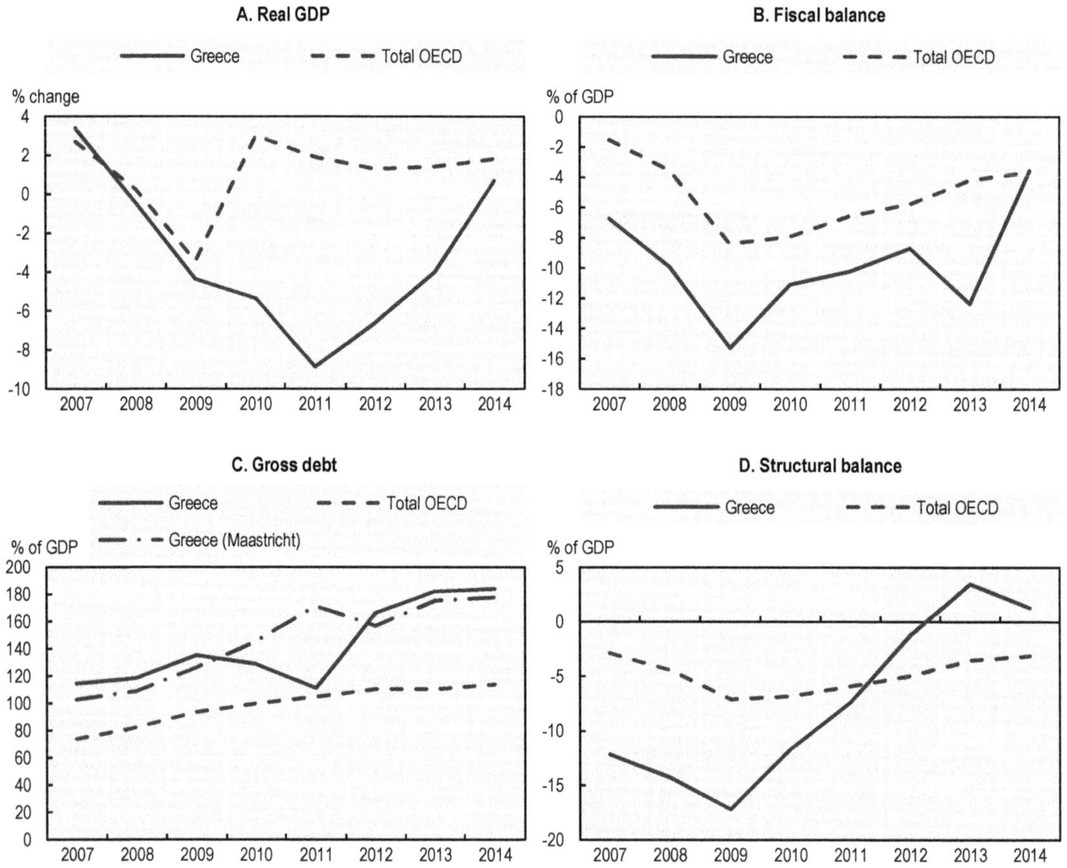

Source: OECD (2015a), "OECD Economic Outlook No. 97 (Edition 2015/1)", *OECD Economic Outlook: Statistics and Projections* (database), http://dx.doi.org/10.1787/data-00759-en.

StatLink http://dx.doi.org/10.1787/888933288136

2. Fiscal policy and budgetary governance

Greece was running an extremely high deficit of -6.7% of GDP prior to the broader crisis in 2007 and its fiscal position in Greece worsened in 2008 and 2009, with the fiscal deficit falling to 15.2% of GDP in 2009. The fiscal deficit has fluctuated since then, sitting at 12.2% of GDP in 2013, although significant fiscal effort since then has brought the deficit back towards the OECD average. The debt level, at over 180% of GDP, is an aggravating factor for overall sustainability however.

Fiscal objectives

Each Medium Term Fiscal Strategy (MTFS) sets specific annual fiscal targets in connection with basic fiscal parameters, such as the general government balance, the primary general government balance and the stock of debt, to be pursued via a package of consolidation measures affecting all the sub-sectors of the general government. According to Law 4270/2014, the fiscal (budgetary) position of the General Government (under ESA) should be balanced or in surplus. This rule is deemed met if the annual structural balance of the General Government has achieved the set medium-term fiscal target. In addition, if the ratio of General Government debt to GDP should exceed 60%, then the difference from the reference value should be reduced by an average of one-twentieth per year.

Spending-side measures

The focus of fiscal consolidation has been on expenditure measures, and this has increased from 60% of fiscal consolidation in 2012 to 70% in the following years. There are three categories of measures: horizontal measures (reduction of operating costs, etc.), targeted measures (addressing specific areas in expenditure, e.g. pharmaceutical expenditure) and structural measures (that increase competitiveness and eliminate rigidities in the long run).

Tax-side measures

There have been a number of targeted tax measures, such as the reduction of illness benefits.

Budget costings and execution

Each General Government entity sets monthly and quarterly goals regarding budget execution. These goals are closely monitored and correction mechanisms are in place to ensure compliance with the targets. In 2012 an overall spending review took place for all major categories of expenses and the proposals led to several measures being incorporated into the budget and the MTFS for 2013-16. In 2014, with external technical assistance, a spending review was again implemented. This focused on six Ministries and specifically on the legal entities supervised by these Ministries. Recommendations regarding savings and rebalancing public spending were incorporated into the 2015 budget.

Protecting economic growth

A number of measures have been put in place to restore economic growth. These include market deregulation and liberalisation, reduction of labour cost, exports and business environment enhancement, opening of closed professions, acceleration of the absorption rate of EU funds, removal of regulatory restrictions identified by the Competition Assessment Toolkit, abolition of nuisance taxes, streamlining the payment process in the public sector and reducing general government arrears to the private sector.

Policy priorities

The top priorities identified in the fiscal plan are:

- Reducing social security contributions by 3.9% as a total (2.9% employer contributions and 1% employee contributions), leading to an increase in corporate income tax and personal income tax.
- Abolishing certain non-reciprocal nuisance charges, leading to a reduction in revenues.
- Rationalising social security expenditure and safeguarding the collection of revenues. The MTFS included interventions in this area worth EUR 6.2 billion.
- Reducing those compensated by the National Organization for Healthcare Provision (EOPYY) by adopting new criterion regarding the issue of medicine.
- Reducing inefficient and expensive medicines, as well as ensuring treatment durations are in line with international standards. Significant incentives are being provided to pharmaceuticals in order to lower prices and increase the competitiveness of their products.

Long-term sustainability and fiscal risks

The amendments initiated for the pension reform are expected to tackle the effect of ageing populations. The reform has introduced a new transparent system to strengthen the link between contributions and benefits. It aims to reduce the projected increase in pension expenditure over the next 50 years. Measures include an automatic adjustment mechanism linking retirement age with increasing life expectancy, a merger of existing pension funds creating a unified new pension system, the development of control systems to combat social insurance contribution evasion, the implementation of a single control system of pension payment and the implantation of a monitoring system for collection of compulsory social contributions. The 2013-16 MTFS also increased the retirement age by two years.

Sub-national budgeting

All general government entities, including those under the social budget and local government, are required to set monthly and quarterly targets for budget execution. Without influencing the autonomy of the entities, execution against targets is closely monitored and, if necessary, corrective mechanisms are implemented to ensure targets are achieved. This process helps safeguard a budget execution that falls within the overall fiscal targets.

Economic forecasting

Economic forecasts produced by the Ministry of Finance but scrutinised and evaluated through "exchange of view" meetings with independent experts such as the Bank of Greece, the Centre of Planning and Economic Research, the Foundation for Economic and Industrial Research and the systemic banks research departments. In addition, an independent fiscal institution is being set up to assess macro and fiscal projections.

Engagement of parliament and citizens

The Ministry of Finance publishes several bulletins on its website, including a monthly state budget bulletin and the General Government bulletin with detailed analysis for each sub-sector.

The government's planned fiscal consolidation: Greece

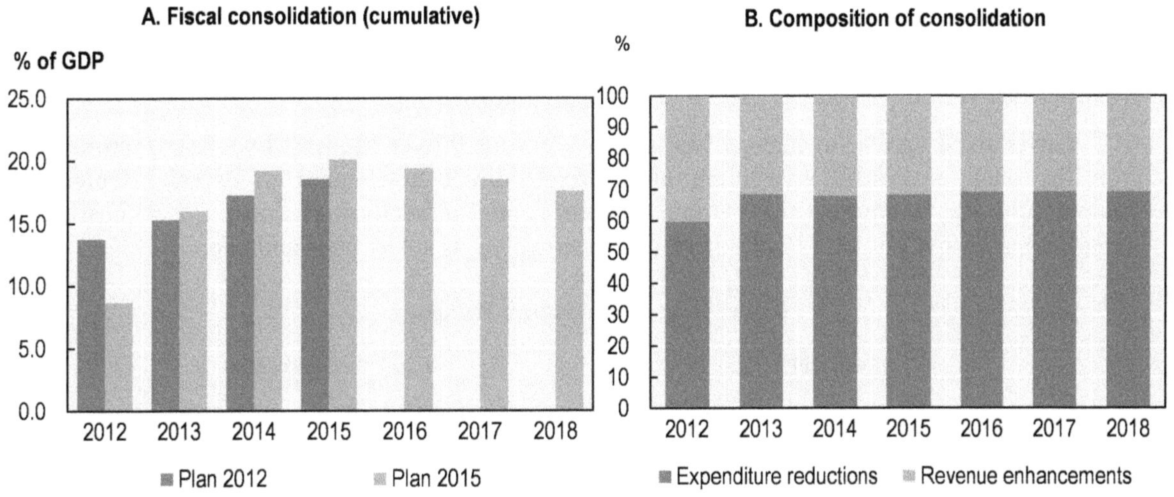

Source: OECD (2015b), *OECD State of Public Finances Survey 2015*; OECD (2011), *Restoring Public Finances*, www.oecd.org/gov/budgeting/47558957.pdf.

StatLink http://dx.doi.org/10.1787/888933288440

Hungary

1. Economic situation

Economic growth is projected to slow but remain fairly robust, and unemployment will decline somewhat further. As the effects of cheaper energy wane and the labour market tightens, inflation should gradually increase. Exports growth will remain dynamic.

After a marked deterioration of the structural fiscal deficit in 2014, the authorities should return to a process of improving their underlying budget position to reduce debt sustainably and expand the fiscal manoeuvre room. By the end of the projection period, there will be little economic slack left, which may require the central bank to raise the policy rate to contain inflation pressures. Pro-competitive structural reforms in product markets are the key to stronger and more inclusive growth.

Gross fixed capital formation has grown vigorously over the past two years, mainly on the back of public investment and foreign direct investment in export-oriented manufacturing. In contrast, investment in housing and in sectors reliant on the domestic market has recovered less. Public investment, however, is set to slow and even decline.

Key economic indicators: Hungary

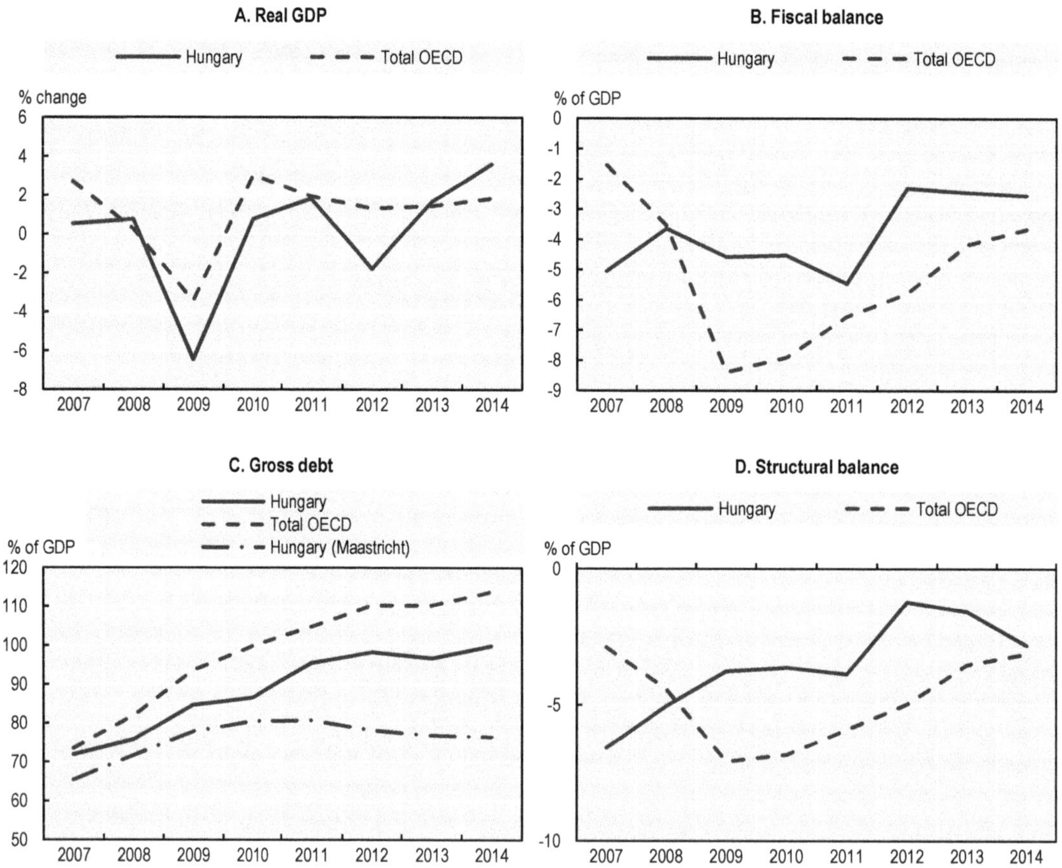

Source: OECD (2015a), "OECD Economic Outlook No. 97 (Edition 2015/1)", *OECD Economic Outlook: Statistics and Projections* (database), http://dx.doi.org/10.1787/data-00759-en.

StatLink http://dx.doi.org/10.1787/888933288143

2. Fiscal policy and budgetary governance

Hungary's public finances were in substantial deficit (around 5% of GDP) in 2007, and – adjusting for one-off items – have improved quite slowly over the period since the financial crisis. From 2012 the deficit has been brought down to around 2.5% of GDP, reflecting in part the *Széll Kálmán* strategic reform plans (named after a distinguished 19th century finance minister) of 2011 and 2012. The deficit is projected to remain at this level, with a modest downward trajectory into the medium term, as the Hungarian Government moves to give equal weight to sustained economic activity as fiscal discipline contraction.

Fiscal objectives

The Hungarian Government, having striven within the European Union's excessive deficit procedure to bring its fiscal deficit below 3% of GDP by 2012, considers it near-term fiscal objectives to have been attained. Fiscal policy must take account of a "debt brake" written into the Fundamental Law in 2012, whereby the debt-to-GDP ratio must be brought down until it reaches the limit of 50% - although the rule does not apply in times of economic contraction (so as to avoid pro-cyclical fiscal policy). New components were added to the system of fiscal rules in 2013 to reflect EU governance rules, notably the concept of the structural fiscal balance that must not exceed the medium-term objective.

Spending-side measures

As mapped out originally in the *Széll Kálmán* reform plans, expenditure consolidation has focused upon the following key areas:

- reduction in pharmaceutical costs/drug subsidies, reflecting health policy changes and increased payments from drug manufacturers
- real-term reductions in public transport costs, including a reduction in the consumer price subsidy
- wage freezes in the public sector, subject to some flexibility to address specific issues that arose in the health sector
- phasing out of early retirement arrangements in the public sector; a measure which produced higher-than-expected savings and provided a boost to the labour supply
- reform of unemployment subsidies, with reduction in benefits introduced in tandem with increased public work schemes, which could be justified by the Hungarian Government under the principle of "giving work instead of social aid".

Tax-side measures

The Hungarian Government made a strategic decision to introduce major structural tax reforms from 2011, whereby the tax burden was shifted from labour to consumption, the cornerstone of this policy being the 16% "flat tax" on personal income. The intention has been to stimulate the demand side of the labour market and thus promote job creation. In 2013, the cap on employees' social security contributions was abolished, thus introducing the "flat tax" principle to this area of revenue policy also. A new "financial transaction fee" was introduced in 2012/2013 to yield a major new source of public revenues.

Flexibility in budget execution

The budgetary rules regarding expenditure reallocation have been revamped to enhance flexibility, consistent with achieving value-for-money. Different areas of expenditure fall under the authority of the National Assembly, the government or of state agencies, and each of these poles of authority have significant freedom to reallocate budgeted resources.

Protecting economic growth

As indicated above, the structural tax reforms between 2011 and 2013 were advanced by the Hungarian Government as growth-promoting measures. In 2013, in the context of its Jobs Protection Action Plan, the Government also introduced a new system of targeted tax credits, to incentivise employment of the most disadvantaged groups in society. In addition, tax simplification measures were introduced for small businesses. Finally in this regard, the decision to pursue a relatively moderate fiscal policy course is justified by the Hungarian Government as a growth-sensitive approach.

Policy priorities

The *Széll Kálmán* plans identified the following top priority areas for reform:

- the flexibility of the labour market
- sustainability of the pension system
- improved public transport
- improved higher education
- reduced and reformed pharmaceutical subsidies
- a reformed local government sector
- reduced administrative burden for businesses.

Long-term sustainability and fiscal risks

The Hungarian Government considered the secure financing of the welfare system as a national priority. The budget of the Pension Fund has been planned accordingly to balance revenues and expenditures over the long term, taking account of the findings of the 2012 Ageing Report. The projected increase in pension expenditure from 2010 to 2060 is 0.5% of GDP, which is small in comparison with other OECD countries.

Sub-national budgeting

From 2011, the finances of the highly-indebted local governments were subject to fundamental restructuring. A new debt rule was introduced for this level of government. The central government assumed the debt of the sub-sector, but the fiscal framework became much more binding and constrictive. Local governments may no longer borrow to finance their operating deficits, and may borrow to finance investments only with the permission of the Government while fulfilling some conditions as for capabilities of repayment. Expenditure savings were realised and the balance of the sector improved considerably. In addition, the balance of responsibilities and functions was rationalised, with the State assuming some of the functions previously carried out by municipalities. In terms of financing the sub-sector, the principle has moved decisively from a "normative" grant allocation to a more specific task-based financing model.

Economic forecasting

The finance minister provides macroeconomic and budgetary forecasts twice a year, on a three-year forward horizon. The Hungarian Fiscal Council examines the feasibility of the State budget in light of the constitutional debt rule, and must give its prior consent in this regard prior to the adoption of the central budget bill or amendments. The Fiscal Council, which is financed from the budget of the parliament, comprises a president (appointed by the President of Hungary for a six-year term), the central bank governor and the president of the State Audit Office. Its work is supported by a five-person secretariat, staff of the central bank and the State Audit Office, and it may commission analysis from external experts.

Engagement of parliament and citizens

The parliamentary approval process was streamlined in 2014: in place of a two-round discussion of the budget, the budget bill is examined by the Fiscal Council (see above) for consistency with the debt brake rule; with the approval by the Fiscal Council on this point, the budget bill is submitted for a final vote of the Assembly. Other than the heightened transparency arising from the role of the Fiscal Council and the clearer fiscal rules, there have been no specific initiatives in Hungary to promote the quality of debate by Parliament, and engagement by the public and civil society in budget policy making.

The government's planned fiscal consolidation: Hungary

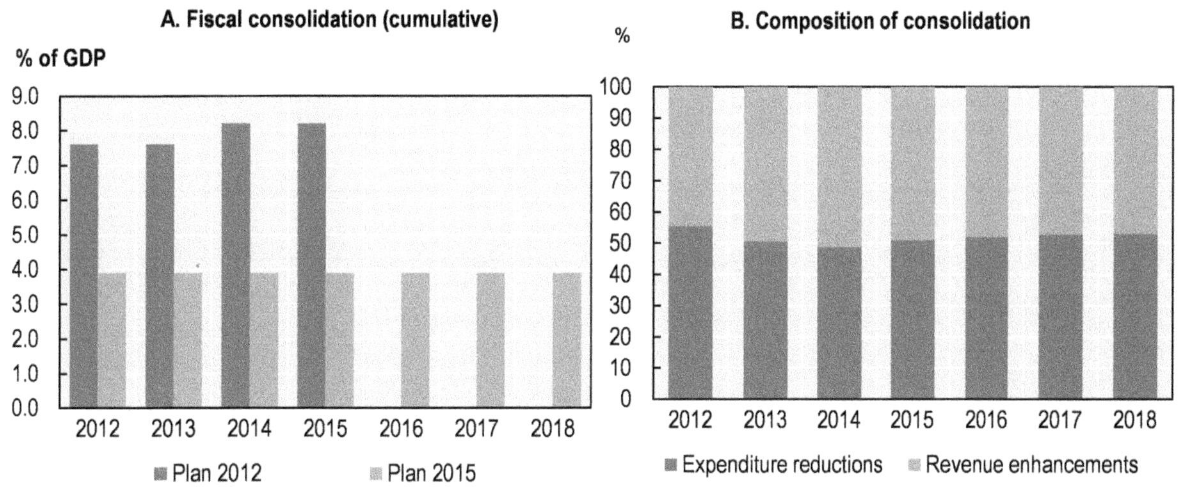

Source: OECD (2015b), *OECD State of Public Finances Survey 2015*; OECD (2011), *Restoring Public Finances,* www.oecd.org/gov/budgeting/47558957.pdf.

StatLink http://dx.doi.org/10.1787/888933288453

Iceland[1]

1. Economic situation

The economy has entered its seventh year of economic growth, with a pick-up in private consumption and fixed investment and a boom in tourism. Large investments in energy-intensive projects and fiscal support for households will sustain growth in 2015 and 2016. Inflationary pressures will mount as the labour market tightens. Fiscal policy has made significant progress in reducing government debt.

The pace of fiscal consolidation will slow in 2015, but debt will still fall further under current plans. Containing public spending pressures will be important in maintaining an appropriate budgetary stance. With spare capacity disappearing, interest rates will need to rise as sizeable wage settlements unleash inflationary pressures. Structural reforms are needed to enhance the investment environment.

Key economic indicators: Iceland

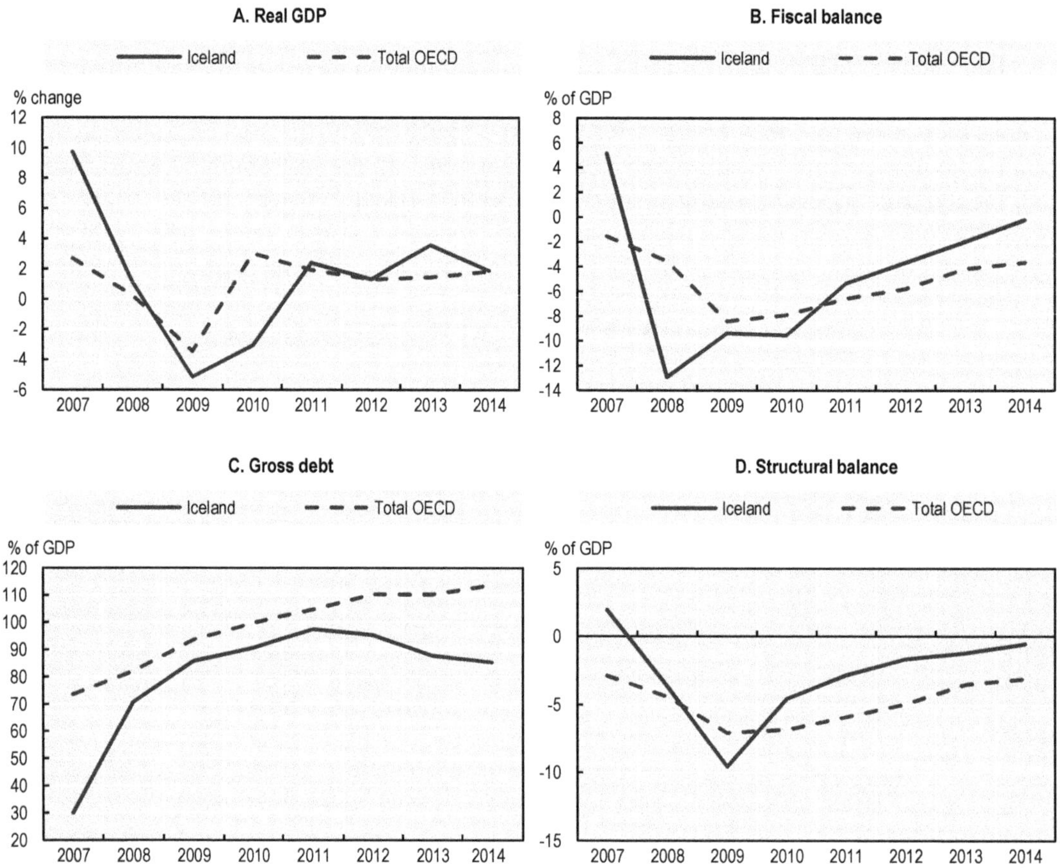

Source: OECD (2015a), "OECD Economic Outlook No. 97 (Edition 2015/1)", *OECD Economic Outlook: Statistics and Projections* (database), http://dx.doi.org/10.1787/data-00759-en.

StatLink http://dx.doi.org/10.1787/888933288156

[1] Iceland did not submit response to the *OECD State of Public Finances Survey 2015* that does not include fiscal policy and budgetary governance section.

Investment slumped after the crisis and is now beginning to recover, but insufficiently to prevent the capital stock from eroding. Public investment was boosted in the 2015 budget, mainly in transportation projects. Making gradual progress in lifting of capital controls would send a positive signal to investors.

Ireland

1. Economic situation

Economic growth is projected to be robust and broadly based in 2015 and 2016. Exports will continue to be strong due to increasing demand in trading partners and the depreciation of the euro. Household consumption will gather pace with employment and wages rising steadily.

Fiscal policy will exert a smaller drag on activity than in past years. Strong revenue growth and low interest costs should be used for more rapid reduction of still-high public debt. Financial conditions have become favourable, but the problem of non-performing loans persists, impeding the full return to normal credit supply. Structural reforms should prioritise getting more people back into work, by making the tax and benefit system more efficient and enhancing activation policy.

Key economic indicators: Ireland

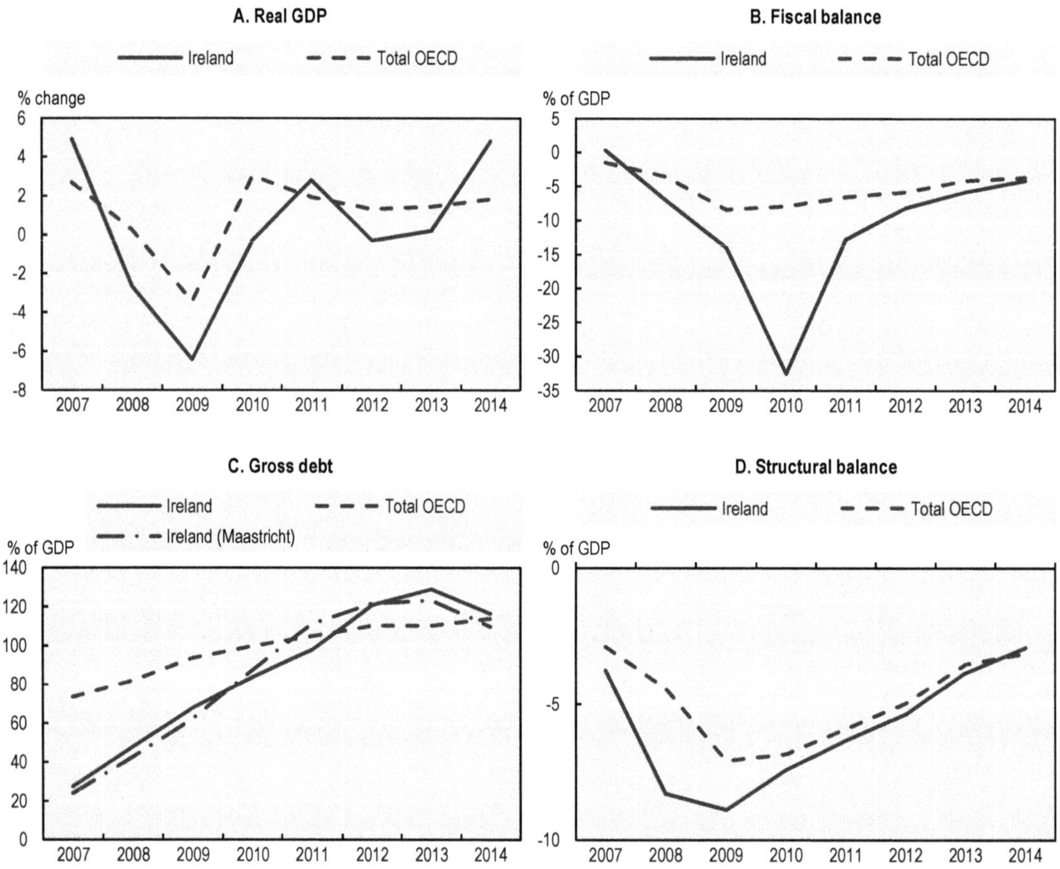

Source: OECD (2015a), "OECD Economic Outlook No. 97 (Edition 2015/1)", *OECD Economic Outlook: Statistics and Projections* (database), http://dx.doi.org/10.1787/data-00759-en.

StatLink http://dx.doi.org/10.1787/888933288162

Business investment will continue to rebound, expanding the capital stock at a pace consistent with robust long-term growth. Fast-rising property prices, both in the housing and office-building markets, are reminiscent of the bubble period of a decade ago. Further macro-prudential tools should be used, if necessary, to prevent investors becoming excessively exposed.

2. Fiscal policy and budgetary governance

Ireland is one of the OECD countries most severely affected by the financial and economic crisis, with its budget swinging from a modest surplus in 2007, with a low debt ratio of 24% of GDP, to a deficit of 6% of GDP in 2008, and around 13% a year in the period 2009-11 and the debt ratio (*Maastricht* definition) peaking at 123.3% of GDP in 2013, as the large cyclical costs were compounded by exceptional bank bail-outs. Remarkable progress has since been made in moving the public finances back onto a sustainable course, with difficult austerity measures coupled with broad-based structural reforms, in the context of the financial support arrangement from the troika of the International Monetary Fund (IMF) and EU bodies. Economic growth is currently rebounding from its low point; with resources becoming available once again, the challenge for the Irish authorities is to manage the recovery phase in a manner that signals respite from the acute period of austerity, while avoiding pro-cyclical fiscal stimulus.

Fiscal objectives

The Fiscal Responsibility Act of 2012 transposed into Irish law the key elements of the EU economic governance framework. The correction of the "excessive deficit" to below the 3%-of-GDP EU norm by 2015 has been the overarching objective of fiscal policy over several years, and is well on course to be achieved. Thereafter, Ireland will be subject to the "preventive arm" of the EU's stability and growth pact, and will aim to achieve a balanced fiscal position over the medium term.

Spending-side measures

Since the original Medium Term Fiscal Strategy was set out in 2011, the composition of the fiscal consolidation has remained broadly in course, with around two-thirds of the overall adjustment coming from the expenditure side. Key features of the Irish Government's approach to expenditure-side consolidation have been as follows:

- sharp reductions in public sector payroll costs (including through staff number reductions and pay cuts) and in social welfare benefits, as well as various targeted reductions across all areas of public spending
- the conduct of "Comprehensive Reviews of Expenditure" every two to three years to generate additional options for policy makers on resource allocation, as part of a range of budgetary reforms including multi-annual expenditure ceilings and performance budgeting
- efficiency measures including through shared services, streamlining of state agencies and a focus on e-government.

Budget 2015 has, however, responded to the economic turnaround by replacing the originally scheduled correction of EUR 2 billion with an overall expansionary budget, including an increase in expenditure of around EUR 630 million. The budget also commenced the process of unwinding some austerity-era measures, and the Irish Government has signalled that certain major savings measures – such as the cuts in public service pay – will be progressively rolled back. The scope for further expansionary budgets will be constrained by the new EU fiscal rules, including the expenditure rule, which links overall spending increases to underlying economic growth (unless offset by tax measures).

Tax-side measures

The dramatic fall-off in revenues from housing-market transactions and from income tax, during the acute budgetary crisis period, led to the introduction of additional broad-based levies on incomes and on residential property. The more recent introduction of charges related to water usage has been a focal point for public protest. For the future, the Irish Government has signalled that it will prioritise the easing of the tax burden on incomes in the lower and middle ranges in particular, in the context of a more general switch from direct to indirect forms of taxation.

Protecting economic growth

A notable feature of Ireland's fiscal correction effort has been the equal attention – at political as well as administrative levels – to introducing broad-based structural economic and public-sector reform. While the structural reforms have been designed to strengthen the longer term responsiveness and capacity of the economy, there have also been shorter term measures to stimulate job creation and labour market activation. Some key points are as follows:-

- The separation of the original Department of Finance into two institutions, the Department of Finance itself remaining in charge of overall fiscal policy, taxation policy and policy for the financial sector, while the new Department of Public Expenditure and Reform is responsible for overall public expenditure policy and public service reform, including in the areas of human resources, public procurement, PPPs and e-government.
- The agreement between the Irish authorities and the IMF and EU institutions on financial support included specific commitments to economic reform and liberalisation across various sectors.
- A Jobs Initiative was launched by the Irish Government in May 2011 with a concerted focus upon employment creation, training and education, and a targeted VAT reduction; since 2012, an annual "Action Plan for Jobs" has been developed, with quarterly monitoring and reporting, and it is credited by the Government with contributing to a relatively "job-rich" recovery over the period.
- In this overall context, a ten-point tax reform plan was announced in Budget 2013 to help small and medium-sized businesses (which account for 70% of people employed); followed up by a EUR 500 million tax package in Budget 2014 containing a suite of 25 measures aimed at the promotion of job creation and economic growth.
- Budget 2015 provided for capital investment to provide more homes for those in need of support, as well as investment in infrastructure and economic capacity. Budget 2015, which marked the end in a series of consolidation budgets, included a suite of tax measures with a net cost of around EUR 390 million in 2015. A significant portion of the measures were designed to alleviate the burden on low and middle income earners. In addition, Budget 2015 provided for capital

investment to provide more homes for those in need of support, as well as investment in infrastructure and economic capacity.

- Spring Economic Statement 2015, outlined that fiscal space of the order of EUR 1.2 billion to EUR 1.5 billion would be available for Budget 2016, while still complying with Ireland's obligations under the Stability and Growth Pact.

Policy priorities

The Irish Government's over-arching priority in fiscal policy has been to correct the excessive deficit and thereafter move towards achieving the medium-term objective of a structural balanced budget, while also encouraging economic growth and promoting employment opportunities. As regards sector-specific priorities, the periodic Comprehensive Reviews of Expenditure are coupled with ongoing evaluations and value-for-money reviews of specific areas, conducted by the newly instituted Irish Government Economic and Evaluation Service.

As regards tax expenditures, various specific reliefs have been reviewed and abolished in recent years with the aim of achieving a more broadly based, transparent and efficient tax system. The Medium Term Economic Strategy (published in December 2013) commits the Irish Government to conducting regular reviews of various tax reliefs using public consultation as appropriate and to publish the results.

Long-term sustainability and fiscal risks

The public pension system has undergone extensive reform in recent years in order to promote long-term sustainability, including the introduction of a Single Public Service Pension Scheme in 2013 and a gradual increase in the minimum retirement age to 68 by the year 2028. As regards fiscal policy, the Irish Government has no specific targets to underpin sustainability, although the medium-term fiscal objective will be designed (in line with EU rules) to reflect long-term demographic and related issues.

Sub-national budgeting

Following a restructuring of local government funding, local government areas have been given greater autonomy in respect to varying the rates of local property tax (+/-15%) with the requirement to produce a balanced budget. The Medium-Term Budgetary Framework, published in July 2014, provides a compendium of how local government budgets will be managed in the context of the (EU-mandated) general government accounting, including the question of how the aggregate-level expenditure rule will have its incidence on local government.

Economic forecasting

The Irish Fiscal Advisory Council (IFAC) was established in 2011 to assess (and more recently to "endorse") the official forecasts produced by the Department of Finance, to assess compliance with fiscal rules and to assess the fiscal stance adopted by the Government. The commentaries provided by IFAC have succeeded in gaining traction in public and political discourse. It is notable that the Irish Government has recently proposed to establish another institution, the Irish Budget Office, with the specific task of providing costings of policy options for political parties.

Engagement of parliament and citizens

A website, www.irelandstat.gov.ie, provides user-friendly information on expenditure allocations, and performance metrics, for key areas of spending.

The government's planned fiscal consolidation: Ireland

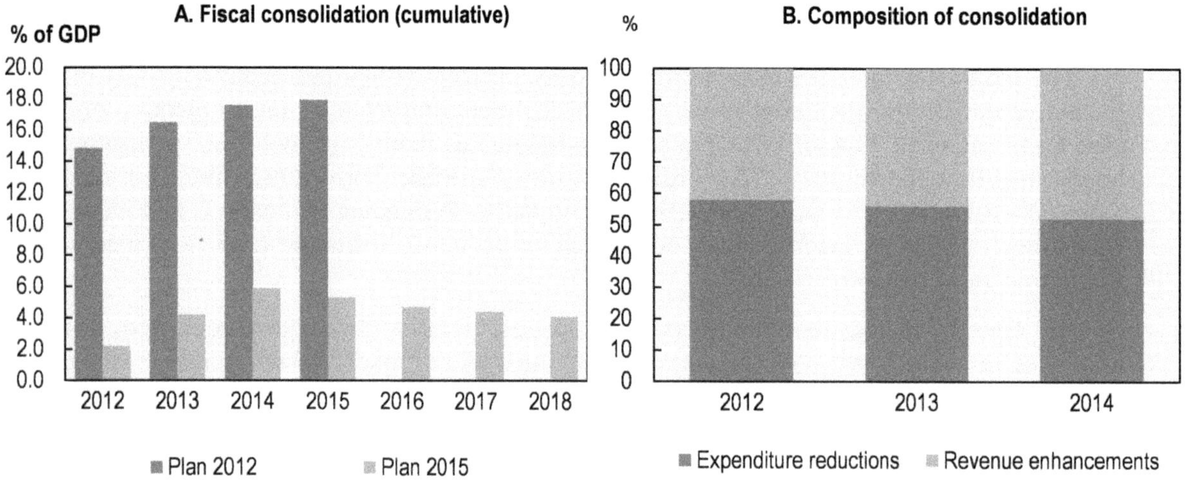

Source: OECD (2015b), *OECD State of Public Finances Survey 2015*; OECD (2011), *Restoring Public Finances*, www.oecd.org/gov/budgeting/47558957.pdf.

StatLink http://dx.doi.org/10.1787/888933288464

Israel[2]

1. Economic situation

Economic growth slowed in 2014, picked up strongly at the end of the year and should strengthen to around 3.5% in 2015 and 2016, helping to keep unemployment low. Lower oil prices, further cuts in interest rates and a significant revaluation of the minimum wage should shore up domestic demand, while the gradual improvement of the global economy boosts exports.

An accommodative monetary policy is still appropriate to support current growth and prevent undesirable appreciation of the shekel. But the likely temporary nature of the price falls in early 2015 argues against further relaxation involving unconventional measures.

Key economic indicators: Israel

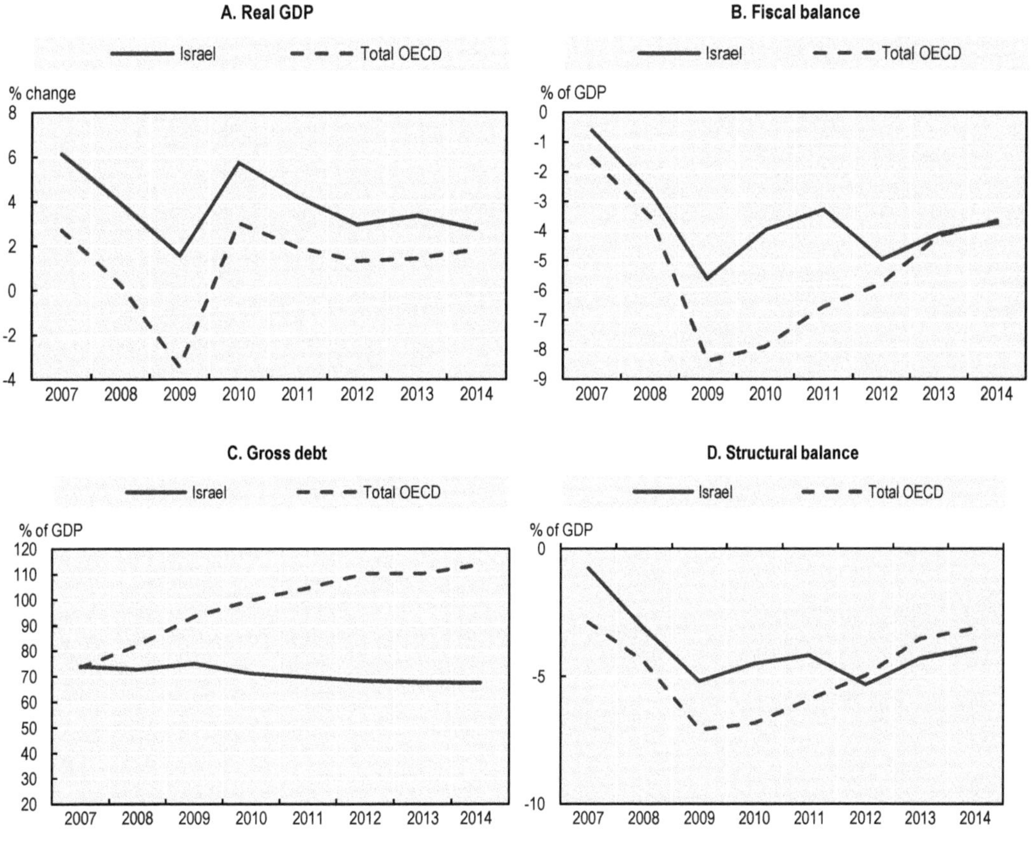

Source: OECD (2015a), "OECD Economic Outlook No. 97 (Edition 2015/1)", *OECD Economic Outlook: Statistics and Projections* (database), http://dx.doi.org/10.1787/data-00759-en.

StatLink http://dx.doi.org/10.1787/888933288173

[2] Israel did not submit response to the *OECD State of Public Finances Survey 2015* that does not include fiscal policy and budgetary governance section. The statistical data for Israel are supplied by and under the responsibility of the relevant Israeli authorities. The use of such data by the OECD is without prejudice to the status of the Golan Heights, East Jerusalem and Israeli settlements in the West Bank under the terms of international law.

The public debt reduction policy is still needed to increase the room for fiscal manoeuvre, but it must draw more on revenue increases, and the current rule constraining spending should be reviewed. Structural reforms are also crucial to enhance competition on product markets and formal education and skills, especially among the Ultra-Orthodox and Arab populations, to stimulate productivity and to make growth more inclusive.

Increased investment in infrastructure – especially public transport and the natural gas distribution network, but also education – is needed to lift some of the barriers to private investment and boost potential growth. The Government should pursue efforts to improve the co-ordination of public intervention in the property sector to better respond to housing demand by increasing supply and thus reducing prices.

Italy

1. Economic situation

After a long recession, the Italian economy has started its gradual recovery. Output is projected to grow by 0.7% in 2015 and by 1.3% in 2016. Exports will continue to support growth, but the recovery will broaden to private consumption. Sluggish private investment will be countered by rising public infrastructure spending. Economic growth will result in employment gains.

Fiscal policy should continue to aim for gradual but steady fiscal consolidation, so as not to strangle the incipient economic recovery, while fully respecting EU fiscal rules and reducing the large debt-to-GDP ratio. The Government should continue to push forward its comprehensive plan of structural reforms, which will boost confidence and lead to higher sustainable and more inclusive growth. Improving the efficiency of the public administration will be key to raising productivity growth.

Key economic indicators: Italy

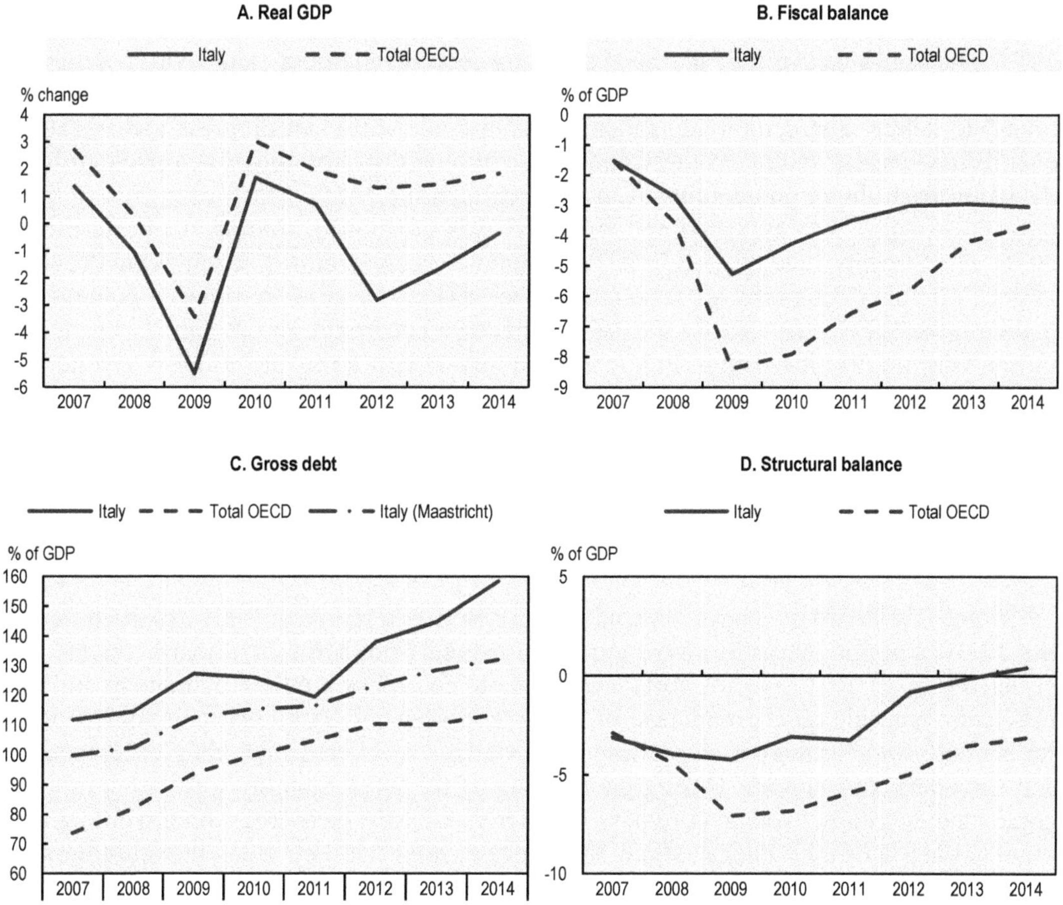

Source: OECD (2015a), "OECD Economic Outlook No. 97 (Edition 2015/1)", *OECD Economic Outlook: Statistics and Projections* (database), http://dx.doi.org/10.1787/data-00759-en.

StatLink http://dx.doi.org/10.1787/888933288182

The crisis hit investment especially hard and gross fixed capital formation has declined by 30% since 2007. To revive private investment, further action is needed to improve the health of the banking system. The planned increase in public infrastructure spending is welcome, but needs to be matched with improvements in the effectiveness of public spending and procurement.

2. Fiscal policy and budgetary governance

The fiscal deficit peaked at 5.3% of GDP in 2009, but has since fallen to 2.8% of GDP in 2013. The fiscal consolidation strategy adopted since 2011 has mainly focussed on increasing revenue and reducing expenditure. Although effective in reducing the deficit, the policies adopted have contributed to the worsening of the macroeconomic outlook. To counter these negative effects, the ongoing fiscal plan has been re-orientated and based on a mix of measures which provide for expenditure cuts against a significant reduction of the tax wedge on labour.

Fiscal objectives

Italy is currently subject to the preventive arm of the Stability and Growth Pact (SGP). The Medium Term Objective (MTO) for a structural balance was originally set for 2013. The preventive arm of the SGP currently requires member states with a debt ratio above 60% of GDP that are not yet at their MTO but are experiencing economic "bad times" to deliver a structural adjustment so as to make sufficient progress towards it. An overall assessment, based on the Commission forecast, points to a risk of a significant deviation from the required adjustment path towards the MTO. Macroeconomic outturns have been worse than expected and the MTO was postponed, first to 2014 and then to 2016. The Stability Law, passed in 2015, contains measures aimed at achieving the fiscal targets. The plan defers the achievement of the MTO until 2017. In order to achieve and maintain the MTO, Law No. 243/2012 introduced a constraint on the public expenditure in line with the EU regulation. Public expenditure in real terms has to grow in line with the medium-term growth rate of potential GDP if the MTO is already achieved. If the country has not yet achieved its MTO, the growth of adjusted general government expenditure is reduced by an amount that ensures a decrease of the structural budget balance of at least 0.5 percentage points per year.

Spending-side measures

Across the board cuts have been adopted as well as a freeze on staff expenditure over the 2011-14 period. Measures have gradually moved from across-the-board cuts towards selected cuts. In 2012, major efforts were made to centralise public procurement and gain efficiency margins on the purchase of goods and services. A crucial component of the Italian budgetary strategy is a spending review aimed to increase spending efficiency and achieve additional savings. During the drafting of the 2015 Stability Law, each ministry conducted an internal spending review in order to identify measures which would enable them to cut 3% of their budget. Using this process, ministries are given the opportunity to prioritise their output targets and to select areas of expenditure for reduction, in compliance with current legislation. Other relevant measures to reduce spending are undertaken by local governments through the Domestic Stability Pact.

Tax-side measures

The Stability Law 2015 includes measures such as:

- an increase to VAT rates in 2016 and 2017
- an increase to excise duties on fuels from 2018.

Budget costings and execution

The main process for designing amendments/updates to the fiscal plan has been the spending review. The Government is committed to conducting these reviews to reduce waste and inefficiency and reallocate expenditure to new priorities. The Ministry of Economy and Finance has been taking a lead role to support the process of reallocating resources from lower to higher priority areas, in coherence with the targets established by the budget packages. There has also been the appointment of a Special Commissioner for the spending review, responsible for proposals on expenditure rationalisation.

Protecting economic growth

Since 2011 the macroeconomic outturns have been worse than expected. Because of this, Italy has had to reconsider its consolidation strategy. In addition, there have also been measures to reduce the tax wedge on labour, such as the full deductibility of regional tax on productive activities for workers hired indefinitely, tax relief for hiring permanent workers and a tax bonus for employees with incomes up to EUR 26 000.

Policy priorities

The top priorities are as follows:

- reducing fiscal pressure and shifting the tax burden from production factors to rents
- promoting public investment
- providing increased protection against unemployment while increasing flexibility of the labour market and improving on ALMPs
- focus on improving efficiency of public spending (through spending reviews).

Long-term sustainability and fiscal risks

There have been no major changes since the previous survey. The pension reform passed by Monti's government is still in place and all parts have been implemented. The Italian pension system is relatively sustainable and ensures higher replacement ratios and average benefits than other European countries.

Sub-national budgeting

Measures to reduce spending are undertaken by local governments through the Domestic Stability Pact. Over the period 2015-18, in net terms the contribution of local authorities amounts to around EUR 10.8 billion obtained through a reduction in the solidarity fund for municipalities, a reduction of current expenditure by provinces and metropolitan cities and appropriations to the fund for doubtful accounts. This is offset by loosening of the bond of the covenant internal stability.

Economic forecasting

The macroeconomic forecasts underlying the Draft Budgetary Plan are endorsed by the Parliamentary Budget Office (PBO), Italy's newly established independent fiscal monitoring institution, which has assessed the forecast as within an acceptable interval given the information currently available.

Engagement of parliament and citizens

The main open data initiatives for higher transparency and participative practices can be found in the MEF-RGS website at the following links:

- www.rgs.mef.gov.it/VERSIONE-I/Dati/OPENDATA/ (central governments expenditures, regional expenditures, local authorities loans)
- www.rgs.mef.gov.it/VERSIONE-I/Dati/Bilancio_in_rete/ (state budget).

The government's planned fiscal consolidation[1]: Italy

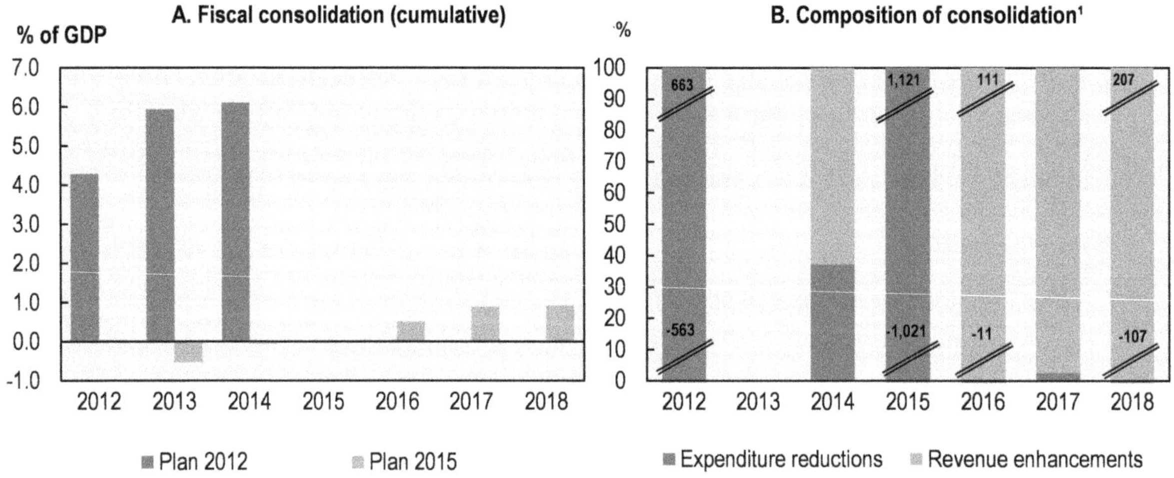

Note[1]: No composition of consolidation data for 2013

Source: OECD (2015b), *OECD State of Public Finances Survey 2015*; OECD (2011), *Restoring Public Finances*, www.oecd.org/gov/budgeting/47558957.pdf.

StatLink http://dx.doi.org/10.1787/888933288477

Japan

1. Economic situation

The economy has now rebounded from the contraction in the wake of the 2014 tax hike. Supported by the fall in oil prices and real wage gains, output growth is projected to reach 0.6% in 2015 and 1.2% in 2016. Export growth is projected to remain buoyant. Inflation, which has fallen close to zero, is projected to begin rising from late 2015, while unemployment continues to fall.

The Bank of Japan's "quantitative and qualitative monetary easing" should continue until the 2% inflation target has been sustainably achieved. The reduction of public debt remains a top priority as gross public debt reaches 230% of GDP. To achieve fiscal sustainability, a detailed and credible fiscal consolidation plan to attain the target of a primary budget surplus by FY 2020 is required, as well as faster output growth through bold structural reforms.

Key economic indicators: Japan

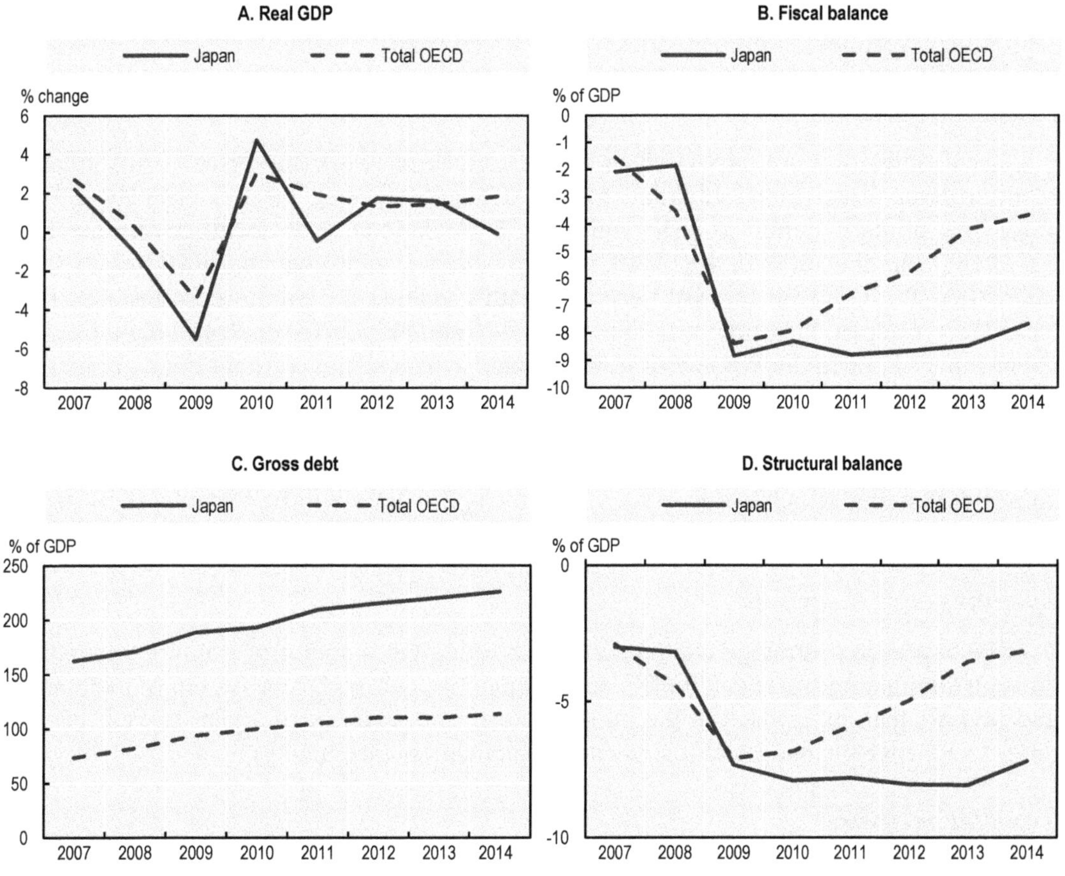

Source: OECD (2015a), "OECD Economic Outlook No. 97 (Edition 2015/1)", *OECD Economic Outlook: Statistics and Projections* (database), http://dx.doi.org/10.1787/data-00759-en.

StatLink http://dx.doi.org/10.1787/888933288199

Business investment is a key to raising labour productivity, which is a quarter below the average of the top half of OECD countries. The planned cuts in Japan's relatively high corporate income tax rate are expected to spur investment, but broader measures are needed. Raising Japan's relatively low rate of firm creation, in part by promoting venture capital investment, is another priority.

2. Fiscal policy and budgetary governance

The Japanese economic strategy continues to be defined by so-called "Abenomics", developed by the Government of Prime Minister Abe, with three "arrows" balancing bold monetary policy, flexible fiscal policy, and a growth strategy to promote private investment and structural reform aimed jointly at overcoming deflation and achieving sustainable growth. The fiscal policy context is shaped by an enormous overhang of public debt (around 230% of GDP). The structure of the debt means it remains serviceable, and fiscal policy efforts are focused on steady improvement in the underlying fiscal position so as to achieve a primary surplus by fiscal year (FY) 2020, and thereafter seek to steadily reduce the public debt-to-GDP ratio. The Japanese Government's fiscal strategy is marked by a pragmatic, flexible approach aiming at achieving both economic revitalisation and fiscal consolidation. The particular focus given to mobilising private capital for investment in infrastructure is also noteworthy.

Fiscal objectives

Fiscal objectives are stipulated in the "Basic Framework for Fiscal Consolidation: Medium-term Fiscal Plan" of August 2013. Under this plan, the Government aims to halve the primary deficit-to-GDP ratio for both national and local governments by FY 2015 from the ratio in FY 2010, and to achieve a primary surplus by FY 2020. Thereafter, the Government will seek to steadily reduce the public debt-to-GDP ratio. Near-term budget measures in the FY 2014 and FY 2015 budget, including the commitment to keep the volume of newly issued Japanese government bonds below that of the preceding fiscal year, are in line with these objectives. The overall budget strategy envisages actions on both the expenditure and revenue sides of the budget. Based on the FY 2015 budget, the FY 2015 target is expected to be achieved. The concrete fiscal consolidation plan to achieve a primary surplus by FY 2020 will be formulated by around the end of June this year.

Spending-side measures

The expenditure strategy is aimed at constraining the increase of primary expenditure through eliminating waste and inefficiency. Japan has put in place a system of evaluations and reviews that are utiliaed in the budget formulation process of a year-to-year basis in order to enhance the budget efficiency and effectiveness (see below).

Tax-side measures

In April 2014, consumption tax was increased from 5% to 8% in order to secure a source of financing for increasing social security expenditure. The planned increase to 10% was however postponed by the Japanese Government in November 2014 to take into account the economic and fiscal conditions.

Protecting economic growth

The three-pronged "Abenomics" policy is fundamentally a growth-centric strategy which provides for co-ordinated and mutually supported actions across the different spheres of policy action. The Japanese Government aims to achieve both economic revitalisation and fiscal consolidation. Specifically:

- As regards monetary policy, the Bank of Japan introduced quantitative and qualitative easing in April 2013 with a view to achieving the price-stability target of 2% inflation within a time horizon of about two years.
- In the area of fiscal policy, within the over-arching fiscal objectives outlined above, there are specific fiscal stimulus measures (notably in the FY 2013 supplementary budget [JPY 5.5 trillion] and FY 2014 budget), which are front-loaded in order to mitigate the potential contractionary impact of the increase in consumption tax from 5% to 8%. An economic stimulus package of JPY 3.5 trillion has been formulated to boost consumption and promote growth in regional areas.
- As regards the growth strategy, the "Japan Revitalization Strategy 2013" and its 2014 revision set out a range of measures for promoting private investment and structural measures, including growth-oriented corporate tax reform and enhancing corporate governance. The growth strategy will be revised again this summer to further promote structural reform.

Policy priorities

The Medium-Term Fiscal Plan stipulates the basic requirements for effective resource allocation while indicating the priority policy areas of social security, public capital investment and local government finance. Moreover, the Cabinet instructions in regard to budget requests limit the budget request for lower priority areas and promote resource reallocation.

As indicated above, the Japanese Government has a range of approaches aimed at facilitating resource allocation with effective and useful evaluation. In this regard, Japan has introduced a PDCA cycle (plan-do-check-action), a kind of performance budgeting which seeks to make use of targets and indicators throughout the budgetary cycle in a continuous/iterative manner. The intention is to provide a continual focus on improving budget efficiency and effectiveness. The PDCA cycle consists of the following four measures:

1. Survey conducted by the budget bureau of the Ministry of Finance, focused on assessing the effectiveness and efficiency of selected policy programmes.
2. Policy Evaluation conducted by the Ministry of Internal Affairs and Communications and by line ministries based on the Government Policy Evaluations Act. This type of evaluation is focused on assessing the achievements of line ministries from the perspective of necessity, efficiency and effectiveness.
3. Administrative Programmes Review is conducted by the Cabinet Secretariat and by line ministries. Under this process, which is regulated by a Cabinet decision, line ministries prepare a comprehensive review of all government policy programmes (over 5 000 in all) in advance of the following year's budget request.

4. The National Audit is conducted by the Board of Audit, which is independent from the Cabinet and constantly audits and supervises public accounts from an accuracy, regularity, economy, efficiency and effectiveness perspective. Audit reports prepared by the Board of Audit, which are routinely published to provide the Government and the Diet with independent critical perspectives, to be reflected in the budget formulation stage.

Long-term sustainability and fiscal risks

The progressive increase in consumption tax has been introduced as a measure to secure the source of financing for increasing social security expenditure, which faces longer-term pressures in Japan (as in other OECD countries) due to population ageing. While the increase to 10% has been postponed, the Japanese Government will apply this increase from 2017. The Fiscal System Council (see below) published its Long-Term Projections on Japanese Public Finances in April 2014, an analysis setting out sustainability and risk assessment to the fiscal year 2060.

Sub-national budgeting

As indicated above, the Medium Term Fiscal Plan and the fiscal consolidation targets that it contains, apply to the central and local governments. The plan stipulates that total local government general revenues in both FY 2014 and FY 2015 should be maintained at the same level as in FY 2013. In this regard, additional grants to local governments will need to be constrained accordingly.

Capital budgeting and public-private partnerships

In light of the tight fiscal situation, and the need to invest in high-priority public works, the Japanese Government is promoting public-private partnership (PPP)/private finance initiative (PFI) approaches to capital procurement and delivery. The Act on Promotion of Private Finance Initiative was amended in 2011 and a new concession scheme was introduced. Moreover, the Government introduced the "Action Plan towards Fundamental Reform of PPP/PFI" in 2013 and set a target to achieve JPY 12 trillion PPP/PFI projects in the period to 2022. In 2014, the Government intensified efforts in this regard with more specific targets laid down for the period FY 2014-FY 2016 (a "Period of Intensive Effort of the Action Plan").

Economic forecasting

In Japan, the Cabinet Office prepares the "Economic Outlook" twice a year and the outlook is approved by the Cabinet. The outlook presents the forecasts for the current year and next year. Japan does not have an official Independent Fiscal Institution along the model of several other OECD countries. Instead, the Fiscal System Council is established as an advisory body to the Minister of Finance, with around 30 members including academics, business leaders and other experts. The Fiscal System Council provides constructive proposals for fiscal consolidation, including expenditure constraining measures, and it produces projections on long-term sustainability (see above).

Engagement of parliament and citizens

The Japanese Ministry of Finance produces easily accessible brochures/fact sheets to enhance the accessibility of public finance information to the public, and briefing sessions are held by the ministry as required. In addition, the Japanese Government submits a summary of the draft budget to the Diet in order to promote the quality of budget scrutiny and debate by parliament. As for the engagement by the public and civil society in budget policy making, the Diet must hold open hearings on the overall budget and important bills concerning revenue based on the Diet Law.

Korea

1. Economic situation

Output growth is projected to slow to around 3% in 2015, reflecting sluggish private consumption in the context of high household debt and stagnant wages. Inflation has fallen to less than 1%, well below the target range of 2.5% to 3.5%, while weak domestic demand is boosting the current account surplus to around 7% of GDP. Lower oil prices are projected to support stronger consumption and investment, boosting output growth to 3.5% in 2016.

With output projected to remain below potential for the fourth straight year, fiscal stimulus is needed to support economic activity and complement monetary policy easing, which has reduced the policy interest rate to a record low. Korea also needs wide-ranging structural reforms, including those in the 2014 Three-year Plan for Economic Innovation, to support its growth potential.

Key economic indicators: Korea

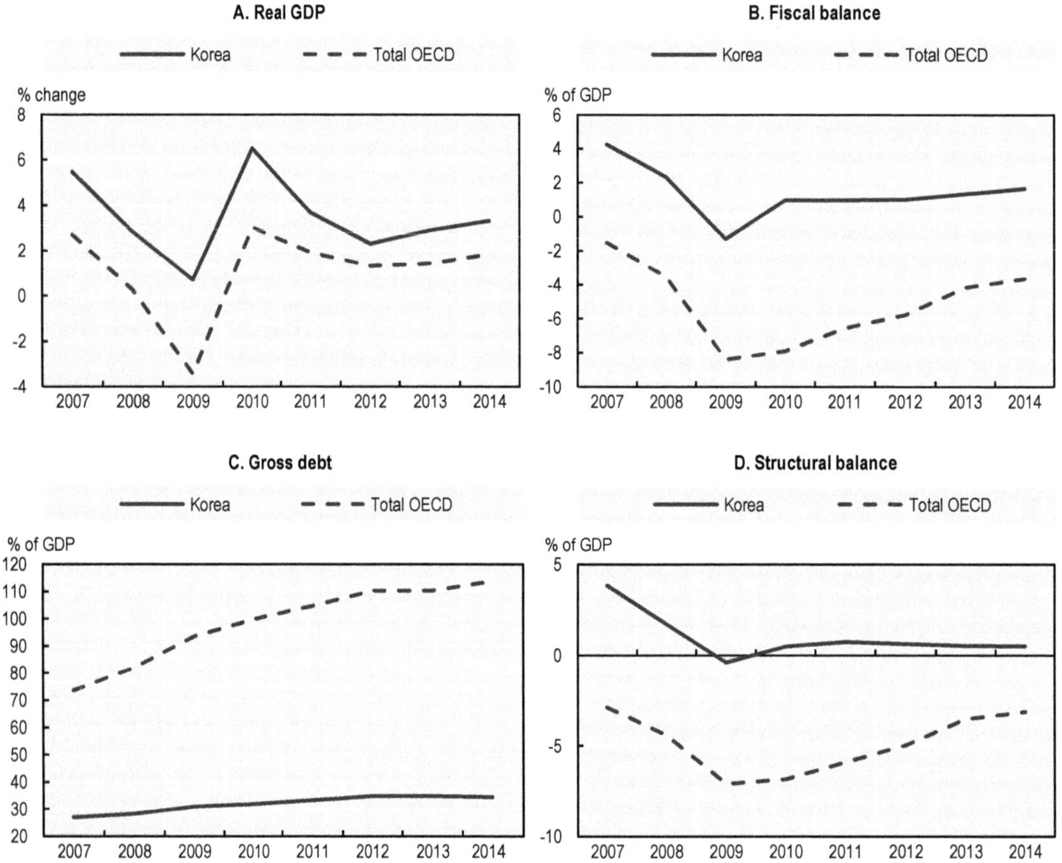

Source: OECD (2015a), "OECD Economic Outlook No. 97 (Edition 2015/1)", *OECD Economic Outlook: Statistics and Projections* (database), http://dx.doi.org/10.1787/data-00759-en.

StatLink http://dx.doi.org/10.1787/888933288203

A top priority is to raise investment to reverse the declining contribution of capital growth to productivity and GDP growth. Implementation of the government reform agenda, which focusses on relaxing regulations and promoting the development of a creative economy, is key.

2. Fiscal policy and budgetary governance

The Korean Government has set out its fiscal strategy in a five-year National Fiscal Management Plan: the 2014-2018 version was submitted to the National Assembly in September 2014. Korea's public finances are in reasonably healthy shape, and Korea is planning to use its available fiscal space for pro-growth policies in 2014 and 2015. The broader strategy is to create a "virtuous circle" of economic recovery leading to higher revenue generation.

Fiscal objectives

Korea is not bound by fiscal rules, but the Fiscal Management Plan envisages that after a relaxation of the fiscal stance in 2014 and 2015, the debt level will be stabilised at around 35-36% of GDP into the future. It is notable that the National Assembly has the power to modify the Government's budget proposals, and indeed exercised this power – both with regard to total expenditure and total revenue – in the course of its 2015 Budget Review, with a net improvement of the fiscal aggregates.

Spending-side measures

To achieve the stabilised debt level, the Korean Government plans to maintain the growth rate of total expenditure at around 4.5% per annum, below the projected growth rate of revenues of around 5.1% p.a. – a *de facto* expenditure rule. Within public expenditures, the Government's strategy is to improve efficiency by eliminating duplication and consolidating similar/redundant programmes.

Tax-side measures

The Government's broad strategy with regard to taxation is to expand the revenue base through the streamlining of tax exemptions and reliefs and a systematic targeting of the underground economy.

Protecting economic growth

As indicated above, the Korean Government has decided to adopt an expansionary fiscal stance for 2014 and 2015, until the effects of the economic recovery are clearly felt. Structural economic reforms are also being introduced to promote market dynamism. As part of this overall strategy:

- Public expenditure has been increased by KRW 20 trillion in 2015, with 58.6% of the extra spending front-loaded to the first half of the year.
- Monetary policy has been simultaneously loosened with rates cut by 75 basis points.
- Three tax packages have been introduced to boost household income.
- A phased increase in the minimum wage is being introduced.

- The cost of living is being reduced by ensuring a timely drop in fuel prices to reflect market movements in the price of oil, as well as though housing subsidies and freezing public utility charges.
- Banking structural reform is being implemented by improving the financial regulatory framework and stimulating technology finance to strengthen the role of the financial sector in supporting the real economy.
- There are measures to mitigate labour market "dualism" between regular and non-regular workers and between conglomerates and small- and medium-sized enterprises (SMEs) to promote high-quality jobs for young people.
- The education system is being reformed by reshaping the school system and introducing a work-study system to ensure students are equipped with the rights skills demanded by industries.

Policy priorities

The five-year National Fiscal Management Plan sets out cardinal directions for public policy under three headings:

- promoting a vibrant economy, through:
  - enhancing the responsiveness of fiscal policy against economic volatility
  - increasing investment to improve economic fundamentals
  - boosting domestic consumption through job creation, revitalising local economies and nurturing promising service-sector industries
  - developing new and emerging industries and markets;
- promoting the well-being and happiness of citizens, through:
  - establishing a framework for key social welfare policies, with expansion of the social safety net and reducing the cost of living
  - improving management and employment conditions for small business owners and temporary workers;
- promoting a safe and secure society, through:
  - expansion of safety inspection for all structures to provide a safe living environment for the public
  - increasing investment for safety equipment and facilities, strengthening the foundation of the public safety industry.

Long-term sustainability and fiscal risks

Korea faces severe longer term demographic pressures, along with several other OECD countries. The Korean Government has been developing a strategy to monitor and address the situation since 2012, in line with the provisions of the National Finance Act of December 2011 which mandates the Minister of Strategy and Finance to prepare long-term fiscal projections at least once every five years, covering a period of more than 40 years. The four major public pension funds – Government Employees' Pension, Teachers' Pension, Military Pension and National Pension – are currently undergoing a fiscal sustainability re-assessment to identify the level of longer term fiscal risk, and to devise appropriate policy/reform responses.

Sub-national budgeting

The fiscal autonomy of local governments has been increased through a series of measures arising from the initiative on "Functional and Resource Allocation Adjustment between Central and Local Governments" of December 2013:

- greater autonomy to levy tax, leading to the local consumption tax being raised from 5% to 11%, and a reform of the local income tax system
- greater autonomy in the use of transfers from the National Treasury, with the previous "decentralisation subsidy" integrated into the general subsidy, and removal of restrictions on the use of these block grants
- improved fiscal soundness of local governments through the amendment of the Local Finance Act of May 2014, which enhances the status of the Medium-term Local Fiscal Management Plan and strengthens the application of financial impact assessment for major projects.

Economic forecasting

The National Fiscal Management Plan for 2014-18 sets out the target of real GDP growth of 4% per annum for the medium term.

Engagement of parliament and citizens

The deadline for submission of the government's budget plan has been brought forward from early October to mid-September, in order to give the National Assembly extra time to review the proposals. Due to a new provision of the National Assembly Law, the budget plan is automatically submitted to the plenary session even if it is not agreed after adjustment negotiations. As regards budget transparency, the national Finance Law now requires each minister to publish the revenue/expenditure budget management status of their ministry on its Internet homepage.

Luxembourg

1. Economic situation

Growth is projected to remain robust at just below 3%, notwithstanding the shift in the EU VAT regime for e-commerce (which makes Luxembourg less attractive for certain export-oriented activities) and higher domestic VAT rates (introduced to partially offset the loss of revenue from e-commerce). Lower oil prices, a weaker euro and an ongoing recovery in the euro area will support exports and investment.

The Government is determined to keep the debt-to-GDP ratio low. This effort would be facilitated by introducing more effective spending control, including a spending ceiling for the general government in the medium-term budgeting framework. Structural reforms should focus at bringing people back to work by adjusting the tax and benefit system and enhancing active labour market policies.

Key economic indicators: Luxembourg

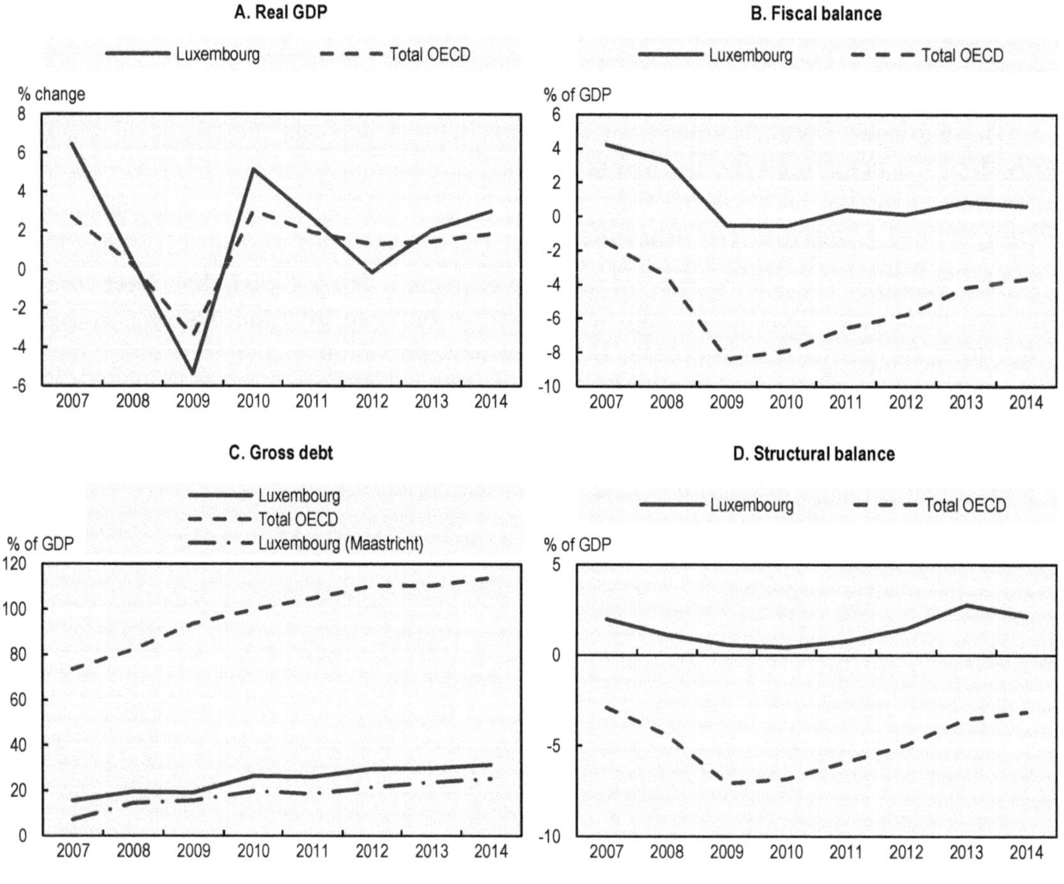

Source: OECD (2015a), "OECD Economic Outlook No. 97 (Edition 2015/1)", *OECD Economic Outlook: Statistics and Projections* (database), http://dx.doi.org/10.1787/data-00759-en.

StatLink http://dx.doi.org/10.1787/888933288215

Going forward, gross fixed investment will contribute positively to GDP growth. The share in GDP of non-residential gross fixed investment is above the OECD average. On the other hand, investment in knowledge-based capital, including overall and business spending on research and development, is lower than in many other OECD countries, with unexploited growth and employment potential.

2. Fiscal policy and budgetary governance

The public finances of Luxembourg were in healthy condition prior to the economic and financial crisis, with a debt-to-GDP ratio of around 19% in 2008 – one of the very lowest in the OECD – and a fiscal surplus of over 3% of GDP. The deficit swung into a modest deficit in 2009 and 2010, and the public debt ratio has risen in 2012 to about 30% of GDP according to OECD standards (21.4% according to *Maastricht* standards). From 2011, a process of budgetary consolidation has brought the public finances back into modest surplus. In the future, Luxembourg will adapt its fiscal objectives to meet challenges arising from EU-wide tax changes. The expenditure review process is a notable new feature of Luxembourg's budgetary framework.

Fiscal objectives

Luxembourg is subject to the new EU economic governance rules which require progress towards a medium-term budgetary objective of achieving structural balance of +0.5% of GDP. However, in light of the underlying central government deficit of 1.2% of GDP, and of the challenges from changes to EU VAT rules (see below), the Government of Luxembourg that took office in late 2013 has set itself two main budgetary objectives:

- to bring the structural budget balance back to its medium-term objective by 2018
- to stabilise gross public debt at below 30% of GDP according to *Maastricht* standards.

Spending-side measures

The consolidation plan since 2011 has involved a broadly equal mix between expenditure and revenue measures. On the spending side, measures included reductions in student loans, pension adjustments, and large-scale reductions in capital transfers and investment.

In identifying further targeted spending reductions, Luxembourg has embarked upon an ambitious expenditure review process. The Government's objective is to make substantial savings up to 2018 across public expenditure as a whole – State, local authorities and social security – while improving the quality and effectiveness of public policies. The expenditure review process is managed by the Minister of Finance and assisted by the *Inspection Générale des Finances,* the budget policy arm of the Ministry. The 2014 process consists of four phases, namely:-

- design phase – from February to March
- preparation phase – from March to June, initiated by letters from the Prime Minister and the Minister of Finance
- decision and consultation phase – from June to September
- implementation phase – from September through to presentation of the budget in October.

In a model similar to that adopted by the Netherlands in 2010, 20 working groups were invited to propose savings relative to 2018 expenditure in the "no policy change" scenario, and the savings proposals were submitted to the Government for consideration as part of the process of formulating the October budget. The proposals submitted by the working groups in their technical deliberations exceeded the savings required for budgetary consolidation, leaving the government with a margin for manoeuvre in selecting measures to adopt during the political decision making phase. The various measures resulting from the spending review are to be implemented via separate bills, named *Zukunftspak* ("Future-Package").

Tax-side measures

As indicated above, Luxembourg has generated additional revenues as part of its consolidation strategy. From 2011, the extra measures included a rate increase in the third (highest) income tax bracket, a rate increase in the solidarity tax, and the introduction of a temporary "crisis levy" which remained in force from 2011 until 2012. A further package of broad-based revenue-raising measures was adopted in 2013, including elimination of tax reliefs, introduction of a new 40% income tax bracket and an increase in the solidarity tax. Further measures were adopted by the Government in 2014 – a package of VAT increases, and a temporary budget adjustment levy – alongside the implementation of the measures from the spending review.

More than any other OECD country, Luxembourg will be affected by changes to EU VAT rules from 2015 onwards: from then, VAT revenues on e-commerce activities will be assigned to the budget of member states based on consumers' country of residence instead of that of the service provider. The negative impact of this change of Luxembourg's revenues is estimated at around EUR 800 million a year – 1.5% of GDP – and this has necessitated the adaptation of Luxembourg's medium-term fiscal objectives as outlined above.

Budget costings and execution

In line with other Eurozone countries, Luxembourg has established an independent fiscal institution whose role is to validate the Government's economic forecasts and assess compliance with the EU fiscal governance objectives.

Protecting economic growth

As indicated above, Luxembourg adopted fiscal stimulus measures in 2010 and 2011 but since then, the focus has been on regaining fiscal balance and there are no specific growth promoting strategies in place that are relevant for the budget process.

Policy priorities

The Luxembourg Government has not set out any particular set of priorities to underpin resource allocation strategy into the medium term.

Long-term sustainability and fiscal risks

The Luxembourg Government has not adopted any particular measures to underpin long-term fiscal sustainability or address fiscal risks.

Engagement of parliament and citizens

Budget documents and data are available to the public on a user-friendly website, http://budget.public.lu.

The government's planned fiscal consolidation: Luxembourg

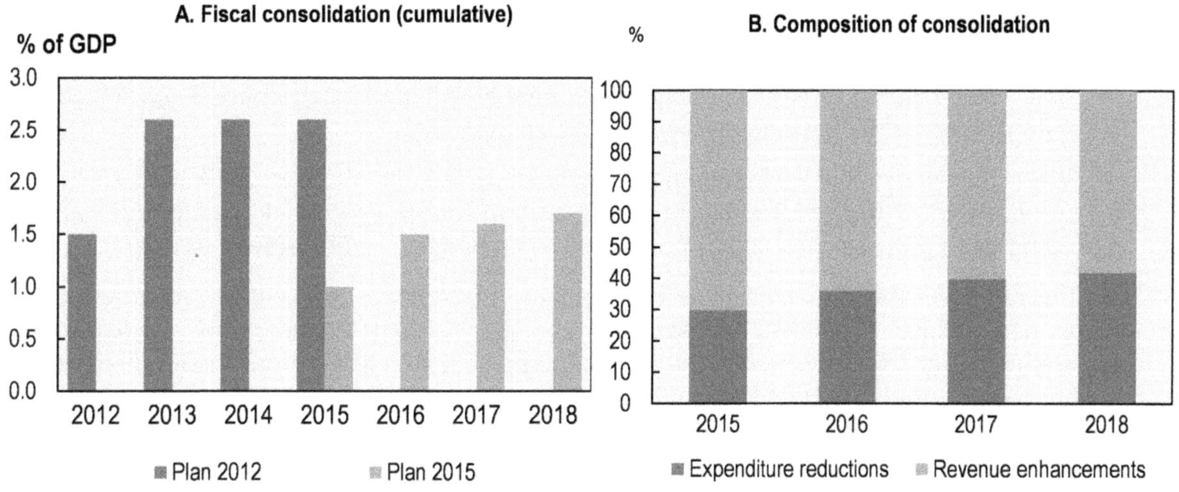

Source: OECD (2015b), *OECD State of Public Finances Survey 2015*; OECD (2011), *Restoring Public Finances,* www.oecd.org/gov/budgeting/47558957.pdf.

StatLink http://dx.doi.org/10.1787/888933288482

Mexico

1. Economic situation

Mexico's economic recovery is strengthening, led by US import demand for manufactures and a weaker currency. Real GDP is projected to grow by 2.9% in 2015 and 3.5% in 2016. Firming exports have finally allowed the rebound to gain speed, and investment has begun to regain lost ground. Notwithstanding lower oil prices, new tenders are attracting considerable interest in the wake of the recent energy-sector reforms. Wide-ranging reforms to competition, energy and market regulation have helped boost confidence while monetary policy has been supportive.

While monetary policy has remained on hold so far, interest rates will need to be raised once the US Federal Reserve raises its rates to forestall potential capital outflows. Spending was tightened early in 2015 and a balanced budget is still foreseen in 2017.

Overall investment spending has been picking up strongly, particularly for durable equipment, while residential construction is also rising, albeit more gradually. Determined efforts to implement the wide-ranging recent structural reforms offer the best chance to boost investment and productivity, helping to ensure more rapid and sustainable gains in well-being going forward.

Key economic indicators: Mexico

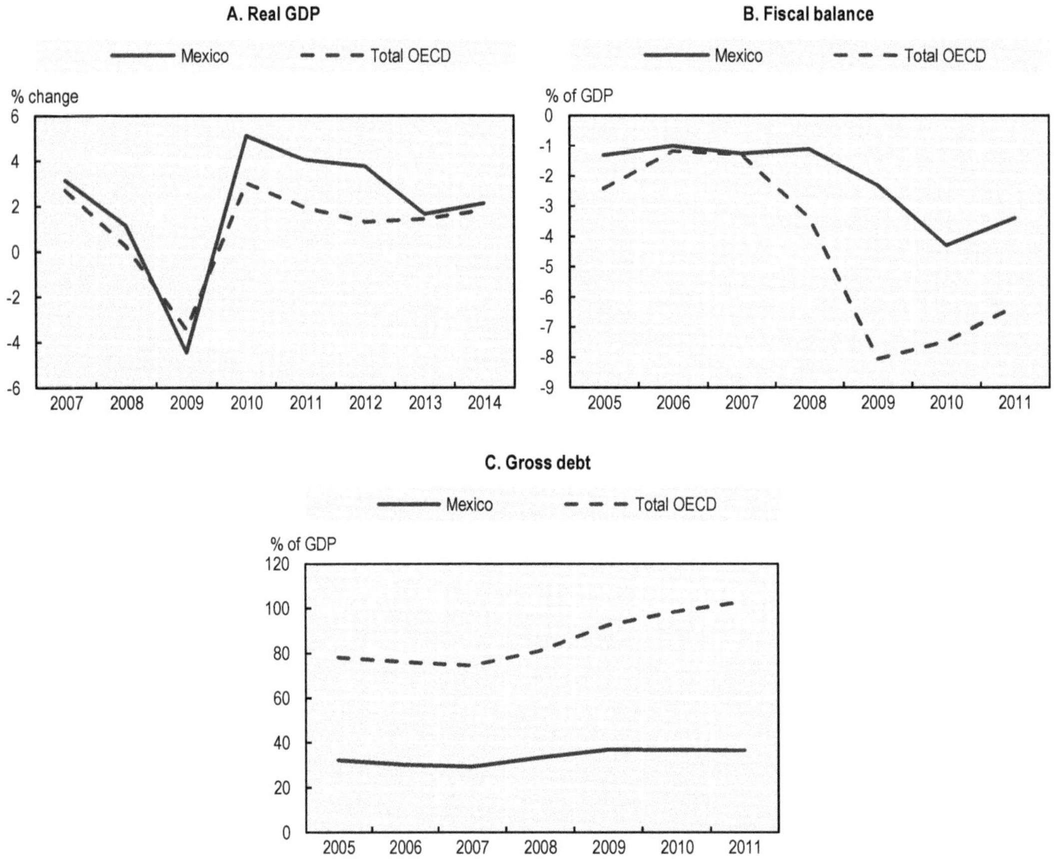

Source: OECD (2015a), "OECD Economic Outlook No. 97 (Edition 2015/1)", *OECD Economic Outlook: Statistics and Projections* (database), http://dx.doi.org/10.1787/data-00759-en.

StatLink http://dx.doi.org/ 10.1787/888933288224

2. Fiscal policy and budgetary governance

The current fiscal plan was established in 2013, in the General Economic Policy Guidelines for 2014. The overall plan has been adapted due to the weak global economic recovery, an increase in financial market volatility and a low oil price situation. The plan lays out two strategies: the implementation of a comprehensive tax reform and a transitory and decreasing deficit path returning to a budgetary balance by 2017 in order to boost economic growth.

Fiscal objectives

A structural balance rule is defined in the current fiscal plan. This new rule allows the implementation of a counter-cyclical fiscal policy throughout the economic cycle. The goal in relation to the deficit path is for the fiscal deficit to be 1% of GDP in 2015, 0.5% of GDP in 2016 and to achieve budgetary balance by 2017. In terms of the public sector borrowing requirement (PSBR), the goal is for borrowing to be 4% of GDP in 2015, 3.5% of GDP in 2016, 3% of GDP in 2017 and 2.5% of GDP from 2017 onwards.

Spending-side measures

The federal government is currently implementing a multi-year public spending adjustment to bring the budget back to balance. This adjustment aims to generate additional fiscal buffers to cope with potential negative shocks during 2015 and beyond. The budget for 2016 will be conducted using a zero-based budgeting approach, meaning that everything will be up for review and each item will need to be justified in order to remain in the budget. An internal exercise to improve administrative processes and eliminate potential duplicities in functions and structures will also be undertaken. The World Bank will support and advise the Mexican Government during this process through a comprehensive Public Expenditure Review that will strengthen the efficiency and quality of the spending policy framework.

Tax-side measures

Tax reform has been fully implemented. Specific measures to assist fiscal consolidation include the Revenue Law 2014 which introduced special taxes, one of them being a tax on the production and consumption of flavoured beverages. The Government has now committed to avoiding increasing taxes given the current economic conditions.

Protecting economic growth

A fiscal stimulus was applied (giving rise to a fiscal deficit above the structural balance) to shield economic growth. The Fiscal Reform also introduced a series of measures aimed at boosting economic development. First, the financial capacity of the state was strengthened through an increase in the resources available to meet its obligations. Second, the equality, progressiveness and fairness of the tax system were improved by eliminating tax privileges. Moreover, the social security contributions process was simplified for small businesses. Finally, a new tax regime for Pemex was established in order to reduce its tax burden and to improve the quality of its expenditure.

Policy priorities

Priorities identified in the fiscal plan include:

- maintaining macroeconomic stability as an essential prerequisite for economic development and the well-being of families
- accelerating the implementation of structural reforms to boost economic potential
- increasing the State's financial capacity to address the primary needs of the population, in particular those with low incomes, in areas such as social security, health and public safety
- improving income distribution, improving progressiveness of the tax system and encouraging formality.

Long-term sustainability and fiscal risks

In the last two decades, reforms to the public pensions systems were made in order to move from a system of defined benefit to a system of defined contribution which helps reduce transitional ageing costs. Benefits from this strategy are already being seen in the medium-term estimations of the General Economic Policy Guidelines.

Engagement of parliament and citizens

The Ministry of Finance has published a new portal relating to budget transparency (www.transparenciapresupuestaria.gob.mx/). It contains information on the performance system, indicators, progress towards targets and programme evaluations. For the first time there is also open data federation expenditure for 2015. There are more than 2 400 files that can be downloaded and used in open data format. There are also other thematic portals. There is a portal for open public investment which provides information on all the programmes of investment funded by the 2015 budget. There is a portal for sub-national government financing where citizens can see the total amount that is allocated to regional and local governments. There is also a portal for the educational reform programme with open data relating to the investment needs of schools and the use of public resources. In addition, some publications, such as the Draft Budget, the proposal for expenditure and the 2013 public accounts that are provided in easy access language for citizens to access.

The government's planned fiscal consolidation: Mexico

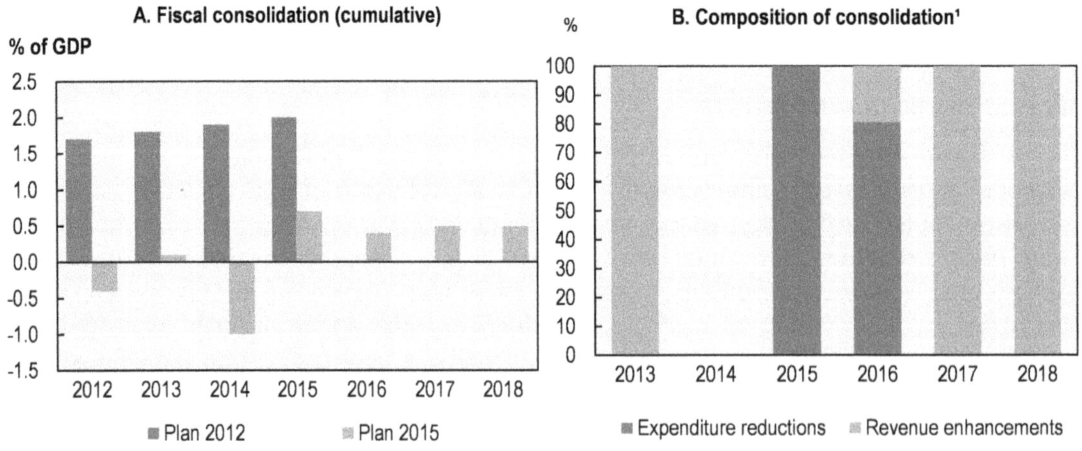

Note[1]: No composition of consolidation data for 2014

Source: OECD (2015b), *OECD State of Public Finances Survey 2015*; OECD (2011), *Restoring Public Finances*, www.oecd.org/gov/budgeting/47558957.pdf.

StatLink http://dx.doi.org/10.1787/888933288493

Netherlands

1. Economic situation

Economic growth is projected to increase to 2.0% in 2015 and 2.2% in 2016. Real wage gains will support higher private consumption, while the improved business outlook and the ongoing recovery of the housing market will support investment. Exports are set to continue to increase steadily, boosted by the recovery in the European Union and the low value of the euro. Employment is set to rise significantly and the unemployment rate to fall gradually.

The planned slow pace of structural fiscal consolidation is appropriate given the strengthening but still uncertain recovery. Further reforming employment protection would support job creation and benefit labour reallocation to more productive uses. The return to trend-based budgetary policy should contribute to budgetary discipline while allowing automatic stabilisers to operate on the revenue side.

Investment is almost 20% lower than it was before the crisis, mostly due to lower residential investment. Business investment has held up quite well since the crisis, although its share of GDP remains moderate compared to other EU countries.

Key economic indicators: Netherlands

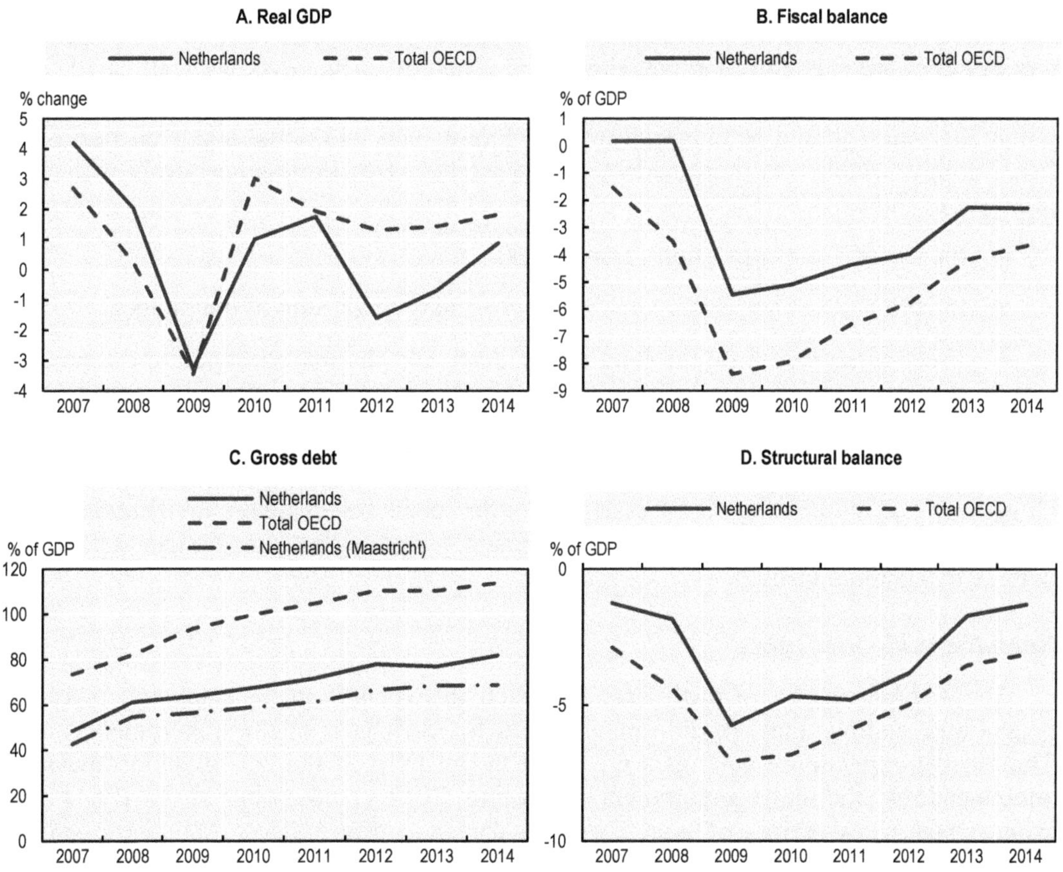

Source: OECD (2015a), "OECD Economic Outlook No. 97 (Edition 2015/1)", *OECD Economic Outlook: Statistics and Projections* (database), http://dx.doi.org/10.1787/data-00759-en.

StatLink http://dx.doi.org/10.1787/888933288236

2. Fiscal policy and budgetary governance

When the Dutch Government assumed office in autumn 2012, it set out three pillars of its socioeconomic policy:

- putting the public finances in order
- ensuring an equitable distribution of benefits and burdens
- working for sustainable growth and an innovative economy.

With regard to the first of these pillars – the correction of the public finances – the Netherlands had suffered an acute rise in its fiscal deficit to above 5% of GDP in 2009-10, remaining at above 4% in 2011-12. In 2013, the Dutch Government was afforded an additional year to correct its "excessive deficit" under EU rules, in return for introducing additional structural measures amounting to 1% of GDP. On this basis, the deficit was brought sharply below the 3% of GDP EU ceiling from 2013. Since that time, the Dutch Government has set its fiscal policy – including in legal terms – in line with the "guard rails" of the EU-wide fiscal governance objectives.

Fiscal objectives

The EU fiscal governance rules have been codified in the Netherlands in the Law on Sustainability of Public Finances, which took effect from December 2013. In essence, the law references directly the EU requirements regarding fiscal balance and debt, and these requirements are therefore applied directly as a matter of domestic as well as EU law. Beyond these EU requirements, the law also specifies how Dutch trend-based fiscal policy discretion should be managed into the future. This additional legal "anchoring" of fiscal policy, which was requested by the lower house of Parliament, deals with three principal elements:

- the use of fixed expenditure frameworks
- the principle of automatic stabilisation on the revenue side of the budget
- fiscal policy based on the long-term figures and the macroeconomic estimates of the relevant variables by the CPB (the official and *de facto* independent Dutch economic forecasting bureau).

In practical terms, the new policy and legal framework is represented by the Dutch Government as combining fiscal discipline with scope for cyclical stabilisation of the economy. On this basis, the Dutch Government foresees that that budget deficit will decline in a gradual fashion.

Spending-side measures

The Netherlands has a distinctive approach to expenditure management, involving expenditure ceilings that are definitively fixed for each year of the government's term. The current expenditure ceilings were fixed in the light of the consolidation measures announced by the new government in spring 2013, amounting to EUR 6 billion (approximately two-thirds of which was on the expenditure side). Actual expenditure within a year may be lower than the mandated "ceiling" amount - any "fiscal space" arising in this way has been used to reduce taxation. The Netherlands has an extensive system of policy evaluation (Schoch and den Broeder, 2013). This comprises both *ex ante* (e.g. cost-benefit analyses) and *ex post* evaluation (e.g. policy reviews). A third aspect of the policy evaluation system concerns (comprehensive) spending reviews. In contrast to *ex post* evaluation, spending reviews are not strictly embedded within legislation, but they have the highest potential impact on the budget. Spending reviews are performed yearly, comprehensive spending reviews only in extraordinary circumstances, such as the financial crises of 2009. Options for savings and spending prioritisation are not only derived from the entire evaluation system, but also from many other sources such as studies by (international) research institutions. These options are used by the Minister of Finance in the annual budget preparation process and may also provide input for the preparation of a new government term (elections and Coalition Agreement).

Tax-side measures

To complement the expenditure-side ceilings, the Netherlands has in place a "revenue ceiling", i.e. an upper limit (likewise set at the outset of a government's term of office) on the revenues from taxes and social contributions, taking account of the government's proposed policy adjustments to the base, rates etc. Any subsequent policy adjustments, which have the effect of increasing or decreasing revenues, must be countered by offsetting measures so that the revenue ceiling is respected. However any cyclically based deviations from the revenue projections are treated as either "windfalls" which are used to improve the fiscal balance, or "setbacks" which are, in principle, not required to be offset. In this way, a cyclically-neutral fiscal policy is facilitated.

In its draft budget of October 2014, the Dutch Government outlined its plans for targeted reductions in income tax to ease the burden on employees, contributing to labour demand, economic growth potential and to improve purchasing power in the economy. Moreover, from 2016 onwards, the Government has reserved fiscal space for implementing this announced revision of the tax system.

Protecting economic growth

The explicitly cyclically sensitive – or trend-related – fiscal policy course adopted by the Netherlands, which aims to fully use the scope for action allowed under the EU governance rules, is the main macro-level instrument for protecting economic growth. In the fiscal consolidation, education and innovation had been spared and received extra funding. Specific policies, both temporary and structural, have been taken to ensure that (potential) economic growth has been protected as much as possible. Examples of structural policies are lowering the transfer tax on housing purchases, lowering the maximum deductible rate on mortgage interest deduction, lowering the maximum loan to value for mortgages, raising the retirement age and lowering the burden on employment (shorter employment benefits, raising the labour tax deduction, limiting severance payments).

Policy priorities

The clarity afforded by fixed expenditure and revenue ceilings requires, as a consequence, clarity on the part of government as to how resources will be prioritised and deployed over its mandate. The Coalition Agreement of October 2012 identifies, alongside its three over-arching pillars, its priorities under 13 policy areas with specific commitments. The government document is therefore a determining factor as line ministries decide each year upon allocation of available resources.

Long-term sustainability and fiscal risks

The Dutch Government has adopted a risk-management policy of reducing *explicit liabilities* to an efficient level; and reducing *implicit liabilities* by identifying them, and including them within a standard Assessment Framework for Contingent Liabilities. In general, the Government will not provide guarantees or accept liabilities unless there is a compelling case for doing so; in any such cases the risk must be priced and a premium extracted; and the overall risk assessment framework must be submitted to Parliament. As regards long-term sustainability, the CPB (Netherlands Bureau for Economic Policy Analysis) calculates a "sustainability balance" showing the gap between the government's medium-term fiscal balance target, and the fiscal balance at which future incomes balance future expenditures. Importantly, this technical analysis assumes that expenditure per capita on various sectors, such as healthcare and education, remains constant over time.

Sub-national budgeting

The Law on Sustainability of Public Finances provides for a new procedure for formal consultation between central and sub-national authorities (municipalities, provinces and regional water authorities), to ensure that the burden of fiscal adjustment – which under EU rules in calculated across the entire "general government sector" – is shared proportionately. The agreements reached with central government envisage an "ambition" for fiscal adjustment in each area, and a "standard" fiscal path which allows some margin of movement relative to the "ambition". When local government in total exceeds its part of the joint deficit on a structural base, a correction mechanism is triggered. It will be addressed in the formal intergovernmental meeting (*Bestuurlijk overleg financiële verhoudingen/Bofv*). The ultimate measure, which is formalised in law, is a cut of the Municipality fund or the Provincial fund.

Economic forecasting

The CPB is a long-established and respected institution, with *de facto* independence, responsible for producing official economic forecasts in the Netherlands. In the context of the Law on Sustainability of Public Finances, the Council of State (Raad van State, RvS) – an advisory body under the Crown – is designated as an "independent budgetary authority", which will exercise adjudicative functions in assessing whether the Government's fiscal plans meet the relevant standards with regard to deficit, debt and the expenditure benchmark. By designating the budgetary assessment to the RvS, the Dutch Government made a distinction between the normative assessment of the RvS and independent budgetary and economic forecasting of the CPB. In its assessment, the RvS uses the economic and fiscal forecasts of the CPB. Dutch budgetary policy, by tradition, is based on independent forecasts and analyses from the CPB. For example, the CPB calculates projections of the (structural) budget balance, the expenditure rule and the debt criterion.

Engagement of parliament and citizens

The Netherlands has no particular initiatives in place to enhance the inclusiveness or participative nature of the budget process.

The government's planned fiscal consolidation: Netherlands

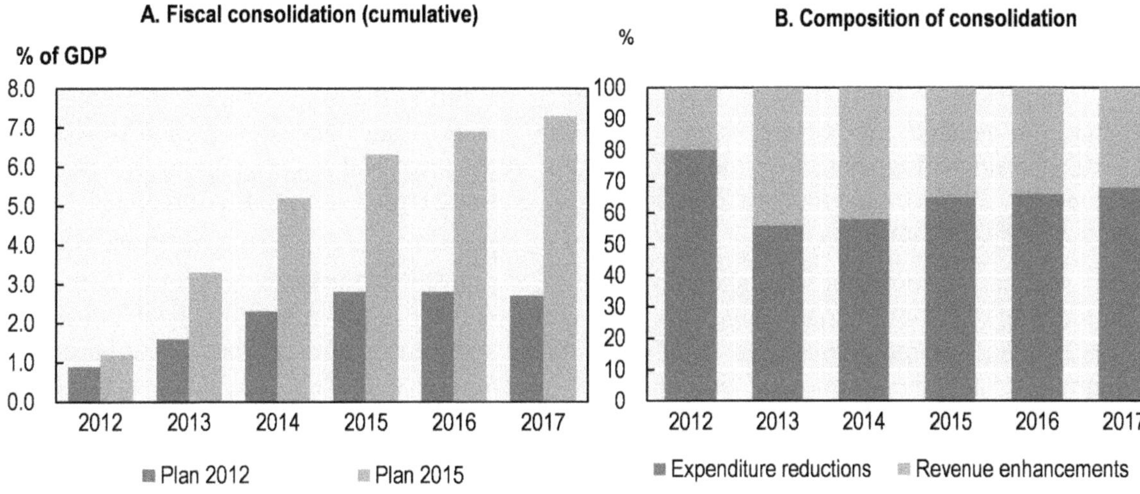

Source: OECD (2015b), *OECD State of Public Finances Survey 2015*; OECD (2011), *Restoring Public Finances*, www.oecd.org/gov/budgeting/47558957.pdf.

StatLink http://dx.doi.org/ 10.1787/888933288503

New Zealand

1. Economic situation

Economic growth is projected to moderate as the fall in the terms of trade depresses domestic demand, the boost from the Canterbury rebuild wanes and immigration slows. Still, the unemployment rate should continue to edge down and wage gains to increase modestly. With economic slack fully absorbed, consumer price inflation is projected to rise to 1.8% by late 2016.

Monetary accommodation should continue so as to allow inflation to return to the middle of the 1-3% target range. To take pressure off the booming Auckland house market, unwarranted barriers to supply should be reduced, macro-prudential measures tightened, and the taxation of trading gains on property extended and more strongly enforced, as planned. Fiscal policy should continue gradually to reduce the debt-GDP ratio over the medium term, while allowing the automatic stabilisers to operate fully. Fiscal priority should be given to continuing efforts to improve the well-being of the most vulnerable members of society.

Key economic indicators: New Zealand

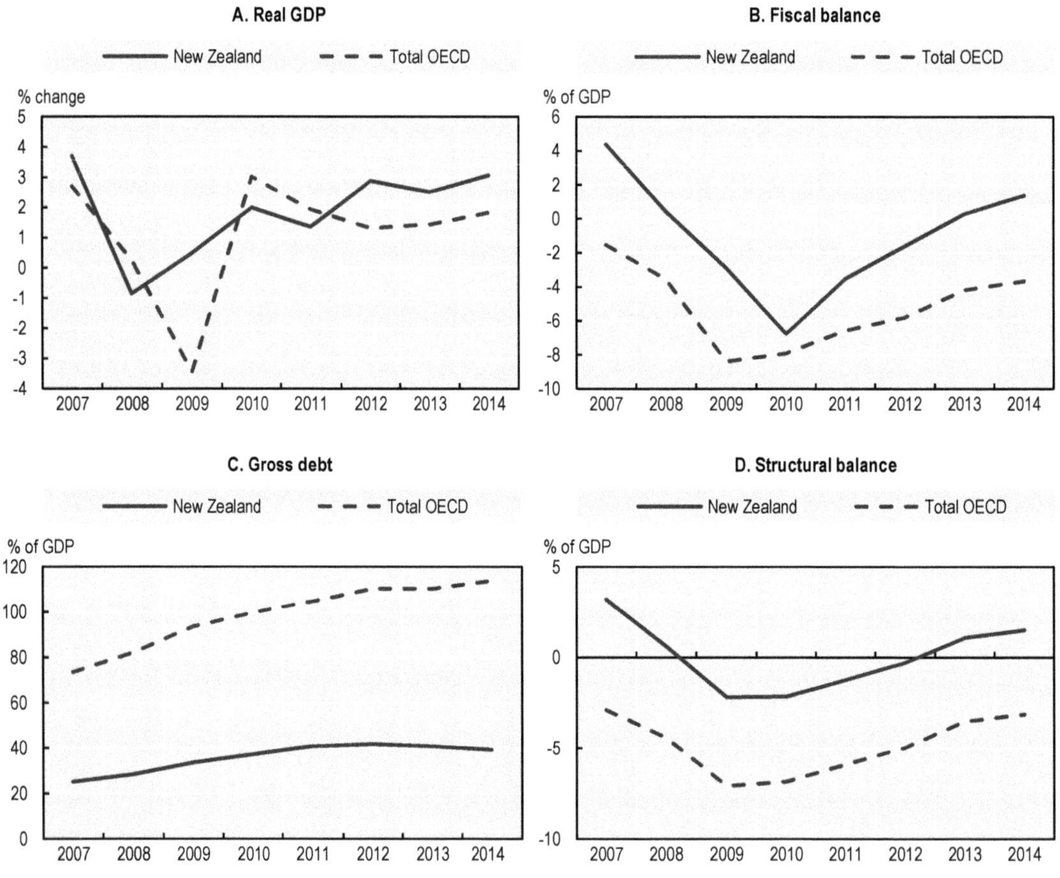

Source: OECD (2015a), "OECD Economic Outlook No. 97 (Edition 2015/1)", *OECD Economic Outlook: Statistics and Projections* (database), http://dx.doi.org/10.1787/data-00759-en.

StatLink http://dx.doi.org/10.1787/888933288249

Residential investment is 13% above its pre-recession peak, boosted by the Canterbury rebuild and demand pressures in Auckland. Business investment has also grown solidly, reaching 10% above the pre-recession peak, buoyed by diminishing spare capacity, high levels of business confidence and the low cost of capital. Growth in government investment has been more modest.

2. Fiscal policy and budgetary governance

The New Zealand Government has run annual budget deficits since 2008/09 as it has permitted automatic stabilisers to support the economy in the short term. However, as early as 2009, it coupled these deficits with a clearly signalled plan to return to fiscal surplus as soon as practical and reduce debt. In Budget 2009 the Government announced a target of returning to surplus in fiscal year 2015/16, subject to significant shocks. In Budget 2011 this was brought forward to 2014/15, despite the region of Canterbury experiencing severe earthquakes in 2010 and 2011. Recovery and reconstruction in Canterbury temporarily added to fiscal expenditures and increased public debt. The general government fiscal deficit peaked at 7.4% of GDP in 2010 but a return to surplus is expected in 2015/16. The biggest contribution to the fiscal turnaround has been considered expenditure restraint that rigorously tests spending for value and results, without resorting to slashing public spending or increasing taxes as other countries have been forced to do.

Fiscal objectives

The New Zealand Government has a target of returning to surplus in fiscal year 2014/15. The latest forecasts published by the New Zealand Treasury in December 2014 show the Government returning to fiscal surplus in 2015/16 – one year later than planned. The Government also has a fiscal objective to control the growth in government spending so that, over time, core Crown expenses are reduced to below 30% of GDP and to reduce net government debt to 20% of GDP by 2020. The forecasts show the Government is on track to meet these objectives, with core Crown expenses forecast to reduce to 29.7% of GDP in 2015/16 and net debt projected to fall to 19.1% of GDP by 2020/21. In 2014, the Government added an additional short-term goal to its fiscal strategy: to manage its spending and revenue so that any changes in fiscal policy settings do not have a material adverse impact on interest rates. It has therefore set allowances for new operating spending and/or revenue initiatives to average NZD 1.5 billion over the next three years.

Spending-side measures

The Government's expenditure restraint has been aimed at slowing the growth of expenditure to below that of tax revenue and GDP through a strong focus on the efficiency and effectiveness of spending. This has included: prioritising spending from lower-value to higher-value activities; reducing the limits on the level of new spending in each budget; reducing cost increases built into existing policies; and driving better results from the public sector by expecting most government agencies to operate within existing baseline budgets. Savings initiatives to slow expense growth have included tightening eligibility requirements for existing student support and welfare policies. Such expenditure restraint has contributed to significant progress being made towards achieving the Government's fiscal objectives. The Government's active financial management means expenditure continues to decline as a proportion of GDP, from 30.5% this year to 29.0% over the next five years.

Tax-side measures

The Government has not implemented significant tax-side measures to deliver fiscal turnaround. However, there have been some initiatives, such as the removal of three tax credits that were no longer fit for purpose. The Government introduced a structural tax reform in 2010 to boost growth that was fiscally neutral, by lowering personal and company income tax rates and increasing the rate of consumption tax. Budget 2012 announced a staggered rise in tobacco excise tax rates of 10% each year from 2013 to 2016, however this is primarily for public health reasons. In 2014, the Government also signalled an intention to introduce modest income tax reductions from 2017/18, subject to economic and fiscal conditions at the time.

Budget costings and execution

The general fiscal strategy continues to be advised by the Treasury, with implementation of the fiscal strategy involving a wide range of key stakeholders, including external experts and government agencies.

Protecting economic growth

The New Zealand economy is continuing to expand at a solid rate and the outlook is for sustained economic growth. The Government is focused on building a more productive, confident and competitive economy that will deliver higher incomes and higher living standards for New Zealanders. In addition, proceeds from the Government's programme of partial share offerings in three state-owned enterprises and Air New Zealand between 2012 and 2014 have been used to fund capital investments in new public assets via the "Future Investment Fund". The Government has also been undertaking microeconomic reforms over the past five years in the areas of taxation, labour-market flexibility, housing supply, oil exploration and an internationally focussed growth package to increase productivity and competitiveness.

Policy priorities

Budget 2015 will continue to progress the Government's programme and priorities, which are: responsibly managing the Government's finances; building a more productive and competitive economy; delivering better public services within tight financial constraints; and rebuilding Christchurch, the second biggest city. The Government intends to reduce its debt to more prudent levels to rebuild New Zealand's resilience to future shocks, lift national savings and reduce future finance costs. The Government's spending restraint also frees up resources to go to more productive uses in the economy. It has committed to get better results from the public services it provides, particularly in the areas of reducing crime, reducing long-term welfare dependency and improving educational outcomes. The strategy has been to bolster frontline services and get more efficiency in back office functions. The Government has also been undertaking welfare reforms for facilitating transition of welfare beneficiaries to work based on an investment approach. Supporting beneficiaries into work is seen as important for lifting their long-term outcomes and for reducing long-term fiscal pressures.

Long-term sustainability and fiscal risks

The New Zealand Treasury is required to publish a statement on the long-term fiscal position at least once every four years. The most recent statement was published in 2013 and contains fiscal projections to 2060. Population ageing and health cost growth are identified as key fiscal challenges in the long term. In 2013, amendments to the Public Finance Act added several new "Principles of Responsible Fiscal Management". This included requirement for governments, when setting fiscal policy, to have regard to the likely impact on present and future generations. The Government has focussed on ensuring that there is a strengthened fiscal position in the short to medium term – controlling government spending and getting debt down – to prepare for an ageing population. Restarting budgetary contributions to the New Zealand Superannuation Fund, once net debt reaches target levels, as planned, will also help to finance future ageing-related liabilities.

Sub-national budgeting

Central government fiscal consolidation has no direct effect on local government fiscal management because their finances are separately run.

Economic forecasting

The New Zealand Treasury provides macroeconomic forecasts and Inland Revenue prepares an independent set of tax forecasts.

Engagement of parliament and citizens

The 2013 amendments to the Public Finance Act focussed on getting the system as a whole better at delivering more meaningful information so that Parliament and the public can more easily see what the taxpayers' money has achieved. The New Zealand Government is also considering how it can be more participative with the budget process. A first step, being trialled for Budget 2015, is the Social Investment Request for Information. Responses were invited from people who work with vulnerable New Zealanders, and others whose input might help the Government invest to get better results. The ideas and information collected will be used to identify where existing services can be improved, or where new local services can be trialled.

The government's planned fiscal consolidation: New Zealand

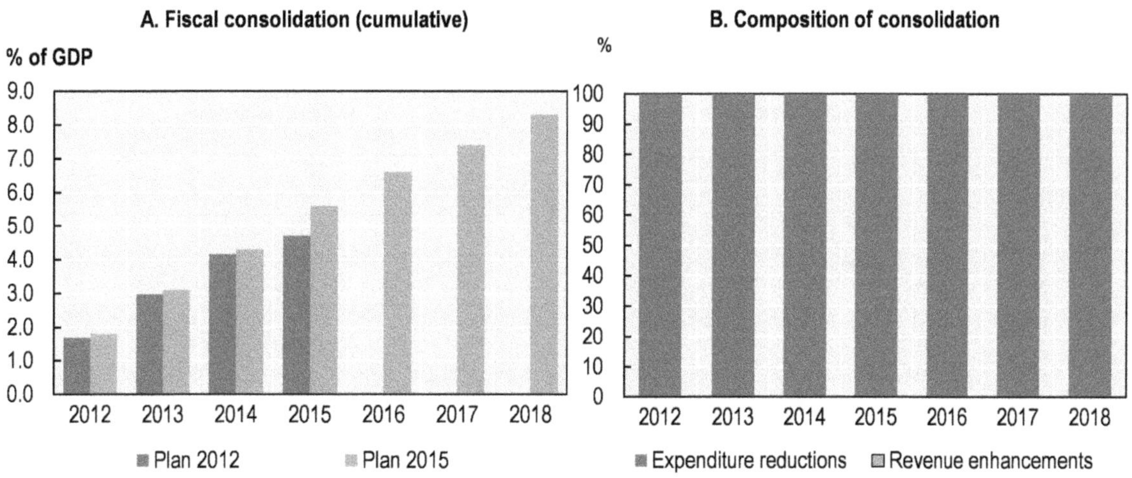

Source: OECD (2015b), *OECD State of Public Finances Survey 2015*; OECD (2011), *Restoring Public Finances*, www.oecd.org/gov/budgeting/47558957.pdf.

StatLink http://dx.doi.org/ 10.1787/888933288511

Norway

1. Economic situation

Growth is projected to weaken in 2015 as the fall in oil prices dents petroleum sector activity and investment, with spillovers on the mainland economy. A gradual recovery in 2016 will be supported by firming business investment in non-oil activities and stronger external demand. The unemployment rate is expected to drift up to slightly above 4% and wage growth is set to moderate. Inflation will remain low given the economic slack.

Monetary policy should remain accommodative, given the absence of inflationary pressures. An expansionary fiscal policy is appropriate in current circumstances. Rising house prices and mortgage lending require continued monitoring given high household debt levels. Improvements in competitiveness and productivity, including through product market reforms and education system improvements, are vital for broad-based growth.

The strong rise in petroleum investment in recent years has now come to a halt. Stimulating investment in the non-resource sector hinges upon a more business-friendly tax system, lower administrative burdens and a more modern infrastructure. Planned improvements in transport and communication networks are hence welcome. Greater public spending efficiency would benefit growth potential.

Key economic indicators: Norway

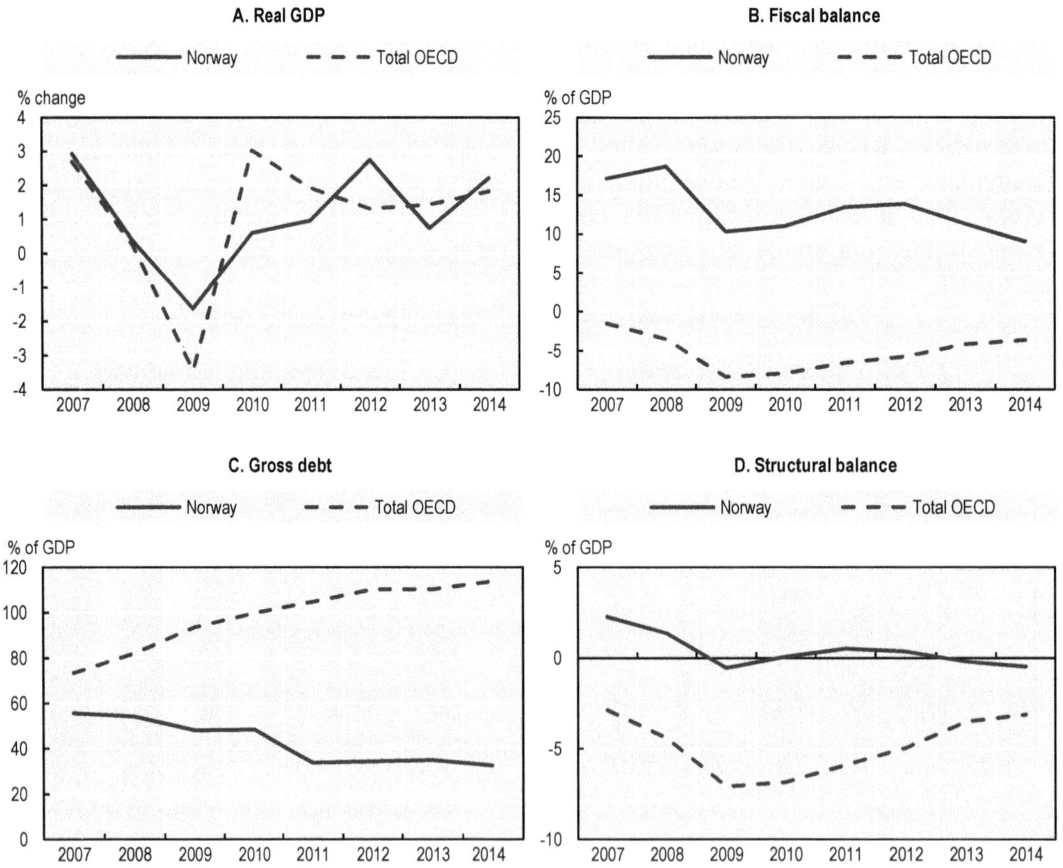

Source: OECD (2015a), "OECD Economic Outlook No. 97 (Edition 2015/1)", *OECD Economic Outlook: Statistics and Projections* (database), http://dx.doi.org/10.1787/data-00759-en.

StatLink http://dx.doi.org/10.1787/888933288250

2. Fiscal policy and budgetary governance

With a budget surplus maintained at 10% of GDP or above over several years, Norway does not have a fiscal consolidation plan. The challenge of fiscal policy is to ensure that large oil revenues are managed prudently, in support of stable economic development over the near and longer term. The rule-based fiscal framework to achieve this objective is complemented, more recently, with a focus by the Norwegian Government on a disciplined approach to public expenditure and some re-prioritisation of resources.

Fiscal objectives

The Government Pension Fund Act stipulates the transfer of the State's oil revenues to the Government Pension Fund Global. In turn, the Fund transfers revenues to the central government budget according to a formula that reflects the real return to the Fund (estimated at 4% a year), and the structural non-oil deficit. The objective is to insulate fiscal policy from volatility in oil prices, and moreover to smooth the effects of the economic cycle by allowing extra revenues to be made available during a downturn, and fewer during an upturn. Norway's well-developed social welfare system amplifies the effect of the automatic stabilisers.

Spending-side measures

While no fiscal consolidation plan is in place, the new government that took office in October 2013 has introduced some budget savings in order to partially finance new initiatives. Budget 2015 accordingly introduces increased automatic productivity cuts across all operational budget appropriations, generating efficiencies of around NOK 1.7 billion (c. EUR 200 million) and further consolidation measures of around NOK 4 billion (c. EUR 500 million), of which around 75% are on the expenditure side. Savings measures include the freezing (non-indexation) of the family allowance. All consolidation measures have, however, been sued to finance additional expenditure in other areas.

Tax-side measures

While the bulk of consolidation efforts have come from the expenditure side, the increased interest rate on student loans is an example of a revenue-enhancing measure.

Long-term sustainability and fiscal risks

The Norwegian Ministry of Finance prepared an analysis paper on "Long-Term Perspectives on the Norwegian Economy" in 2013, highlighting the fact that the oil fund's contribution to financing public expenditures is due to start declining in 15-20 years, and that Norway faces similar long-term demographic challenges as other OECD countries. The Norwegian Government's broad-based strategy to address these longer term challenges centres upon promoting domestic economic capacity, including through incentives to improve labour supply, education and investment.

To improve public sector efficiency, the Government has announced several public sector reforms. These include reforming the police, the transport system and local governments. The reforms also include a new framework for PPP projects. The framework emphasises the use of PPP for the purpose of ensuring efficient project execution, while project financing over the fiscal budget is largely independent of whether a particular project is organised as PPP or as traditional public procurement. This captures the possible benefits from PPP while the current fiscal rule is met.

Engagement of parliament and citizens

Norway has not adopted any particular initiatives to promote the quality of scrutiny and debate by parliament, and accessibility of the budgetary process to the public.

Poland

1. Economic situation

Output growth, supported by strengthening private consumption, is projected to continue to rise, reaching 3.7% in 2016. The labour market will make further progress, and exports will benefit from firmer international trade and faster growth in the euro area. Energy and food prices have started to turn around following sharp falls and consumer prices will pick up after the recent spate of deflation.

Monetary policy should remain supportive, and it is assumed that the central bank will not start to raise interest rates before late 2016. The slightly restrictive fiscal stance is broadly appropriate and the European Council is likely to approve Poland's exit from the European Union's Excessive Deficit Procedure in June 2015, but further medium-term consolidation would help prepare for rising long-term costs.

Key economic indicators: Poland

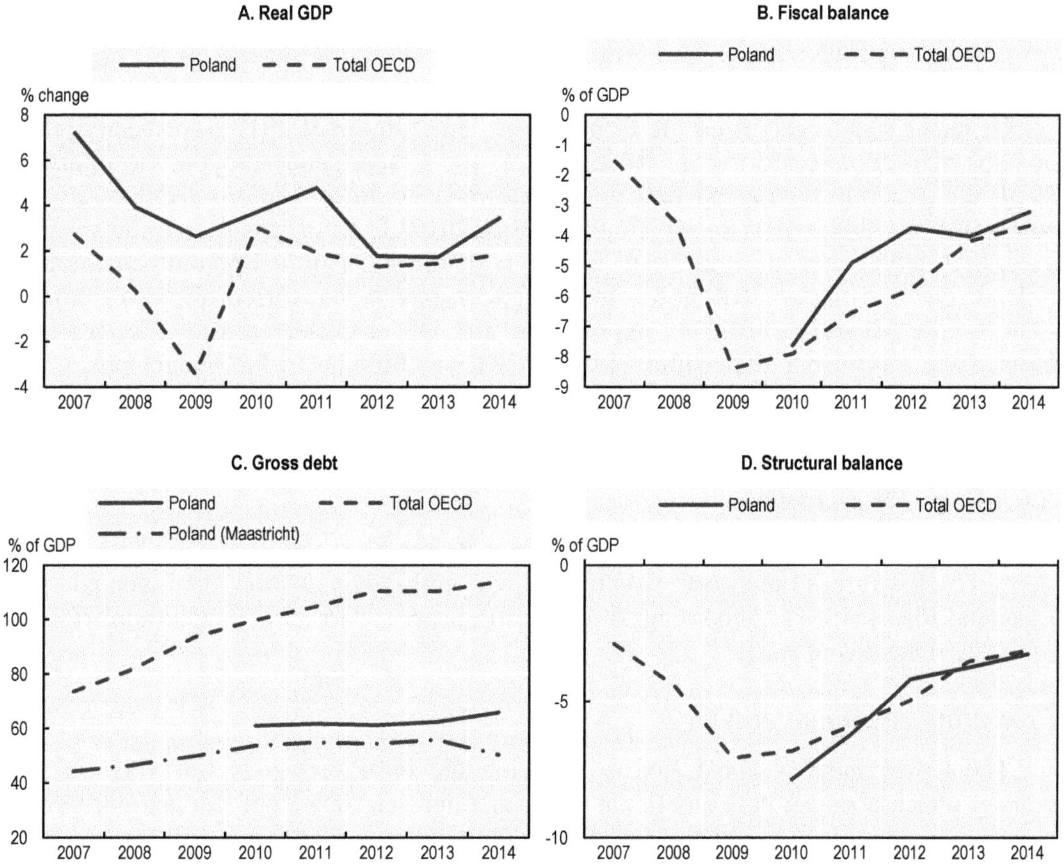

Source: OECD (2015a), "OECD Economic Outlook No. 97 (Edition 2015/1)", *OECD Economic Outlook: Statistics and Projections* (database), http://dx.doi.org/10.1787/data-00759-en.

StatLink http://dx.doi.org/10.1787/888933288266

Notwithstanding remarkable GDP increases over the past 25 years and solid investment growth in 2014, the private sector investment share of GDP has been lower than in neighbouring countries. To sustain rising living standards and move to higher value-added production activities, regulatory investment barriers need to be lifted and skills upgraded. Investment policies should be better targeted at strengthening workers' mobility, and thus productivity, as well as at greening the economy through improved energy and transport infrastructure and access to housing.

2. Fiscal policy and budgetary governance

Poland already had a relatively high fiscal deficit of -1.9% of GDP prior to the economic crisis in 2007, and has since experienced a prolonged period of "excessive deficit". However the deficit has improved from its low point of -7.6% of GDP in 2010 to just over 3% of GDP in 2014. Significant economic slowdown has led to the postponement and re-phasing of extensive consolidation measures. Taking these circumstances into account, in 2013 the European Commission defined a new deadline for correction of the excessive deficit, postponing the deadline for exiting the procedure until 2015.

Fiscal objectives

Official fiscal targets from the Convergence programme of 2012 have been updated in light of economic slowdown. According to the Convergence programme update of 2014, the general government deficit is to be reduced from 4.3% of GDP in 2013 to below 3% of GDP in 2015 and 1.2% of GDP in 2017. The target is to exit the so-called excessive deficit procedure in 2016, in line with the EU Council recommendation for Poland. The revenue-to-GDP ratio is to remain constant in that period (37.5%), while the share of the general government expenditure in GDP is to decrease by 3.2 percentage points. The Stabilising Expenditure Rule (SER) was binding in the budget process for 2015. The goal is to ensure the sustainability of public finances and the correction of their possible excessive imbalance.

Spending-side measures

Fiscal consolidation is implemented mainly through expenditure cuts. The Medium Term Expenditure Framework (MTEF) is currently part of the Multiannual State Financial Plan (MSFP). According to this, ceilings are set for total expenditure for each of the 22 functions of state.

Protecting economic growth

The Government is committed to reducing the imbalance in public finances in a manner which does not pose any threat to the medium-term development prospects of the country. In accordance with the Excessive Deficit Procedure report of October 2014, fiscal consolidation is to be implemented with regard to limiting the impact of expenditure reductions on GDP. The stabilising expenditure rule has a built-in mechanism preventing it from working pro-cyclically.

Policy priorities

The main strategic document in the medium-term is the National Development Strategy 2020. It defines strategic tasks for Poland that are crucial for accelerating the development process. There are three strategic areas where operations will be focussed: effective and efficient state, competitive economy and social and territorial cohesion.

Long-term sustainability and fiscal risks

The retirement system was reformed in 1999. In 2011 the Government was obliged to conduct a periodical review of pension system performance. The first review took place in 2013 and a number of decisions were taken to improve the effectiveness of the general pension system. These were included in the Act of 6 December 2013 which amended the principles underpinning pensions benefit payments from contributions gathered in the Open Pension Funds.

Economic forecasting

Macroeconomic forecasting is handled by the Polish Ministry of Finance; there is no independent fiscal institution in place.

Engagement of parliament and citizens

Poland has not adopted any particular initiatives to promote the quality of scrutiny and debate by parliament, and accessibility of the budgetary process to the public.

The government's planned fiscal consolidation: Poland

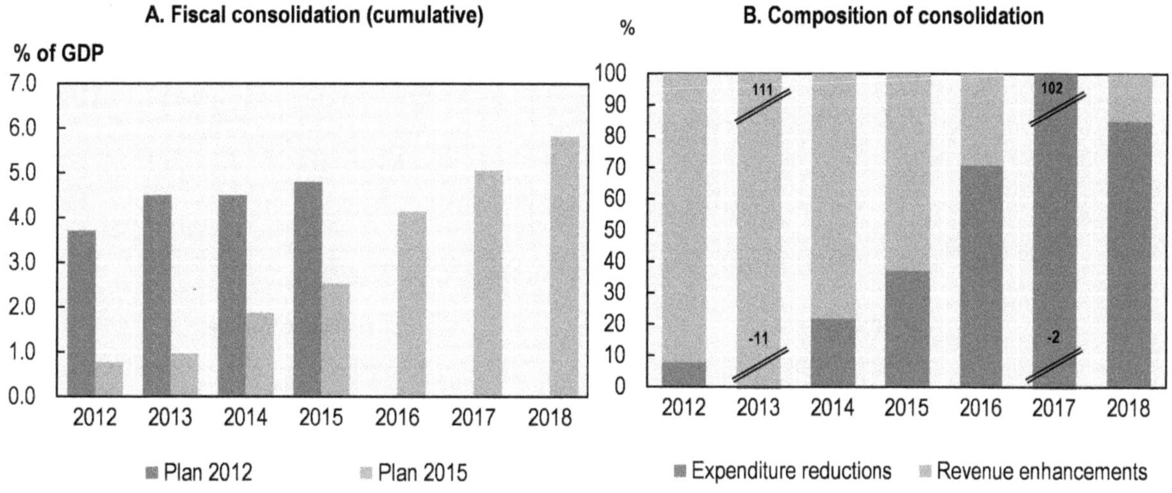

Source: OECD (2011), *Restoring Public Finances*, www.oecd.org/gov/budgeting/47558957.pdf.

StatLink http://dx.doi.org/10.1787/888933288527

Portugal

1. Economic situation

The recovery is projected to strengthen in 2015 on the back of strong external demand, a weaker euro and lower oil prices. After having contracted for three years, domestic demand has started to rise, and business investment is projected to pick up further in 2016. However, considerable economic slack will remain, as the unemployment rate will continue to fall only moderately.

As the recovery remains fragile, the more moderate pace of fiscal consolidation is welcome. Further tax reforms, such as an additional, revenue-neutral, reduction in the effective corporate tax rate could strengthen business investment. Structural reforms are needed to boost competitiveness. Private sector indebtedness remains high; new insolvency procedures should be reviewed, in the context of seeking to improve bank credit and investment.

Key economic indicators: Portugal

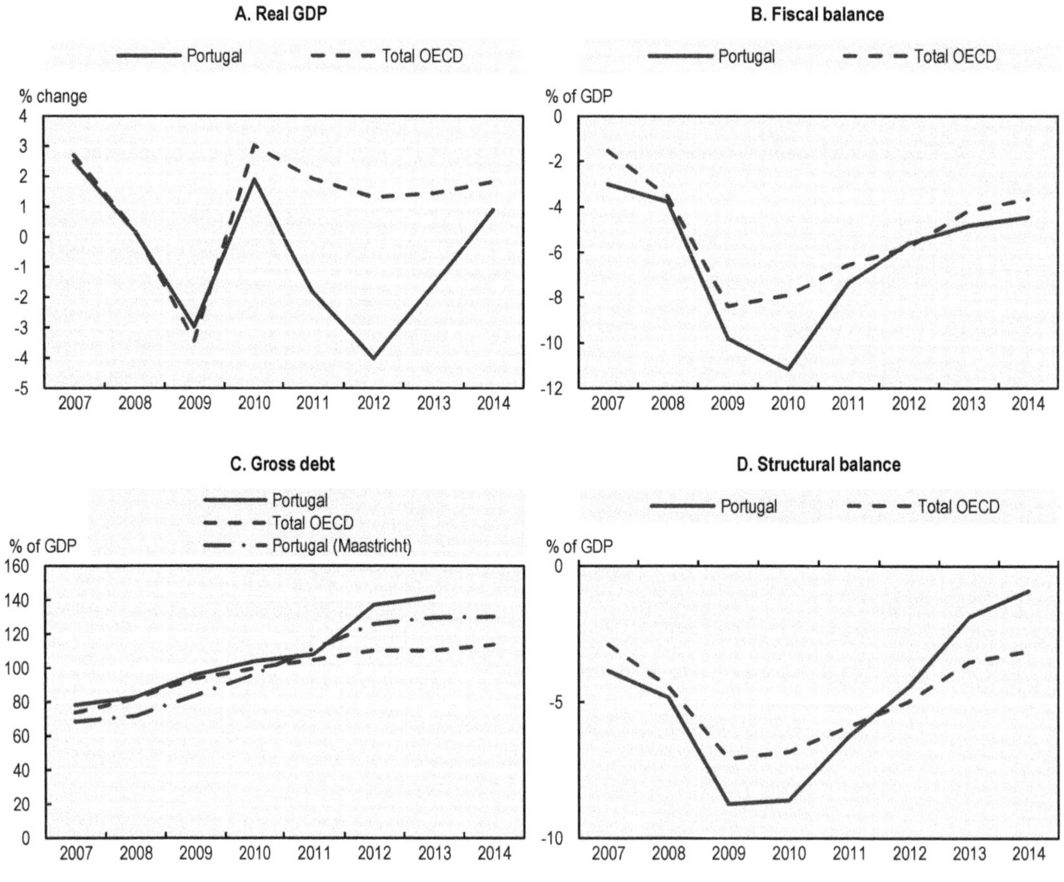

Source: OECD (2015a), "OECD Economic Outlook No. 97 (Edition 2015/1)", *OECD Economic Outlook: Statistics and Projections* (database), http://dx.doi.org/10.1787/data-00759-en.

StatLink http://dx.doi.org/10.1787/888933288278

Investment fell by nearly 35% between 2007 and 2014, more than twice the decline in the European Union as a whole. Business investment has started to increase again, driven by stronger prospects for internal and external demand, higher capacity utilisation and the need to renew depleted capital stock. Still, the pick-up in investment observed in key euro area economies has yet to materialise in Portugal. Public and residential investment will continue to stay subdued, reflecting fiscal consolidation needs and high leverage ratios of households and firms in the construction sector.

2. Fiscal policy and budgetary governance

Portugal is one of the OECD countries most severely affected by the economic and financial crisis: while it was already running a high fiscal deficit of 3% of GDP before the crisis, the deficit reached over 11% of GDP in 2009. Through sustained fiscal consolidation and economic reform, the deficit is on course to fall back below 3% of GDP in 2015. The state budget for 2015 is the first under the "post-programme" period, following the expiry of the Economic and Financial Assistance Programme in June 2014. The priority for the period ahead will be to stabilise and reduce the debt ratio, which has almost doubled to 140% of GDP over the crisis period.

Fiscal objectives

As a euro area country, Portugal has transposed the Fiscal Compact Treaty into its domestic law, with amendments to the Budget Framework Law introduced in both 2013 and 2014. The changes concern the introduction of a structural balance rule, a correction mechanism, and the requirement to reduce the debt level when it exceeds 60% of GDP. A further amendment to the Budget Framework law requires the multi-annual budgeting framework to include projections over a four-year period, for both central government bodies and the social security sub-sector.

Spending-side measures

The envisaged expenditure reductions in 2014 and 2015 have had to be adjusted to reflect decisions of the Constitutional Court, which disallowed certain proposed salary reductions and additional pension contributions. More generally, the medium-term expenditure framework has been progressively improved, with technical and procedural refinements arising from the central government expenditure review in 2013. The framework incorporates Portugal's ten-year experience of "top down budgeting", coupled with bottom-up input in determining expenditure ceilings, so that overall expenditure management is quite disciplined.

Budget execution and performance

As a general rule, government bodies in Portugal have freedom to reallocate funds within the same budget programme. Line ministries have indeed been afforded a growing degree of autonomy over recent years in the reallocation of budget appropriations, with increased decentralisation of authority from the Ministry of Finance. While carry-over of funds from one year to the next is possible *de facto,* this practice must be ratified during the budget implementation process. Public expenditure control is also enhanced through a new methodology based on "available funds", which constrain the assumption of commitments and thereby control the generation of arrears. Moreover, budget classification is being streamlined, with better integration between budget and financial accounting.

As regards performance, the framework law for the state budget requires the Government to submit to Parliament, by 31 March each year, a report on the implementation of the previous year's budget programme, explaining results and resources used. Since 2012, the budget authority has conducted monthly meetings with programme co-ordinators to analyse ongoing implementation by reference to performance forecasts.

Protecting economic growth

The priority for the Portuguese Government over recent years has been fiscal correction, but some measures have been introduced with a view to promoting economic growth:

- The Corporate Income Tax reform, initiated in 2012, reduced the rate from 23% to 21% to boost private and foreign investment.
- 2014 saw the introduction of a tax credit (costing EUR 225 million) aimed at promoting investment in enterprises.
- In 2015 the Green Taxation has been introduced, to promote eco-innovation, efficient energy use, and promote more sustainable production and consumption patterns.

With the accomplishment of the key fiscal objectives now in sight, the Portuguese Government will be turning its attention to a more broad-based, growth-promotion strategy.

Policy priorities

Within the over-arching priority of restoring sustainability to the public finances, the priority has been to re-structure the public sector and to rationalise social payments.

Long-term sustainability and fiscal risks

Portugal faces long-term demographic challenges, as in the case of many other OECD countries. The 2012 Strategic Budget Document (DEO) included detailed analysis of long-term fiscal sustainability. The budget for 2015 includes measures to improve the sustainability of the social welfare system, notably an increase in the retirement age to 66.

As regards fiscal risks, considerable progress has been made in reporting since a risk analysis first appeared in the 2012 fiscal report. Greater attention is now paid to contingent liabilities, including in respect of PPPs and state-owned enterprises. Specialist technical support units have been established for both of these sectors, and their roles include advice on financial sustainability issues.

Sub-national budgeting

Since 2011, local and regional levels of government in Portugal have been more dependent on central government assistance, with loan arrangements put in place for many regions linked to specific reform/public financial management commitments. The Local Finances Law and Regional Finances Law were approved in 2013 to limit the indebtedness of sub-national levels of government and to promote consolidation. The major changes involved revenue sharing between central and local governments, among municipalities, debt monitoring and insolvency procedures and sanctions. In this overall context, a Fiscal Co-ordination Council has also been established to promote exchange of information and forecasts, in particular in regard to multi-annual budgeting frameworks; as well as a Financial Policies Monitoring Council to ensure co-ordination among the autonomous regions and the central government.

Economic forecasting

In 2015 the role of the Portuguese Public Finance Council (CFP) in budget monitoring was enhanced. This independent fiscal institution now provides an opinion on the macroeconomic forecasts underlying the annual State Budget Proposal. In addition, Portugal has in place since 2006 a Technical Budget Support Unit (UTAO) within Parliament, to provide technical analysis mainly in support of the standing parliamentary committee for budgetary and financial matters.

Capital budgeting and PPPs

A technical support unit for PPP projects was created in 2012, responsible for appraisal, structuring, tendering and supervision of PPP contracts across the public sector. The State Budget report includes a chapter on containing the estimated costs of PPP projects over a long-term horizon (until 2041, in the case of the 2015 budget). The Budget Authority has tightened to provisions regarding PPP proposals so that budgetary costs are made clear from the outset, and to ensure that multi-annual commitments are registered and managed at aggregate level.

Engagement of parliament and citizens

As indicated above, the Technical Budget Support Unit (UTAO) has been operating since 2006 to assist parliamentary committees in engaging on budgetary matters, and its competencies have been developed in recent years. For the public more generally, a "citizen's budget" was introduced in 2013 (for the 2014 state budget) aimed at making technical budget material more accessible and user-friendly. The 2015 citizens budget was complemented by a new initiative, "To know the 2015 Budget", which provides a simple and dynamic analysis of the 2015 Budget, namely the programme, ministry and function of expenditure, and the economic categories of revenue.

The government's planned fiscal consolidation: Portugal

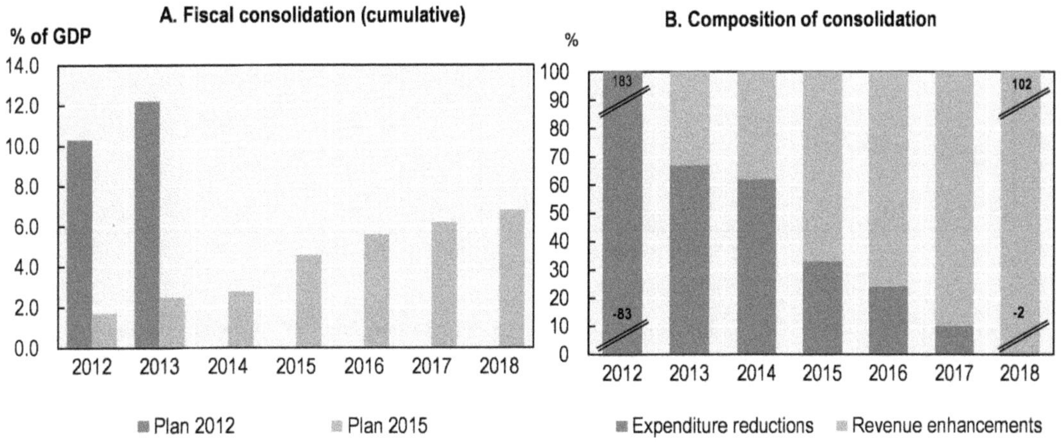

Source: OECD (2015b), *OECD State of Public Finances Survey 2015*; OECD (2011), *Restoring Public Finances*, www.oecd.org/gov/budgeting/47558957.pdf.

StatLink http://dx.doi.org/10.1787/888933288534

Slovak Republic

1. Economic situation

Economic growth is projected to accelerate further in 2015. Labour-market performance will continue to improve and increasingly confident households should spend more out of rising real incomes. Export markets are set to recover, raising business sentiment and investment.

The slowdown in the pace of fiscal consolidation in 2014 was appropriate, given the economic slack. Nevertheless, budgeted further consolidation efforts are welcome to build fiscal buffers. In that regard, implementing multi-annual binding spending ceilings will reinforce budget discipline, while improving the efficiency of tax administration will support revenue collection.

Key economic indicators: Slovak Republic

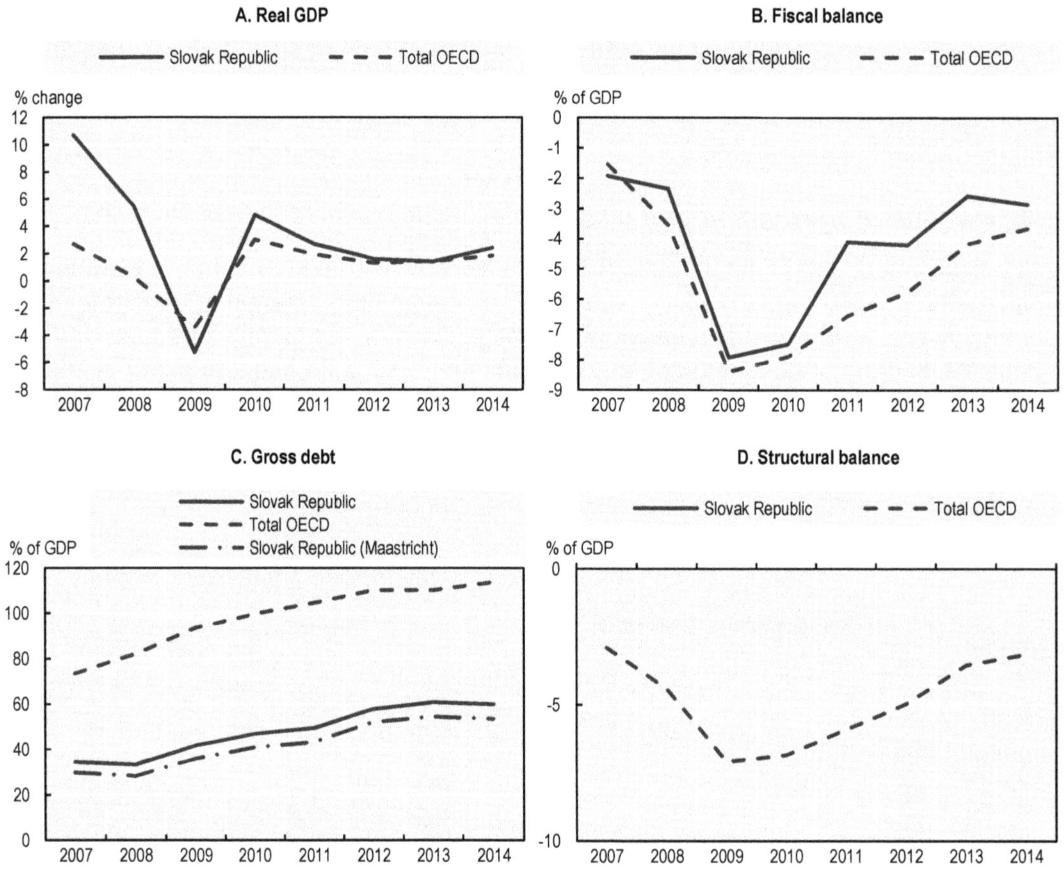

Source: OECD (2015a), "OECD Economic Outlook No. 97 (Edition 2015/1)", *OECD Economic Outlook: Statistics and Projections* (database), http://dx.doi.org/10.1787/data-00759-en.

StatLink http://dx.doi.org/ 10.1787/888933288282

Investment is still well below the pre-crisis level. Foreign investment, which has been an important driver of capital accumulation (the foreign direct investment [FDI] stock is

60% of GDP), has been subdued due to the sluggish growth of the Slovak Republic's trading partners and competition from low-cost countries in the region. Policies to improve business climate, infrastructures, innovation and skills can give impetus to more broad-based FDI. Strengthening administrative capacities and expanding the use of simplified procedures will help to increase the use of EU structural funds.

2. Fiscal policy and budgetary governance

The fiscal deficit in the Slovak Republic, which was already high at -1.9% of GDP before the crisis in 2007, reached -7.9% of GDP in 2009, but after significant consolidation efforts this was reduced to 2.6% of GDP in 2013. The next year, the Slovak Republic successfully exited the EU's Excessive Deficit Procedure. The Government has since relaxed the pace of fiscal consolidation, and indeed the budget deficit increased to 2.9% GDP in 2014. This is expected to be compensated for by a stronger consolidation effort in 2015. The primary objective of fiscal policy in the Slovak Republic is to ensure effective and sustainable public finances that facilitate further improvement in the quality of life in the Slovak Republic, which demands continued efforts towards revitalising public finances in the next years.

Fiscal objectives

The Government has set a medium-term target for the fiscal balance to be 0.5% of GDP in 2017, confirmed in the Stability Programme 2015-18. The latest government estimate is that the budget deficit will be 2.55% of GDP in 2015, slightly above approved budget (2.49% of GDP) but still within EU fiscal limits. The targets for ongoing years were set at 1.93% of GDP in 2016, 0.88% of GDP in 2017 and 0.53% GDP in 2018. Nearly three-quarters of the consolidation efforts in 2015 are focused on the expenditure side of the budget.

Spending-side measures

The majority of expenditure reductions will be achieved through ESO public administration reforms (effective, reliable and open public administration). In particular, the Government is looking to rationalise the number of state organisations, improve their service processes and increase their effectiveness. Other measures include increasing efficiency in the healthcare sector.

Tax-side measures

The Government is making efforts to improve the efficiency of tax collection. This will partly be achieved through introducing an obligation to record revenues in electronic cash registers into new economic sectors. Efforts will also extend to evasion relating to corporate income taxes. In addition, VAT will be maintained at the current rate of 20% from 2015 and the Income Tax Act is being amended to broaden the tax base and eliminate various exceptions.

Budget costings and execution

The planned expenditure savings are not specified in detail and cannot be expected to be implemented in full. Additional measures are expected in the context of the state administration reform (ESO), which according to the Draft Budgetary Plan would yield savings mainly from freezing wage bill growth. Savings from planned efficiency increases in the healthcare sector may be overestimated in the short-term.

Protecting economic growth

Fiscal consolidation in 2015 is expected to slow GDP growth down by 0.5 percentage points. However, the Government has prepared a set of structural measures focused on supporting economic growth and employment. The labour market is the greatest challenge for the Slovak economy and the Government is planning significant reforms. For example, the health contribution allowance and concurrence of material need benefits and wages should help increase employment among low-income employees.

Policy priorities

Government priorities include:

1. state administration reform (ESO programme)
2. improved efficiency of tax administration and collection
3. implement structural reform to improve functioning of the labour market.

Long-term sustainability and fiscal risks

The risks to the macroeconomic scenario underpinning the Draft Budgetary Plan appear to be balanced and the scenario is deemed realistic. The budget which was adopted for 2015 included a reserve of EUR 155 million in case the macroeconomic scenario worsens.

Sub-national budgeting

Overall, the government budget proposal for 2015 is expected to worsen the fiscal performance (net of taxes) of local governments by EUR 28 million. For example, significant savings in public expenditure are expected from capital expenditures where the primary source of savings is expected to come from local governments.

Economic forecasting

Forecasting is completed by the Ministry of Finance and approved by the Macroeconomic Forecasting Committee. This committee was established under the constitutional Fiscal Responsibility Act (Act No. 493/2011) as an advisory body to the Minister of Finance. The role of the committee is to ensure greater transparency, objectiveness and quality of macroeconomic forecasts. The committee consists of representatives of private banks, the central bank, the fiscal council and independent economic analysts. Its independence from government influence is anchored in the committee's statutes.

Engagement of parliament and citizens

The Government has created a web portal to show the general government budget and explain how it is compiled. The website is managed by the Ministry of Finance and also acts as a source of information on the budget and its regulatory framework.

The government's planned fiscal consolidation: Slovak Republic

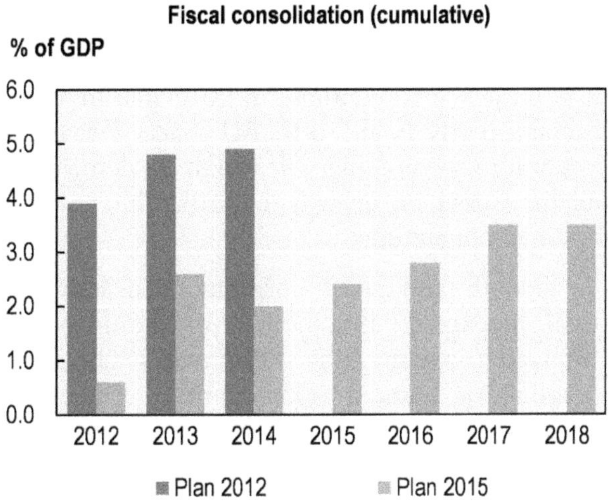

Source: OECD (2015b), *OECD State of Public Finances Survey 2015*; OECD (2011), *Restoring Public Finances*, www.oecd.org/gov/budgeting/47558957.pdf.

StatLink http://dx.doi.org/ 10.1787/888933288549

Slovenia

1. Economic situation

Economic growth is projected to continue in 2015 due to strong exports and public investment in infrastructure, partly financed by EU funds. Fiscal consolidation, still high unemployment and corporate deleveraging will weigh on domestic demand. A decline in public investment will be a drag on growth in 2016, although private investment and consumption will gain some momentum.

A key priority is smooth and swift corporate restructuring and reducing non-performing loans. Fiscal slippage in structural terms should be avoided but automatic stabilisers should be allowed to operate fully. Continued structural reforms are needed, in particular to lower regulatory burdens and improve efficiency in public services. Strengthening active labour-market policies would enhance growth and its inclusiveness. Privatisation and greater openness to FDI would be appropriate.

Key economic indicators: Slovenia

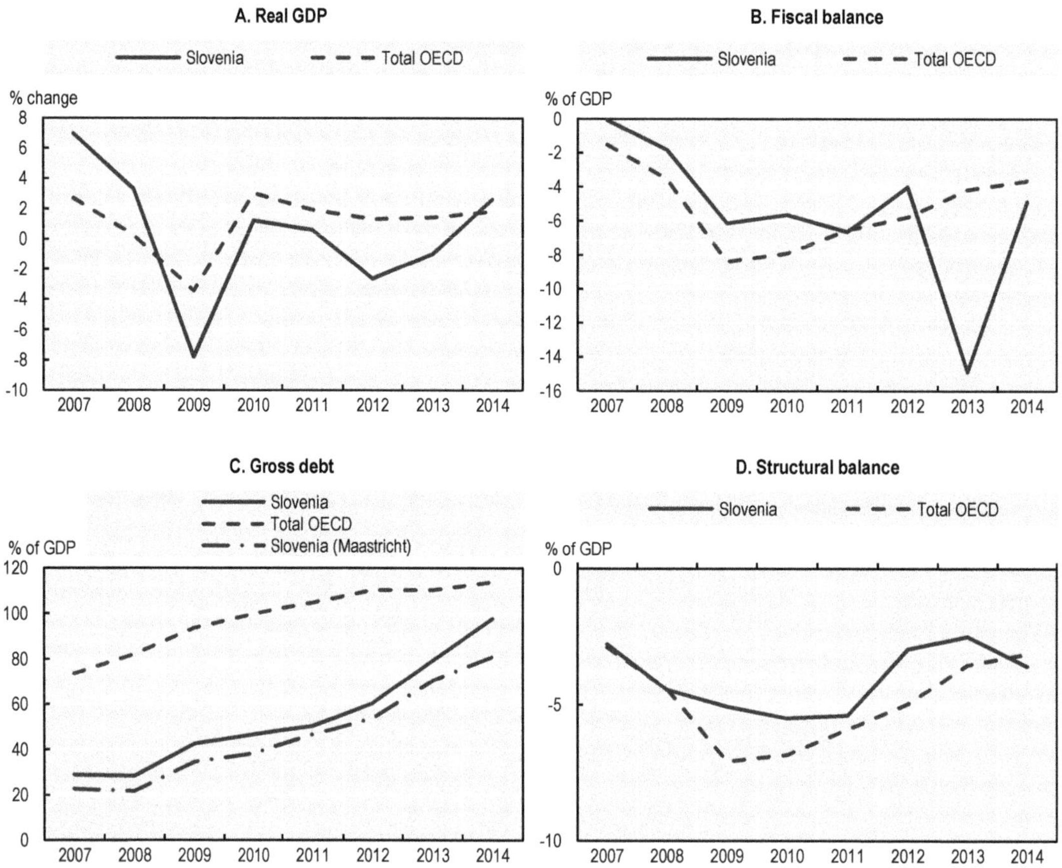

Source: OECD (2015a), "OECD Economic Outlook No. 97 (Edition 2015/1)", *OECD Economic Outlook: Statistics and Projections* (database), http://dx.doi.org/10.1787/data-00759-en.

StatLink http://dx.doi.org/10.1787/888933288294

Investment dropped substantially following the 2009 crisis, dragged down by deleveraging in the corporate sector and restructuring of bank balance sheets. As the EU Multiannual Financial Framework comes to an end in 2015, reducing inefficient public spending will be needed to sustain public investment. While residential investment is expected to recover gradually as the economy improves, stronger business investment would require faster progress with corporate restructuring and, to ease credit conditions, reducing non-performing loans in banks.

2. Fiscal policy and budgetary governance

Slovenia's public finances were at a broadly balanced position before the crisis in 2007. After a sharp decline to –6.1% in 2009, in line with the broader trends across the OECD, public finances have remained vulnerable and major bank recapitalisation requirements caused the deficit to plummet to -14.6% of GDP in 2013, before recovering to -4.9% in 2014. The Slovenian Government is therefore prioritising public finance sustainability at present. The proposed Fiscal Rule Act stipulates the manner and timeframe for achieving this medium-term balance and will be fully implemented by 2016. In addition the new Government has introduced a supplementary budget to reduce the excessive government deficit to below 3% of GDP in 2015. The Government is currently engaged in medium-term fiscal framework goals within a new Stability programme from 2016.

Fiscal objectives

The Slovenian Government has set a target of reducing the fiscal deficit to 4.4% of GDP in 2014 and to 2.9% of GDP in 2015. This is in line with the final goal of reducing general government net borrowing to below 3% of GDP in 2015. Fiscal consolidation will largely be achieved through reducing government expenditure, with more minor changes on the revenue side.

Spending-side measures

The Government intends to achieve large savings in public expenditure (EUR 205 million) by reducing public sector wage costs. This is to be achieved through a freeze on promotions, a freeze on regular performance payments, a freeze of premia for supplementary collective pension insurance and a reduction in the number of employees. Furthermore, the Government plans to lower the bonuses for working years, Sunday work and academic titles. Additional spending measures that the Government has adopted for the year 2015 include:

- centralising procurement (expected savings of EUR 80.5 million)
- replacing some grant subsidies in return assets (expected savings EUR 27 million)
- centralising government IT and establishing an IT cloud (expected savings EUR 9 million)
- streamlining the provision of public utilities (bus and rail) (expected savings EUR 6 million)

To ensure the consolidation of general government expenditure in 2016, measures will be adopted in 2015 (with the purpose of achieving financial effects in 2016), based on which the effects of short-term saving measures will be replaced with the effects of appropriate long-term structural measures in systemic legislation:

- In the field of salaries and other labour costs in the public sector, measures will be adopted in collaboration with public sector unions which ensure that the amount of funds to cover labour costs in the public sector in 2016 (integral expenditure) will be maintained at the level of expenditure to cover labour costs in the public sector (integral expenditure) in 2015, increased by the realisation costs under Item III of Paragraph 1 of the Agreement on measures in the field of salaries and other labour costs in the public sector for the purpose of balancing public finances for the year 2015, and reduced by the range of differences between salaries in order to eliminate the second quarter of disparities of basic salaries in 2015.
- Measures will be adopted concerning the financing of pension and disability insurance which will ensure that the amount of transfer from the state budget in ZPIZ in 2016 does not increase with consideration of realisation compared to 2015; in the future, a gradual reduction of this transfer in accordance with the adopted pension reform will be ensured.
- In the area of transfers to individuals and households, measures will be adopted which, with a consideration of medium-term structural balance goals (prolonging the validity of individual savings measures) will ensure appropriate socio-economic situations for individuals and enhance domestic spending.
- The general government consolidation includes structural measures and the rationalisation of expenditure which must become permanent. These measures will be achieved by combining improved management, centralisation and lean public administration:
  - CVB Renovation of the public procurement system
  - centralisation of the state's real property management
  - adoption of the Strategy for Slovenian Public Administration Development 2015–20 to improve efficiency
  - further reduction of court backlogs and further IT development of the judicial system
  - centralisation of the state information system
  - increasing the efficiency of the general public sector.

Tax-side measures

In the Draft Budgetary Plan 2015, the Government proposes several measures that would generate an additional 0.3% of GDP in revenue. Key revenue measures include:

- changing the system of student work (expected to generate EUR 51 million)
- increasing environmental taxes relating to CO2 emissions (expected to generate EUR 30 million)
- increasing the efficiency of public tax collection (expected to generate EUR 24 million)
- increasing sales tax on insurance services (expected to generate EUR 17 million)

- preserving the fourth personal income tax bracket (expected to generate EUR 16 million)
- increasing the rate of tax on financial services (expected to generate EUR 13 million).

In the next programming period (from 2016), the Government will strive to prepare changes in the payment of public duties, especially by eliminating administrative burdens and restructuring tax burdens:

- Elimination of administrative barriers when fulfilling tax obligations and enhancing the efficiency of the collection of public duties – an amendment to the Tax Procedure Act is planned.
- Modernisation and restructuring of tax on real property – in this next programming period, the Government will prepare a proposal for the taxation of real property, while consistently taking into account the constitutional framework.
- Restructuring of the burden of public duties – to enhance the competitiveness of the Slovenian business environment and reduce burdens on labour.

Budget costings and execution

The Government has had to adapt its previously announced fiscal consolidation measures, but the overall fiscal target for 2015 remains unchanged. The main changes relate to:

- a lower planned target for interest expenditures
- a lower planned transfer to the Pensioner Fund
- a lower planned target for EU funded expenditures (due to beginning of new financial period).

Protecting economic growth

The Slovenian Government has tabled an investment oriented budget to promote economic growth. This includes measures to attract FDI and accelerated investments in R&D.

Policy priorities

The Slovenian Government is prioritising restricting the public sector wage bill, rationalising social transfers and improved targeting of investment so that it remains a growth orientated and social country.

Long-term sustainability and fiscal risks

Risks to public finance projections are tilted to the negative side for several reasons. There are risks that the estimated yield of the measures underpinning the draft budgetary plan, particularly in relation to compensation of employees, are not fully realised. The deadline for the recapitalisation of Gorenjska Banka was extended until end 2015 and the newly established Resolution fund may have to provide capital if private sources cannot be found. In July 2014, the European Court of Human Rights in Strasbourg ruled that Slovenia has to repay deposit holders of Ljubljanska Banka within one year of the ruling (but this has been included in 2014 general government balance already as a one-off item). There has been further improvement and development of models for estimating the impact of ageing on public finance and the effects of different social policy measures. Pension reform was implemented in 2013 and results show positive effects in the first year. The Long-term Care Act is also under preparation, along with the White Book on the future pension system.

Sub-national budgeting

The Government intends that the new Public Finance Act will focus more on general government planning and development (i.e. pension fund, health fund, local communities) which will include sub-national levels.

Economic forecasting

Macroeconomic forecasts are produced by the Institute of Macroeconomic Analysis and Development (IMAD), an independent government office. The authorities are currently preparing an overhaul of the legislation underpinning Slovenia's fiscal framework, including independent bodies, in order to comply with the EU legal requirements on fiscal governance as well as the Treaty on Stability, Co-ordination and Governance in EMU. Whereas this overhaul will include the establishment of a fiscal council, it is expected that IMAD will preserve its role of a producer of macroeconomic forecasts underlying budgetary planning documents.

Engagement of parliament and citizens

Slovenia has no particular initiatives in place to enhance the inclusiveness or participative nature of the budget process.

The government's planned fiscal consolidation: Slovenia

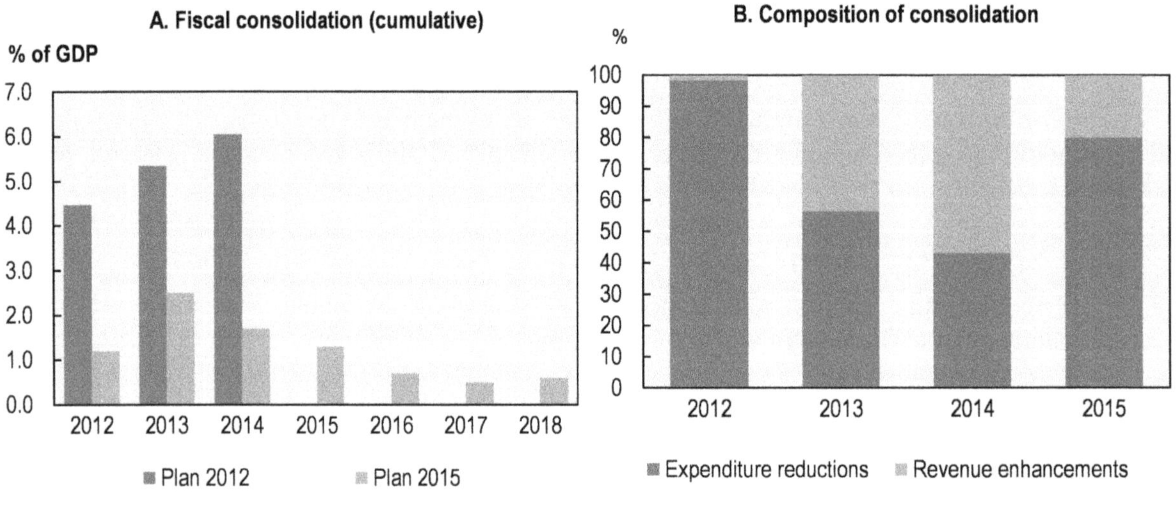

Source: OECD (2015b), *OECD State of Public Finances Survey 2015*; OECD (2011), *Restoring Public Finances*, www.oecd.org/gov/budgeting/47558957.pdf.

StatLink http://dx.doi.org/10.1787/888933288552

Spain

1. Economic situation

Robust growth is projected over the next two years, driven by very supportive financial conditions, the depreciation of the euro, lower oil prices and strengthening trading partner growth. The fiscal stance is assumed to be mildly contractionary. Private consumption growth will be supported by rising employment and incomes, household tax cuts, and lower fuel prices and interest rates. Export growth will be underpinned by cost competitiveness gains, and slack will keep inflation low.

The Government should continue to bring down the fiscal deficit in order to put public debt on a downward path. Business-friendly structural reforms are needed to move towards a knowledge-based economy and ensure strong inclusive growth. High unemployment, which has pushed up income inequality, is a key concern and will require labour-market reforms and interventions.

Key economic indicators: Spain

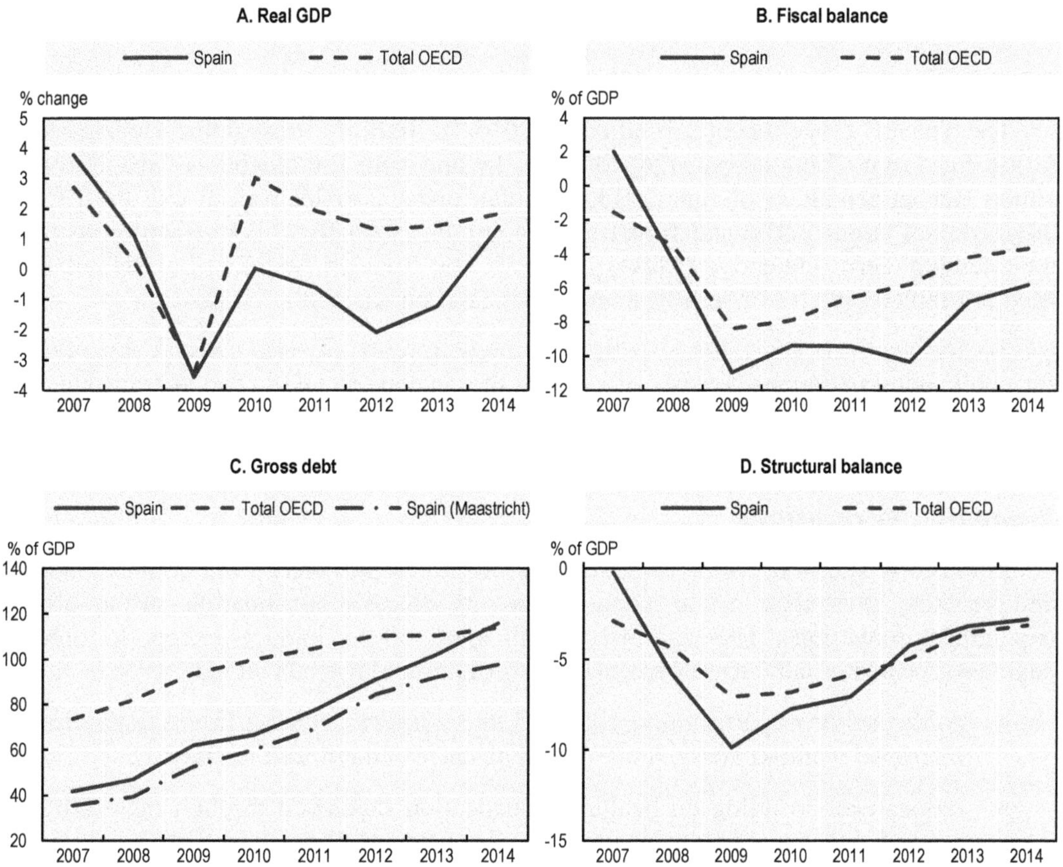

Source: OECD (2015a), "OECD Economic Outlook No. 97 (Edition 2015/1)", *OECD Economic Outlook: Statistics and Projections* (database), http://dx.doi.org/10.1787/data-00759-en.

StatLink http://dx.doi.org/10.1787/888933288300

The collapse of the property bubble and the recession led to a fall in total investment from a historical peak of 31.0% of GDP in 2007 to a trough of 18.5% of GDP in 2013. Machinery and transport equipment investment has however been growing strongly. The bubble left an excess of housing in coastal resorts and satellite towns as well as excessive investment in regional airports. It also contributed to high corporate leverage but this is now declining. Continued investment in cross-border electricity transmission would increase energy market efficiency in Spain and the European Union.

2. Fiscal policy and budgetary governance

From an apparently healthy fiscal position in 2007, with a fiscal surplus of 2% of GDP, Spain was severely affected by the economic and financial crisis, and elements of its economic narrative – the bursting of a property bubble, with repercussions for confidence in the banking sector – reflect those of some other OECD countries. After remaining in the range 9-11% of GDP in the period 2009-12, Spain's fiscal deficit has since steadily improved as the Government has focussed on restoring budgetary stability. Fiscal consolidation has been based both on measures to reduce expenditure and to improve the tax system efficiency, which has enabled a substantial reduction in the public deficit to 5.7% of GDP in 2014.

Fiscal objectives

The Spanish Government submitted its 2015-18 Stability Programme Update (SPU) to the European Commission in April 2015. In line with the Council of the European Union Recommendation of June 2013, this plan presents objectives to exit the EDP in 2016 (deficit target 2.8%) and furthermore continues with fiscal consolidation to reach the Medium Term Objective (MTO) in 2019. The Spanish Stability Law stipulates a Medium-term Objective of zero structural balance to be reached in 2020.

To achieve these goals, the SPU fiscal strategy in terms of revenues and expenditures for public administrations consists of keeping the revenue to GDP ratio at approximately 38% of GDP and reducing the ratio of spending to GDP by 5 points, from 43.5% in 2014 to 38.4% of GDP in 2018.

Spending-side measures

In the early stages of the consolidation process, although there were both expenditure and revenue measures, Spain concentrated its fiscal consolidation effort around expenditure reductions. This has affected all areas of the budget (except for interest payments, pensions and unemployment). Areas of particular focus include:

- public sector wage restraint (achieved through a recruitment freeze, a pay freeze, increased working hours, limitation of absence and reduced holidays)
- rationalised spending on health and education (achieved through increasing the ratio of students per class, centralising pharmaceutical purchases, etc.).
- reform of the pension system (achieved through increasing the retirement age and removing the inflation index for pensions).

In addition to expenditure cuts, the Spanish Government has been looking to improve expenditure efficiency, investing in areas that lend greater growth returns.

Tax-side measures

On the revenue side, Spain has adopted several modifications of the tax system in recent years. Tax reform has focussed on two main areas: the first area is geared towards reduction in direct taxation and a push towards environmental taxation and fighting fraud; the second area focusses on the long term and is centred on fiscal devaluation.

Over the period 2012-14, Spain introduced changes to different taxes to rebalance public finances. In line with EU recommendations, taxation is moving gradually from direct to indirect taxes, new environmental taxes are being introduced and special attention is being paid to fighting fiscal fraud.

Key revenue measures introduced over the first period include:

- a temporary increase in personal income tax for the period 2012-14
- an increase in the standard rate of VAT from 18% to 21% and an increase in the reduced rate from 8% to 10%
- an increase in real estate property tax
- an extraordinary and limited Fiscal Amnesty in 2012
- an increase in effective rates of corporate income tax through elimination of several deductions and benefits
- the introduction of new environmental taxes and other new taxes such as taxes on lottery, banking deposits, etc.
- an increase in resources for fighting against tax and social security fraud.

More recently, in 2015 an ambitious tax reform entered into force which includes changes to the main taxes and a reduction in social security contributions, focussing on creating growth and jobs in the long term and fostering a fiscal devaluation that improves the competitiveness of Spanish enterprises. Tax reform in Spain plays a crucial role in closing the fiscal gap in labour income, increasing consumption and investment, encouraging the capitalisation of businesses and improving the competitiveness of the economy. The *ex-post* effects of the tax reform are estimated to approximately amount to a EUR 7 billion reduction in tax collection over the 2015-16 period.

Key revenue measures introduced in this last tax reform include:

- A reduction in personal income tax to increase the disposable income of families. The tax burden on taxpayers has been reduced, particularly for middle and low income earners and those with greater family responsibilities. The tax rates applicable to the general tax base have been decreased, the tax has been simplified, the number of tax brackets for the general base has been reduced from seven to five and the treatment of savings has been improved.
- A general reduction in Corporate Income Tax to set it in line with most EU countries. The nominal rate is being lowered gradually: to 28% in 2015 and 25% in 2016. To make this reduction compatible with the stability path, measures are being adopted to broaden the tax bases, reducing tax benefits.
- New social security benefits to reduce unemployment and to foster new jobs and growth. In 2014 a flat fee of EUR 100 per month for social contributions for permanent contracts was introduced. In 2015 this incentive was transformed into a

new and more progressive measure, a minimum exemption for social contributions of EUR 500 for new permanent contracts that generate net employment.

Budget costings and execution

The Commission for Public Administration Reform (CORA) has made a detailed assessment of the Spanish public sector to identify opportunities to improve efficiency, to eliminate the existence of duplications and to simplify procedures and administrative burdens through the use of new technologies. In addition, where there have been specific reforms, Committees of Wise Men have been appointed to analyse the situation and put forward proposals.

Protecting economic growth

A number of structural reforms have been put in place to improve competitiveness and generate economic growth and job creation in the last three years. In 2012 there were three major reforms in relation to the labour market, the financial sector and the budgetary framework. In 2013, measures were introduced in different productive sectors aimed at increasing efficiency and reducing costs, to enable them to compete more effectively internationally and to achieve more sustainable public finances. In 2014, new reforms were put into place with an emphasis on tax reform to liberate resources to the private sector and a job strategy to strengthen the economic recovery and the labour market.

Policy priorities

The early years of fiscal consolidation were focussed on rebalancing public accounts and guaranteeing the long-term sustainability of the public sector. Fiscal consolidation was a key cornerstone of the Spanish economic recovery. However, over this period social spending has been preserved, with education, healthcare, pensions and unemployment benefits being considered as priority areas. The fiscal plan has also prioritised those policies with a larger impact on growth, competitiveness and employment. The objective is to increase the efficiency of the budget so that conditions conducive to investment, production and employment are generated while fulfilling the commitment to reducing public deficit.

Long-term sustainability and fiscal risks

The pension system was reformed over the period 2010-12 to ensure future sustainability of the system. This included a gradual increase in the retirement age and increased incentives to work beyond the legal retirement age, as well as an extension to the reference period for calculating pensions. In 2013, further measures were adopted to increase the effective retirement age and continue to ensure long-term sustainability.

Sub-national budgeting

Spain is the OECD country with the most decentralised spending. All the public administrations have faced up to their fiscal commitments, substantially improving their budgetary balances. The Government also put in place extraordinary liquidity measures to support the financing of sub-national governments, providing liquidity to them and establishing stricter additional fiscal commitments to fiscal consolidation. All of the autonomous communities plan to incorporate public revenue and expenditure measures so that upcoming stability targets are met.

Economic forecasting

This macroeconomic scenario that accompanies the General State Budget for 2015 were produced by the Spanish Government and have been endorsed by the Independent Fiscal Responsibility Authority (AIREF), according to Article 14 of Organic Law 6/2013 of 14 November and Article 4 of Council Directive 2011/85/EU of 8 November 2011 on Member States requirements for budgetary frameworks. After its evaluation, the forecasts have been qualified as likely by the AIREF and the Authority has made a series of recommendations that the Government will take into account.

Engagement of parliament and citizens

Law 19/13 (transparency, access to public information and good governance) introduced in December 2013 has three main purposes. Firstly, it increases and strengthens transparency, secondly it recognises and guarantees access to information and thirdly it sets forth the good governance obligations to be met by public authorities, as well as the legal consequences of non-compliance. In addition, in December 2014 the Spanish Government launched a new transparency website that will make over 500 000 details of public interest freely available to all citizens.

The government's planned fiscal consolidation: Spain

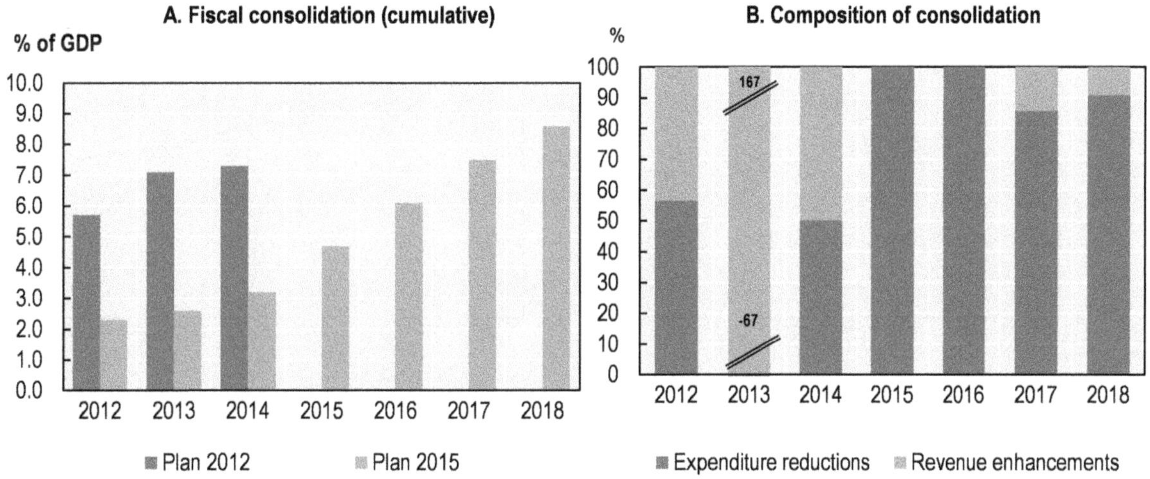

Source: OECD (2015b), *OECD State of Public Finances Survey 2015*; OECD (2011), *Restoring Public Finances*, www.oecd.org/gov/budgeting/47558957.pdf.

StatLink http://dx.doi.org/10.1787/888933288567

Sweden

1. Economic situation

Private consumption and investment continue to grow briskly, while foreign trade will make a significant but modest contribution to growth. Unemployment is projected to recede only slowly, as integrating the substantial flow of immigrants takes time and labour force participation increases. Inflation is set to pick up gradually, as wages increase and the disinflationary effect of falling oil prices fades out.

Monetary policy is highly expansionary and should remain so until inflation is clearly moving towards target. Macro-prudential policies should be strengthened and complemented by measures to increase housing supply to reinforce financial stability. Fiscal policy is reverting towards a broadly neutral stance. Structural policies to improve immigrant integration, skills and innovation are needed to boost long-term growth.

Residential investment is growing rapidly from a low level, responding to strong housing demand. Business investment growth is robust. Intangibles, notably software and R&D, account for a large share of corporate investment. Public investment is increasing at a moderate pace, with a focus on enhancing rail and road infrastructure.

Key economic indicators: Sweden

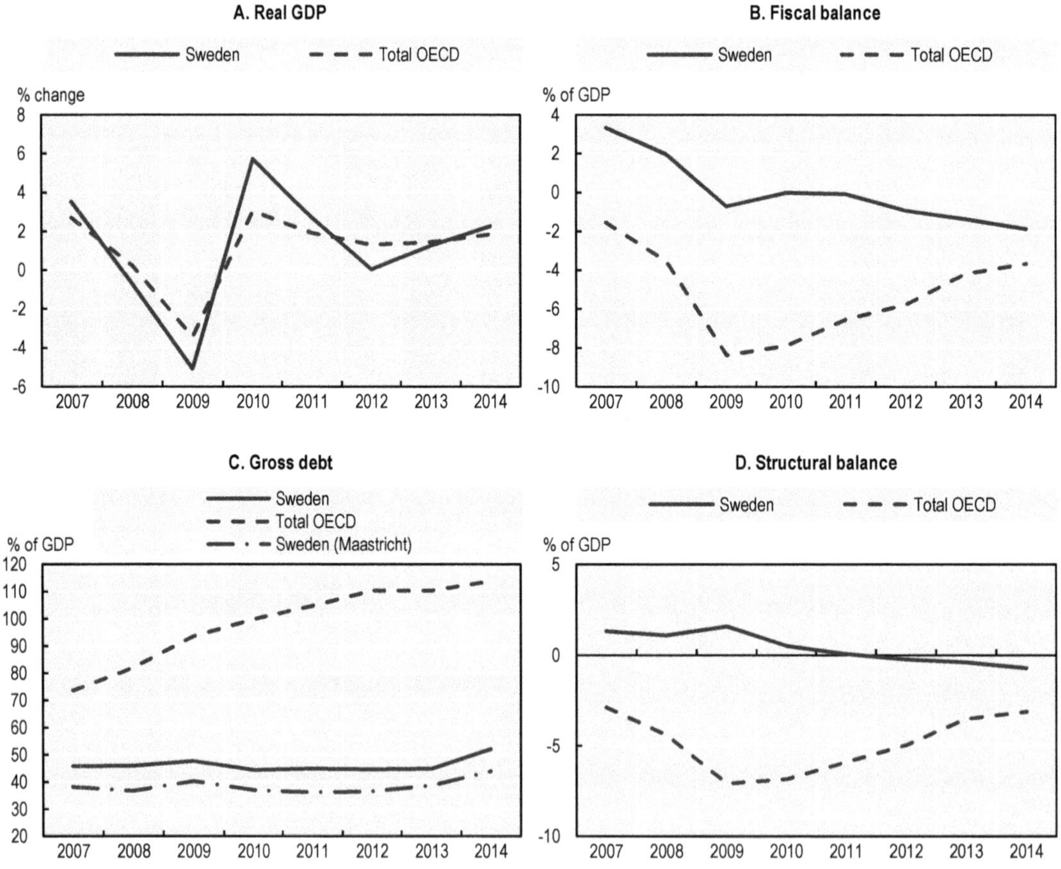

Source: OECD (2015a), "OECD Economic Outlook No. 97 (Edition 2015/1)", *OECD Economic Outlook: Statistics and Projections* (database), http://dx.doi.org/10.1787/data-00759-en.

StatLink http://dx.doi.org/ 10.1787/888933288312

2. Fiscal policy and budgetary governance

Sweden was running a healthy budget surplus of over 3% of GDP in 2007, and its public finances absorbed the fiscal shock from the economic crisis as part of a counter-cyclical "active stabilisation" policy. However Sweden's deficit figures have slipped again over recent years. The Swedish government's 2015 Budget Bill aims to steer the public finances back towards fiscal balance. Sweden's budget framework, which is marked by a strong rules-based approach and a series of automatic consolidation mechanisms, should assist the Government in closing the deficit. The Government has also undertaken that any new policy initiatives must be fully financed.

Fiscal objectives

Sweden's fiscal policy is governed by a target for a surplus of 1% of GDP, on average over the business cycle. The latest figures show a deficit in structural terms and the objective can only be realised over the medium term. The Government is obliged to present a fiscal adjustment path showing how the fiscal objective will be attained. By default – i.e. in the absence of discretionary policy action by government – Sweden's public finances are automatically strengthened each year by up to 0.5% of GDP, as various corrective measures in the indexation provisions serve to exert downward pressure on the expenditure ratio.

Spending-side measures

The new Swedish government which assumed office in late 2014 intends to increase overall public expenditure, to be financed through additional tax measures. In practical terms, the Swedish Government has proposed an increase in the multi-year "expenditure ceiling" which limits the central government budget. This key political decision sets the scene for the medium-term fiscal framework with multi-annual ceilings for almost all areas of expenditure.

Tax-side measures

To fund its new policy priorities, the Swedish Government is proposing the phasing-in of a range of revenue-raising measures, including:

- discontinuation of social security reliefs for young people
- ending of tax deductions for private pensions
- less generous tax reliefs for certain domestic services and renovation and rebuilding of private homes
- additional payroll tax for older people to increase uniformity of taxation of earned income
- increased environmental taxes building upon the "polluter pays" principle
- introduction of a tax on the financial sector (no specific proposal yet).

Policy priorities

The new Swedish government has laid down policy priorities in the following areas:

- education
- labour-market reforms

- infrastructure
- health and medical care.

The process for bringing these priorities to bear upon the resource allocation process is not yet explicit, but will be handled in the context of the annual budget process rather than through any new extrinsic process.

Long-term sustainability and fiscal risks

According to the Organic Budget Law, the Swedish Government is obliged to publish an analysis of the sustainability of the public finances each year in the Spring Fiscal Policy Bill. The dimension of longer term fiscal and economic sustainability is also assessed by the Fiscal Policy Council (see below) in its regular reporting.

Sub-national budgeting

Sub-national governments are obliged to run balanced budgets, and therefore must budget revenue to meet or exceed expenditures.

Economic forecasting

The Swedish Fiscal Policy Council was established in 2007 to provide an independent assessment of whether the Government's fiscal policy objectives are being achieved, and to promote public debate on fiscal policy. It may also evaluate the quality of the Government's economic forecasts and the models on which the forecasts are built.

Engagement of parliament and citizens

Sweden has taken no new initiatives to promote the quality of scrutiny and debate by parliament, or of accessibility of budget policy making to the public. However, the Parliament Act (2014) codifies some existing practices how Parliament decides on the annual budget and on supplementary budgets during the year. In addition, information on appropriated amounts for each line item in the budget as well as budget execution per line item on a monthly basis are publicly available.

The government's planned fiscal consolidation: Sweden

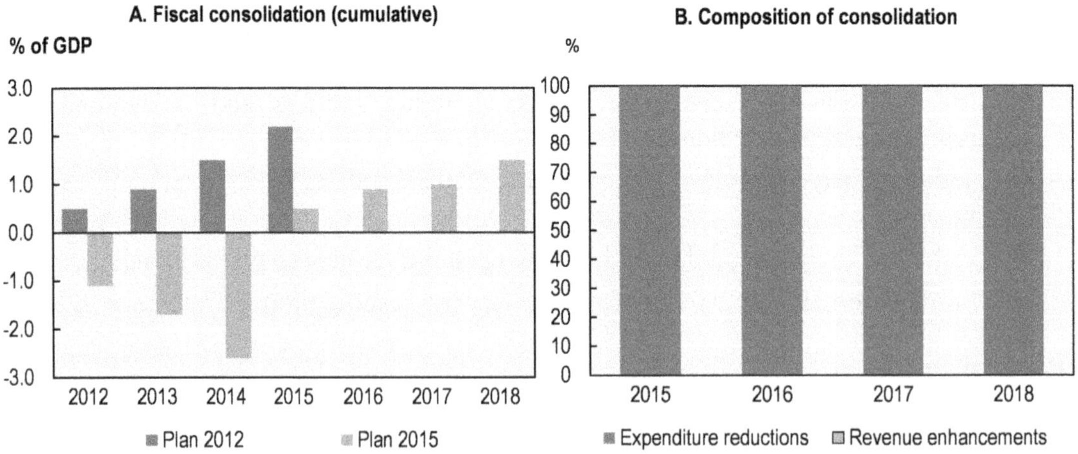

Source: OECD (2015b), *OECD State of Public Finances Survey 2015*; OECD (2011), *Restoring Public Finances*, www.oecd.org/gov/budgeting/47558957.pdf.

StatLink http://dx.doi.org/10.1787/888933288574

Switzerland

1. Economic situation

The economy has weakened thus far in 2015, but growth is projected to rise gradually into 2016 as the recent large exchange rate appreciation is absorbed. Private consumption should hold firm on the back of rising real wages and very favourable financial conditions, but exports and business investment will suffer. Lower oil prices combined with the higher Swiss franc are bringing inflation back into negative territory.

Policy interest rates will remain negative for the foreseeable future. Should growth slow further, healthy public finances leave ample room for fiscal support. Stepping up funding for childcare and education for migrant children would boost job opportunities for women and increase growth. Raising competition and efficiency in healthcare could free up consumer spending for other items.

Key economic indicators: Switzerland

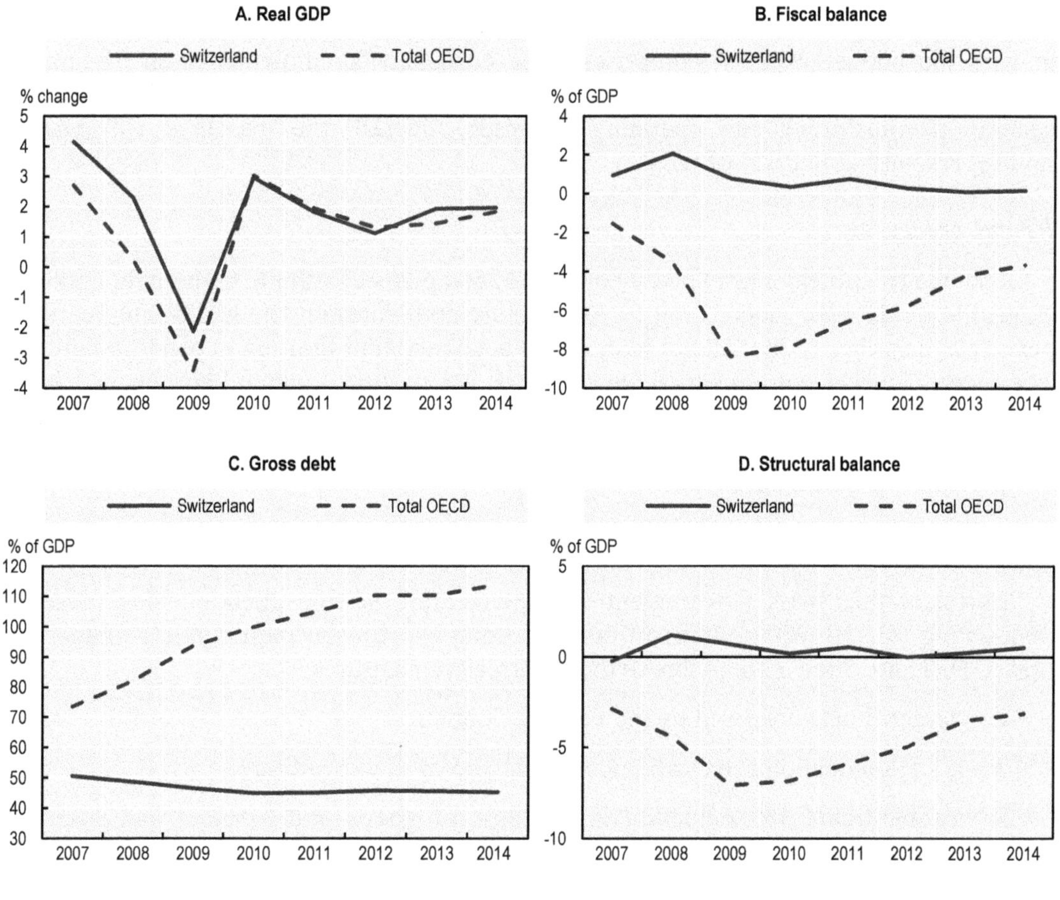

Source: OECD (2015a), "OECD Economic Outlook No. 97 (Edition 2015/1)", *OECD Economic Outlook: Statistics and Projections* (database), http://dx.doi.org/10.1787/data-00759-en.

StatLink http://dx.doi.org/ 10.1787/888933288328

Investment will be hit by lower business confidence, exchange rate volatility and the uncertainty surrounding the implementation of immigration quotas in 2017. In the medium term, as the country phases out its nuclear power plants, investment in other forms of energy will need to increase, which should boost domestic demand. Transport infrastructure is already well developed, but implementing peak-load pricing in motorway and train transportation could help reduce congestion and boost productivity.

2. Fiscal policy and budgetary governance

Although Switzerland has weathered the global financial and economic crisis relatively well, the recession in 2009 had a noticeable impact on public finances. Therefore, in the summer of 2010 the federal government announced a consolidation programme (KOP 12) in order to meet the requirements of the debt brake rule. The various measures of the programme were implemented from 2012 onwards and resulted in budget reductions totalling 0.2% of GDP.

As the fiscal outlook started to deteriorate again in 2012, the Swiss Parliament instructed the federal council to present new programme measures to relieve the federal budget further. Thus, a new consolidation programme (KAP14) was initiated and factored in with the budget 2015. It comprises three components: implementation of targeted reductions; across-the-board reductions justified by lower inflation; and reductions in general, administrative and operating expenses. Overall, the measures will provide savings amounting to 0.1% of GDP.

Fiscal objectives

The budget strategy has two key objectives: compliance with the Swiss debt brake (an expenditure rule which sets a limit on expenditure both during boom and during recession periods and applies to the federal budget and accounts) and limiting expenditure growth. The Swiss Government aims to achieve a CHF 186 million structural surplus in relation to the federal budget and for spending growth to be 1.3% in 2015. This target is below the expected level of economic growth (3.1%) because of the need to take measures to comply with the Swiss debt brake.

Spending-side measures

Currently the Swiss Government is implementing several spending-side measures (amounting to CHF 700 million) in order to comply with the requirements of the debt brake. There are three main pillars to these corrective measures:

1. targeted cuts proposed by the Federal Council
2. a 1.1% reduction across all uncommitted areas of expenditure
3. an additional 1% reduction in the cost of goods and services and operating expenditure.

Tax-side measures

Tax-side measures have not been envisaged as part of the consolidation programme 2014 (KAP 14). However, in 2012 the tax rates on tobacco products have been increased as part of the consolidation programme 2012 (KOP 12).

Protecting economic growth

The debt brake does not require budgets to be balanced on an annual basis, but only over an entire economic cycle. Therefore, what is relevant to the annual controlling process is the structural fiscal balance, i.e. the balance that has been adjusted for cyclical influences. The application of the debt brake thus leads to a stabilisation of expenditure development and enables the automatic stabilisers in the federal budget to exercise their impact freely. In a recession, cyclically related shortfalls in receipts do not have to be compensated for by corresponding cuts in expenditure. The resulting budget deficits have the effect of supporting aggregate demand in the economy (and prevent pro-cyclical expenditure cuts), and thereby contribute to the stabilisation of economic development. The reverse is the case when the economy is booming. The debt brake therefore allows for a passive anti-cyclical fiscal policy, i.e. a rule-based and cyclically stabilising fiscal policy.

Policy priorities

The debt brake is a key pillar of the Federal Council's budgetary policy. It sets the maximum level of expenditure and brings a top-down element to budgeting. However, the debt brake is silent about the composition of the budget. The Federal Council therefore defined medium-term target growth rates for expenditure by task area. In the 2011–15 legislative period plan, it resolved to elaborate expenditure policy priorities for the medium term (i.e. over an eight to ten-year period) too. This allows the Government to set different policy priorities within the framework of the debt brake. Currently education and research, social security and development aid are among the tasks with the highest growth rates.

Long-term sustainability and fiscal risks

The Swiss Government published a report on the long-term sustainability of public finances in 2012. It was calculated that annual savings or additional receipts of 1.8% of GDP would be required to prevent the debt ratio from rising by 2060. The Swiss Government also faces ongoing risks in relation to ongoing turbulence in the financial markets and the ongoing dialogue with the EU on tax issues.

Economic forecasting

Within the administration, the macroeconomic forecasts are made by a Committee of Economic Experts with the participation of experts from the State Secretariat for Economic Affairs, the Statistics Office, the Central Bank as well as experts from the Ministry of Finance.

Engagement of parliament and citizens

Switzerland has no particular initiatives in place to enhance the inclusiveness or participative nature of the budget process.

The government's planned fiscal consolidation: Switzerland

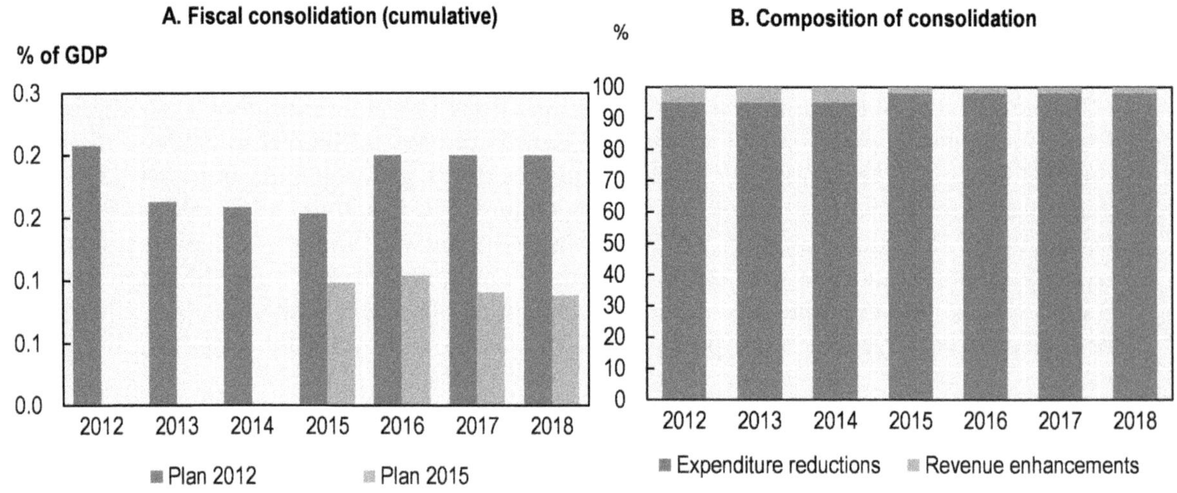

Source: OECD (2015b), *OECD State of Public Finances Survey 2015*; OECD (2011), *Restoring Public Finances,* www.oecd.org/gov/budgeting/47558957.pdf.

StatLink http://dx.doi.org/10.1787/888933288581

Turkey

1. Economic situation

Growth weakened in early 2015, after a short-lived upturn in late 2014. The uncertainties associated with the forthcoming legislative elections and ongoing geopolitical tensions in the region are holding back investment and consumption spending. GDP growth is projected to pick up gradually over 2015 and 2016, after the "wait and see" attitudes of businesses and households dissipate.

Against the backdrop of large foreign financing needs and volatile capital flows, inflation – which remains far above target – will need to be brought down. To further rebalance demand from domestic to external sources, freeing up the productivity potential of the business sector and achieving durable competitiveness gains is crucial. The implementation of key product and labour-market reforms would spur growth.

Key economic indicators: Turkey

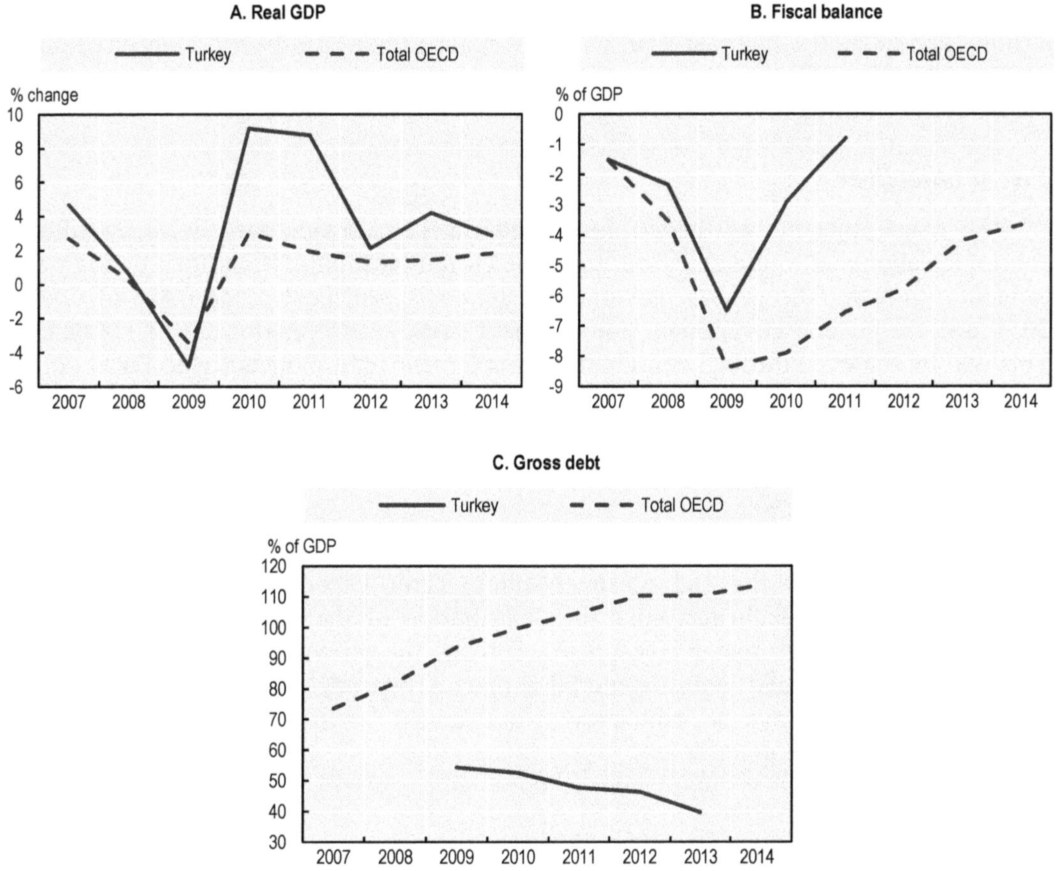

Source: OECD (2015a), "OECD Economic Outlook No. 97 (Edition 2015/1)", *OECD Economic Outlook: Statistics and Projections* (database), http://dx.doi.org/10.1787/data-00759-en.

StatLink http://dx.doi.org/10.1787/888933288339

Private investment peaked in 2011 after a swift recovery following the global crisis, but has since been sluggish. In contrast, government investment, mainly in infrastructure, continued to increase until the end of 2013 and provided support during a time of volatile economic activity. Exchange rate uncertainty, corporate leverage and foreign exchange exposures, and regional geopolitical tensions will influence the pace of recovery of investment.

2. Fiscal policy and budgetary governance

After the global financial crisis, Turkey implemented a series of temporary expenditure and revenue measures such as temporary tax rate cuts and increased public investments. However, the economy recovered sooner than expected and the fiscal deficit decreased from 5.5% of GDP in 2009 to 0.4% in 2011. In addition, the general government nominal debt stock was 46.0% of GDP in 2009, but receded to 39.1% of GDP in 2011. From 2012, the fiscal policy focus shifted and achieving sustainable growth rates to curb the current account deficit became the top priority. In addition, increased emphasis was given to the public sector's role in meeting the Central Bank's inflation target in 2013. Since then, there has been a new structural reform agenda and the introduction of a Development Plan with two main primary transformation programmes (PTPs). The first PTP is a Programme of Rationalising the Public Expenditure and the second PTP is a Programme of Raising the Quality of Public Revenues.

Fiscal objectives

The main objective of the 2015-17 Medium Term Programme is to continue to control inflation and to gradually decrease the current account deficit, thereby increasing economic growth. The general government deficit is projected to be 0.8% of GDP in 2014, and the general government nominal debt stock is projected to be 33.1% of GDP. This will be achieved through continuing to implement tight monetary and fiscal policies and accelerating structural reforms. There is a target for the general government balance to yield a surplus of 0.1% in 2017.

Spending-side measures

General government expenditure is estimated to decrease from 38.7% of GDP in 2015 to 37.2% of GDP at the end of the Medium-Term Programme. Spending will be prioritised in areas which maximise the contribution of the public investments to the growth, support private sector investments, activate the growth potential of the regions, increase employment and increase overall country prosperity. In addition, activities will be carried out to improve the efficiency of the services of the public administrations in fiscal management and control.

Tax-side measures

The tax burden as a percent of GDP is expected to increase by 0.4 percentage points in 2015 as a result of restructuring social security premiums, but then to decrease gradually towards the end of the Medium-Term Programme. Revenue policies will be focussed on collecting tax revenues from buoyant and permanent sources in a way which improves income distribution, contributes to sustainable development, raises domestic savings and enhances the competitiveness of the economy. Measures include:

- Increasing direct tax collection relative to indirect tax collection (in particular, transaction taxes will be reduced).
- Introducing policies which support R&D activities and the production of high value-added products.
- Improving voluntary tax compliance.
- Prioritising environmental tax policies.

Budget costings and execution

A Fiscal Management and Control Centre Harmonisation Unit exists and it is planned that its monitoring function will be strengthened. In addition, internal audit within Government will be strengthened with the goal of increasing public administrations' level of compliance with the Internal Auditing Standards.

Protecting economic growth

Fiscal policy is implemented in line with the goal of supporting economic stability and boosting economic growth potential. To achieve this, spending programmes in infrastructure investments will be prioritised, along with programmes to promote regional development, education and R&D support. Infrastructure investments will include spending on rail and maritime transport and logistics centres to support productive private sector activities. Projects that can be completed in the short term will be prioritised, as well as maintenance-replacement, maintenance-repair and rehabilitation spending.

Policy priorities

The main goals of the current fiscal policy are to support economic stability, increase domestic savings, curb the current account deficit, fight inflation and boost economic growth potential.

Long-term sustainability and fiscal risks

The main fiscal risks are considered to be the current account deficit and high levels of inflation. To mitigate against this, tight monetary and fiscal policies will continue. In addition, structural reforms are being accelerated.

Sub-national budgeting

Local government revenues will be increased. This will be done by reviewing the property tax system and harmonising local taxes within the general tax system.

Economic forecasting

There are no specific details on how macroeconomic forecasts are produced. However, in general public finance statistics are published in compliance with the international standards.

Engagement of parliament and citizens

Turkey has no particular initiatives in place to enhance the inclusiveness or participative nature of the budget process.

The government's planned fiscal consolidation: Turkey

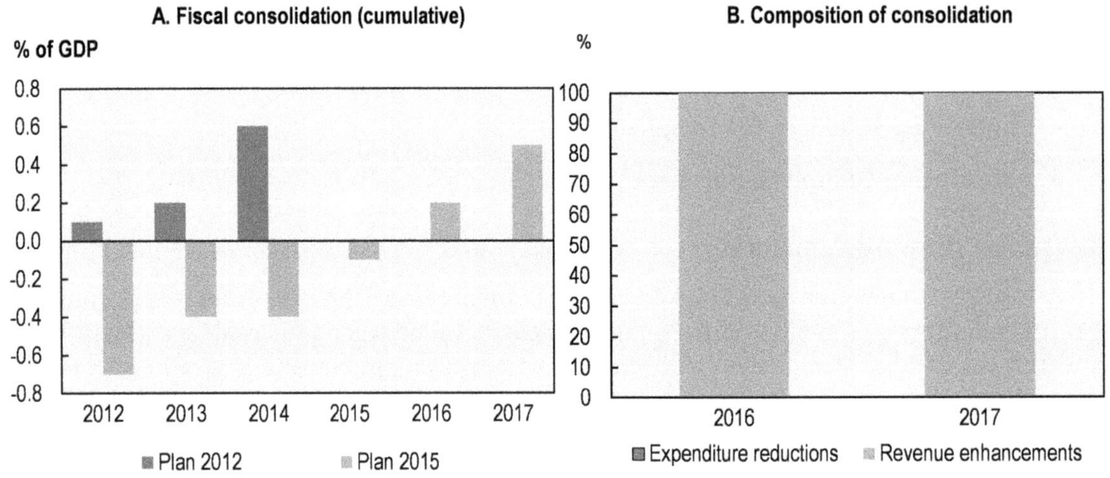

Source: OECD (2015b), *OECD Fiscal Consolidation Survey 2015;* OECD (2011), *Restoring Public Finances,* www.oecd.org/gov/budgeting/47558957.pdf.

StatLink http://dx.doi.org/10.1787/888933288592

United Kingdom

1. Economic situation

Economic growth was strong in 2014 and is projected to continue at a solid pace in 2015 and 2016, boosted by domestic demand. The unemployment rate is projected to fall further towards 5%. As spare capacity wanes, inflation is expected to pick up towards the 2% inflation target. The current account deficit, which has widened to above 5% of GDP, should narrow as the euro area recovers.

According to the March 2015 budget, bolder fiscal consolidation is planned by the authorities in 2016 and 2017, with the adjustment mainly on the spending side. It is important that adjustment measures that are yet to be defined be fair. The normalisation of interest rates is projected to start in early 2016 as spare capacity narrows and inflation pressures rise. Planned bank stress tests are welcome, but extending future exercises to shadow banks would provide fuller information.

Key economic indicators: United Kingdom

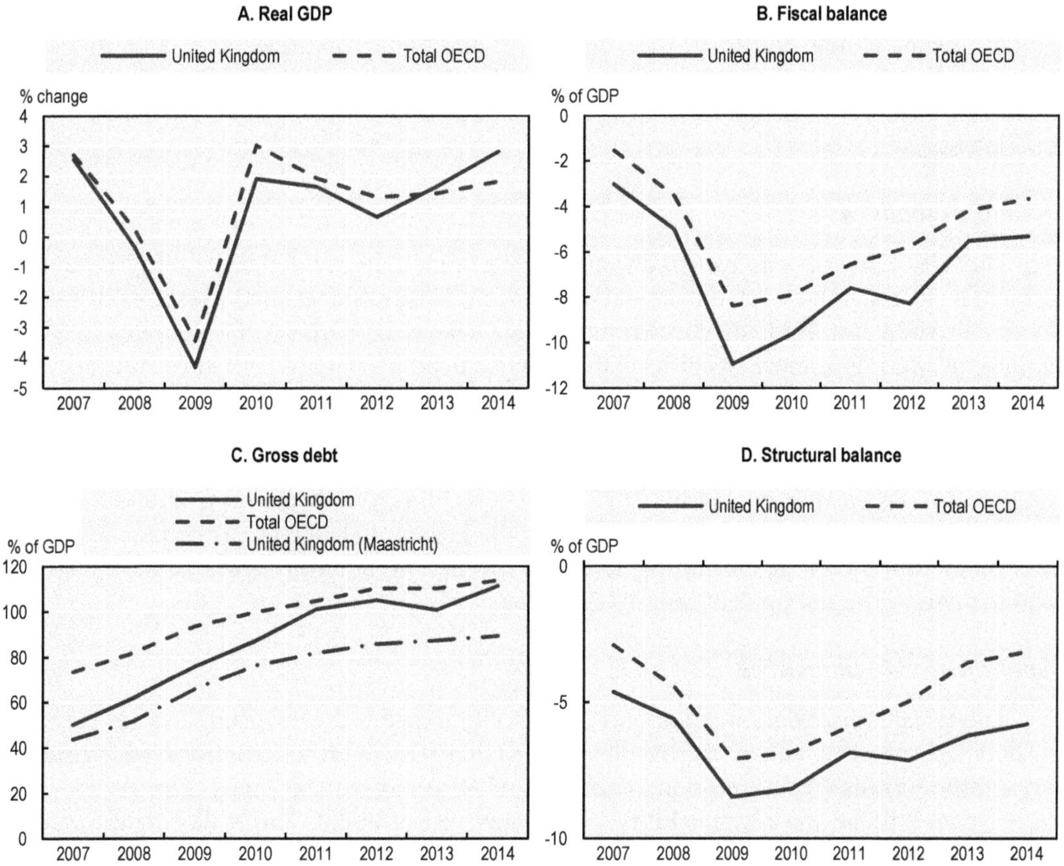

Source: OECD (2015a), "OECD Economic Outlook No. 97 (Edition 2015/1)", *OECD Economic Outlook: Statistics and Projections* (database), http://dx.doi.org/10.1787/data-00759-en.

StatLink http://dx.doi.org/10.1787/888933288349

Stronger investment is needed to revive labour productivity, wages and competitiveness, and to balance the housing market. This requires greater access to finance for businesses, relaxed land planning regulations, and improved infrastructure. The perceived quality of infrastructure is lower than in other G7 countries, and the investment ratio is comparatively low. Infrastructure could be enhanced by strengthening long-term government strategy and planning in order to attract private investors, and by leveraging limited public resources with private investment.

2. Fiscal policy and budgetary governance

The United Kingdom ran a high fiscal deficit of almost 3% of GDP in 2007, and with the onset of the financial and economic crisis, the deficit swelled to over 10% of GDP by 2009. The UK Government (2010-15) has set fiscal sustainability as a primary policy goal, to be effected through demanding targets for fiscal consolidation. While the fiscal correction has made gradual progress – the deficit remaining at over 5% of GDP in 2013-14 – the Government has managed to retain the confidence of markets that fiscal sustainability is being restored. The new government will need to pursue further, sustained fiscal correction; although the strong underlying performance of the UK economy should help to mitigate the overall fiscal effort required. Given policy commitments which constrain the raising of additional tax revenues, and given the significant efficiency savings that have contributed to the consolidation effort to date, identifying further expenditure-side cost savings will present a major challenge for the coming years.

Fiscal objectives

The UK Government has traditionally determined its own fiscal policy course by reference to objectives set out at national level. Under the Budget Responsibility and National Audit Act 2011, the Government must set out its high-level objectives for fiscal policy, as well as a more specific mandate (fiscal policy targets) for the Treasury, in a Charter for Budget Responsibility to be submitted to Parliament. The initial Charter (April 2011) laid down a demanding target of achieving cyclically adjusted current balance by the end of the rolling five-year forecast period, and to bring the debt-to-GDP ratio onto a downward course by 2015-16. These objectives were revised and approved by Parliament in January 2015 to require that the current balance target be reached by the end of the third year of the rolling five-year period, creating a tighter fiscal constraint; and to achieve the falling debt ratio by 2016-17.

Spending-side measures

The fiscal consolidation objectives are heavily expenditure-focused, and are reflected in detailed spending consolidation plans up to 2015-16, with assumptions for aggregate expenditure limits ("total managed expenditure") for subsequent years. Details for those later years will be the responsibility of the new government, and will be informed by further spending review.

A principal budgetary policy lever of the UK Government, and of HM Treasury, is the setting-down of multi-annual spending caps for departments on the basis of periodic spending reviews. A notable addition to the UK Government's expenditure-containment policy has been the "welfare cap", an upper limit on overall forecast expenditure on the broad social welfare area. The objective of this measure is to balance the cyclical increase in this area of expenditure with a strengthened requirement to prioritise and rationalise within fixed resources.

Tax-side measures

The UK Government specified from the outset of its fiscal consolidation plan (2010) that the bulk of consolidation would come from the expenditure rather than revenue side of the budget, consistent with international research that this approach would be most conducive to maintaining growth. However, the Government also committed to rebalancing the economy through fairness, and recent budgets have sought to generate increased revenues from higher earners and corporations through curtailment of tax reliefs and of aggressive tax avoidance.

As regards future fiscal consolidation beyond 2015-16, this is currently expressed in terms of a reduction in aggregate expenditure, although it will be open to an incoming UK government to specify the aggregate revenue/expenditure contribution to fiscal correction.

Flexibility in budget execution

From 2011-12, the former system of end-year flexibility (whereby departments could carry over unlimited amounts of their unspent budget into the following year) was replaced with "budget exchange", whereby departments are allowed to surrender an underspend in advance of the end of the fiscal year, in return for a corresponding increase in the following year's allocation, subject to a prudent limit.

Protecting economic growth

As a matter of policy, the UK Government credits a firm commitment to fiscal discipline and fiscal sustainability as an important underpinning of economic confidence and growth. In parallel with this approach, however, the Government has sought to boost productivity through a range of structural economic reforms, including a strong commitment to reducing the regulatory burden, and tax reform aimed at lowering corporation tax rates and reducing the burden on low-paid employees. In addition, the Government has prioritised and protected capital investment that supports long-term economic growth: the Government added GBP 10 billion to its capital investment plans in autumn 2011; and more recently, public sector gross investment is planned to be held constant in real terms in 2016-17 and 2017-18, and to increase in line with GDP in the following year.

Policy priorities

The Government's medium-term policy priorities were established in the context of the 2010 Spending Review, which allowed for priority to be afforded to the National Health Service, schools and early years provision, as well as protecting capital investment. Official development assistance has also been a protected area of spending.

Long-term sustainability and fiscal risks

The over-arching fiscal objective identified by the UK Government in its Charter for Budget Responsibility is "to ensure sustainable public finances" that support economic growth, inter-generational fairness and effectiveness of overall policy. To address future fiscal pressures, the Government has introduced pension reforms including a progressive increase in the State Pension age and adopting a guiding principle that adults should expect to spend, on average, up to one-third of their adult life in retirement.

The independent Office for Budget Responsibility produces an annual Fiscal Sustainability Report which sets the analytical basis upon which policy responses can be formulated by government.

Sub-national budgeting

The largest innovation in sub-national budgeting is the proposed new dispensation regarding enhanced fiscal autonomy for Scotland, in the wake of the "no" vote on the independence referendum in 2014. Following recommendations from the Smith Commission, the UK Government proposed in November 2014 that the Scottish Parliament will in future be responsible for more than 50% of its funding, and the Smith Commission agreement builds on the Scottish Parliament's existing powers so that welfare provision can be better tailored to local needs.

Economic forecasting

The Office for Budget Responsibility (OBR) was established in 2010 on an interim basis, introducing independence, greater transparency and credibility to the economic and fiscal forecasts on which the Government's fiscal policy is based. Since then, the OBR has been placed on a permanent, statutory footing through the Budget Responsibility and National Audit Act 2011, which received Royal Assent on 22 March 2011. The OBR is an independent fiscal institution, formally attached to HM Treasury, tasked with assessing and monitoring fiscal sustainability, and preparing official forecasts for use by government. In December 2013 the OBR was also asked to take on additional responsibilities in terms of monitoring compliance with the government's "welfare cap", and publishing information about the drivers of welfare spending. More generally, it is notable that the OBR's assessments of the fiscal outlook, and implications for aggregate budgetary management, have been influential in public and political debate.

Engagement of parliament and citizens

The traditional parliamentary debate on budget day is usually followed by four days of debate, structured by different policy areas such as health, education and defence. With regard to citizen engagement, the Government invites members of public and external organisations to submit policy ideas ahead of the budget as part of its open policy-making agenda. External stakeholders are invited to submit policy ideas to the Treasury via the GOV.UK website.

The government's planned fiscal consolidation: United Kingdom

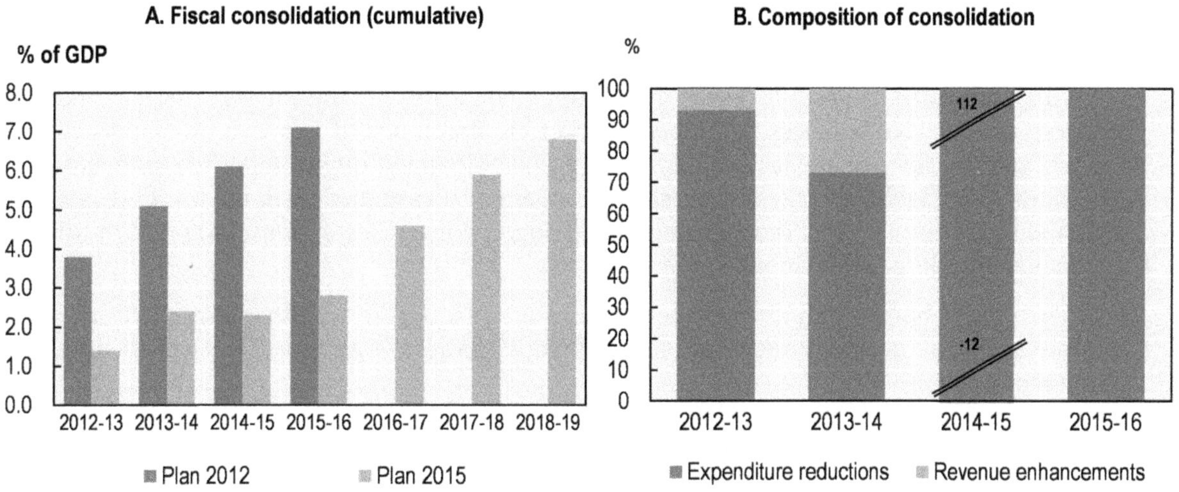

Source: OECD (2015b), *OECD State of Public Finances Survey 2015*; OECD (2011), *Restoring Public Finances*, www.oecd.org/gov/budgeting/47558957.pdf.

StatLink http://dx.doi.org/10.1787/888933288607

United States

1. Economic situation

Output growth paused in early 2015, weighed down by the stronger dollar and adverse weather. Nonetheless, the labour market has continued to improve, as evidenced by job gains in the private sector and a falling unemployment rate. Supportive monetary conditions and lower energy prices should underpin a sustained pick-up in aggregate demand as the fiscal policy drag dissipates and ongoing increases in household wealth lift consumer spending and residential construction.

The federal budget deficit continues to narrow, reflecting consolidation measures and the advancing recovery. Policy actions to directly address long-term fiscal challenges remain desirable.

Key economic indicators: United States

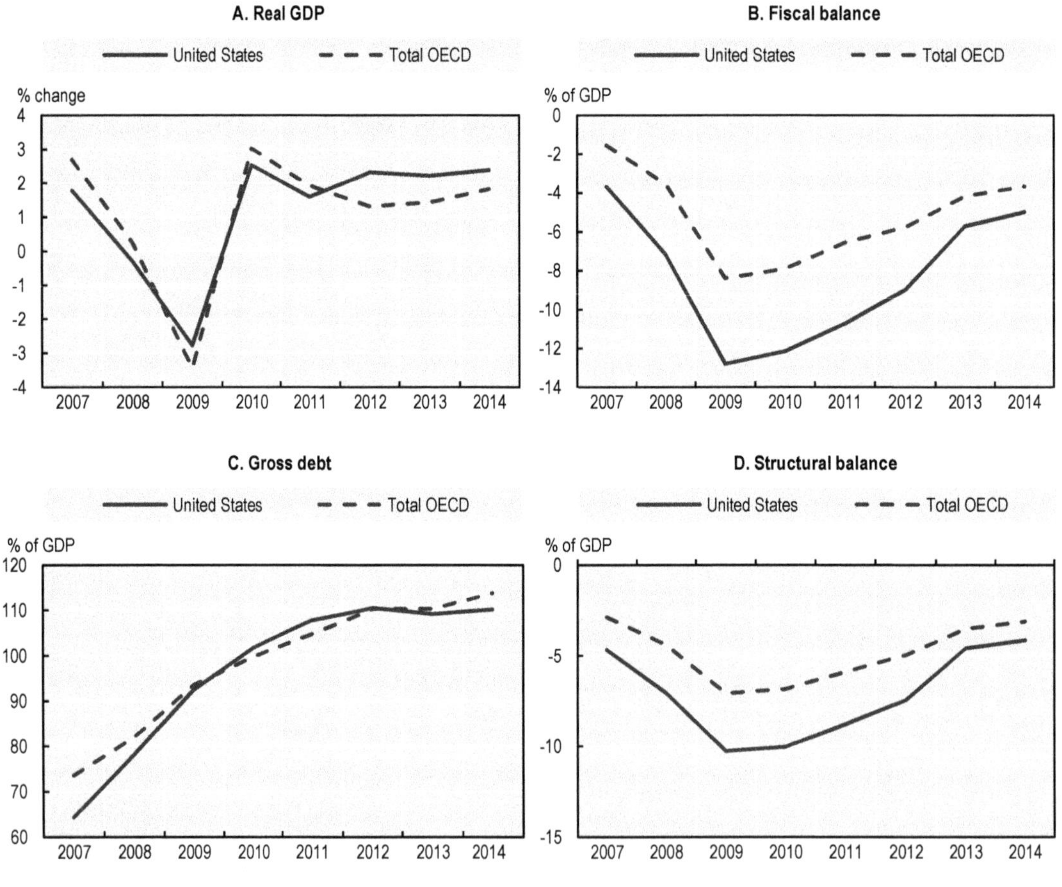

Source: OECD (2015a), "OECD Economic Outlook No. 97 (Edition 2015/1)", *OECD Economic Outlook: Statistics and Projections* (database), http://dx.doi.org/10.1787/data-00759-en.

StatLink http://dx.doi.org/10.1787/888933288359

The recovery of investment spending has been sluggish so far, reflecting the weakness of the demand outlook, the overhang of construction from the housing boom, and a sustained public spending squeeze. Low public and private capital investments have reduced productivity and weakened production capacity. With real long-term interest rates historically low, the federal and state and local governments have scope to accelerate infrastructure investment spending.

2. Fiscal policy and budgetary governance

With a high federal deficit of 3.7% of GDP in 2007, the public finances in the United States absorbed much of the initial strain of the economic and financial crisis with the deficit rising to above 10% of GDP each year in the period 2009-11, and the debt ratio rising by almost 50 percentage points to its current level of around 110% of GDP, where it has plateaued since 2012. The US Government has an overall goal of bringing deficits to a more sustainable fiscal path, and with the combination of steady economic growth and strict budgetary discipline, federal deficits have shrunk to below 5% of GDP in 2015. Public budgeting in the United States is notable for the strong roles exercised by the co-equal branches of government, and by the reliance in recent years upon strict statutory limits on appropriations.

Fiscal objectives

The Budget Control Act of 2011 put statutory limits on annual appropriations and a requirement to reduce spending by USD 109 billion per year through to 2021, referred to as "sequestration". However, since 2012 short-term budget agreements have increased spending limits and have been paid for by a combination of changes to the tax code and alternative spending reductions. The Bipartisan Budget Act of 2013 replaced a portion of sequestration cuts in 2014 and 2015 with long-term reforms. The 2013 budget included USD 3 trillion in net deficit reduction over the subsequent ten years. Combined with the approximately USD 1 trillion in savings from the provisions in Title I of the Budget Control Act, this would generate more than USD 4 trillion in deficit reduction over the next decade. Sequestration is due to return in full in 2016 through to 2024.

Spending-side measures

Measures such as the Affordable Care Act and the Budget Control Act, along with proposals in each budget, are credited by the US Government with reducing public spending and helping to narrow the deficit. In addition, in 2014 the Executive Branch initiated strategic reviews for the first time. These help agencies use evidence to inform resource allocation from lower to higher priority areas. There have also been significant savings from winding down of military commitments overseas.

Tax-side measures

The American Taxpayer Relief Act of 2012 brought about revenue increases by restoring higher tax rates on the wealthiest Americans. Measures included extending the current tax rates on income tax and capital gains and dividends tax except for taxpayers with high incomes and increasing the top rate of estate, gift and generation skipping transfer tax to 40%.

Budget costings and execution

The Congressional Budget Office (CBO) produces independent analyses to support the Congressional budget process. For example, periodically the CBO produces a reference volume examining numerous options for reducing budget deficits. The volume includes a wide range of options, derived from many sources, for reducing spending or increasing revenues. For each option, CBO presents an estimate of its effects on the budget and a discussion of its benefits and drawbacks but makes no recommendations.

Protecting economic growth

After the financial crisis the Recovery Act helped stimulate the economy and create jobs. Congress also took bipartisan action in 2010 to temporarily reduce payroll taxes and continue emergency unemployment benefits. However, since the Budget Control Act of 2011, sequestration has had a large impact on publicly funded programmes and has curtailed the Executive's discretion to undertake further large-scale public investments that could contribute to future growth. While the Bipartisan Act of 2013 replaced a portion of the sequestration cuts in 2014 and 2015 with long-term reforms allowing for higher investment levels, sequestration is due to return in full in 2016.

Policy priorities

The budget for fiscal year 2016 increases investments that will accelerate growth and expand opportunity. For example, it proposed pro-work, pro-family tax reforms and mandatory investments in surface transportation infrastructure, universal pre-kindergarten, childcare assistance for middle-class and working families. It also focuses on finishing the task of putting the nation on a sustainable fiscal path. A USD 1.8 trillion deficit reduction over ten years is to be achieved primarily from health, tax and immigration reform.

Long-term sustainability and fiscal risks

The key drivers of the long-range deficit are the Government's major health and retirement programmes: Medicare, Medicaid and Social Security. Revenues rise somewhat relative to GDP, but not enough to keep pace with the increase in health and retirement programme spending. The Affordable Care Act introduced reforms aimed at slowing growth in medical costs into the future. In addition, there have been annual reductions of 2 percentage points to Medicare spending due to the sequestration required by the Budget Control Act of 2011. Resolving the long-run fiscal challenge will require a comprehensive approach involving consideration of all budgetary tools and levers available to policy makers.

Sub-national budgeting

State governments are independent entities in the US constitutional framework.

Economic forecasting

The US Government publishes its own economic forecasts that underpin the budget estimates. It compares these forecasts with those of the Federal Reserve's Open Market Committee (FOMC), the CBO, and the Blue Chip Consensus of private forecasters.

Engagement of parliament and citizens

As indicated above, the public budgeting system in the United States provides for very significant parliamentary engagement in and control over the public budgeting process, as a co-equal branch of government. A series of reforms over recent years, notably on foot of the Government Performance and Result Act (GPRA) Modernization

Act of 2010, has brought additional clarity to the objectives of government agencies and managers, including through a public-facing website.

The government's planned fiscal consolidation: United States

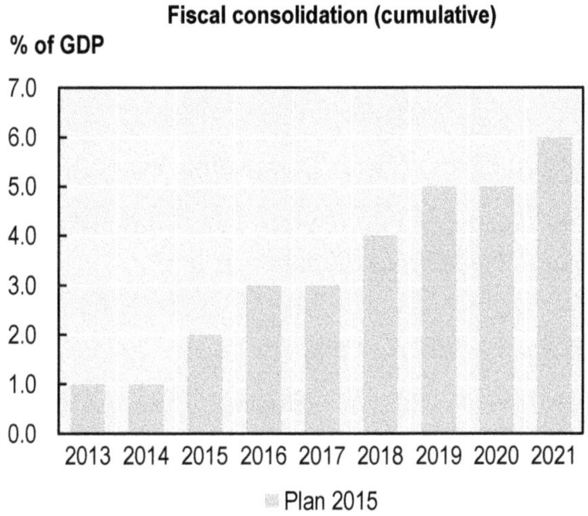

Source: OECD (2015b), *OECD State of Public Finances Survey 2015.*

StatLink http://dx.doi.org/10.1787/888933288613

References

Government of Canada (2015), *Economic Action Plan 2015*, http://actionplan.gc.ca/en.

OECD (2015a), "OECD Economic Outlook No. 97 (Edition 2015/1)", *OECD Economic Outlook: Statistics and Projections* (database), http://dx.doi.org/10.1787/data-00759-en.

OECD (2015b), *OECD State of Public Finances Survey 2015*, OECD.

OECD (2015c), *Government at a Glance 2015*, OECD Publishing, Paris. DOI: http://dx.doi.org/10.1787/gov_glance-2015-en

OECD (2011), *Restoring Public Finances,* www.oecd.org/gov/budgeting/47558957.pdf.

Chapter 3

Monitoring and managing the finances of sub-national governments

In most OECD countries, the finances of sub-national governments (SNGs) form a significant component of overall national finances. SNGs have also been significantly affected by the recent economic and financial crisis. This chapter discusses recent trends in the management of SNG finances and of fiscal relations across levels of government, including the main drivers of SNG debt levels, the limitations on SNGs' capacity to improve their fiscal situation, the various types of fiscal rule and models such as "rainy day funds" that govern and stabilise SNG finances, and related issues and challenges for monitoring and managing SNG finances.

1. Introduction

Sub-national government (SNG) debts represented on average 13% of GDP and 17% of total public debt in OECD countries in 2013. This chapter analyses the main drivers of sub-national government debt, and how they have evolved since the beginning of the financial and economic crisis in 2007. It examines strategies adopted to monitor and control sub-national government debts, and raises some principal challenges and tentative recommendations.

2. Limitations on sub-national governments' capacity to improve their financial situations

SNGs enjoy less autonomy for improving their fiscal situation than central governments (CGs) (Vammalle and Hulbert, 2013). First, the revenue base of SNGs is smaller and SNGs' autonomy to increase revenues is usually limited, with little or no power over tax rates or tax bases, high reliance on transfers, etc. Therefore, for SNGs, it is more relevant to look at deficits and debt as a share of their revenues, rather than as a share of gross domestic product (GDP). On this measure, SNG deficits (as a share of revenues) increased from 1.5% in 2007 to 4.5% in 2010, while the average SNG debt-to-revenue ratio rose from 70% to 83% during the same period. In 2010, it represented more than one-and-a-half years of revenues in countries such as Canada (Provinces), Germany (*Länder*) or Japan.

Second, an important share of SNG expenditure is mandatory and/or difficult to cut, because reductions entail high social and political costs:

- A particularly large share of SNG spending is in critical sectors. On average, SNGs spend 50% of their budgets on education, health and social protection, i.e. sectors where cuts are particularly visible, unpopular, or may be costly in the long run.
- Some SNG expenditures are expected to rise due to demographic factors. Population ageing implies increases in health and elderly care expenditures in the coming decades, which in some countries represent a large share of SNG spending.
- Rules and standards of SNG expenditure are often dictated by higher levels of government. This gives SNGs very little autonomy in deciding to reduce the levels or standards of services delivered in order to reduce their deficits.

Finally, fiscal rules often constrain SNGs' room for manoeuvre, as they have less opportunity to use debt to adjust their budgets. Decreases in revenues therefore rapidly lead to expenditure cuts. The most noteworthy example is in the United States, where almost all US states have a balanced budget rule in their constitution. This led to wide-ranging expenditure cuts in 2008-09 during the global financial crisis, which further amplified the effects of the crisis (Blöchliger et al., 2010).

Therefore, looking at the ratio of SNG debt to SNG revenues gives a better picture of the reimbursement capacity of SNGs (Figure 3.2)

3. Recent trends in SNG finances

In most OECD countries, SNGs have been affected by the recent financial and economic crisis, and were active players both in the initial stimulus phase, and in the subsequent consolidation policies.

During the first phase of the crisis (2008-10), SNGs actively contributed to the stimulus policies, and CGs often helped SNGs cope with the crisis, in order to prevent them from running pro-cyclical policies and undermining national recovery plans (Blöchliger et al., 2010). During this period, SNG finances experienced a "scissors effect": tax revenues decreased, while transfers from CG, SNG public investment and SNG spending on social benefits increased (Figure 3.1). As a result, the ratio of SNG deficits to revenues increased from 1.5% in 2007 to 4.5% in 2010 (Vammalle and Hulbert, 2013), and the SNG debt-to-revenue ratio rose from 70% to 83% during the same period.

Figure 3.1. **Evolution of SNG finances since 2006**

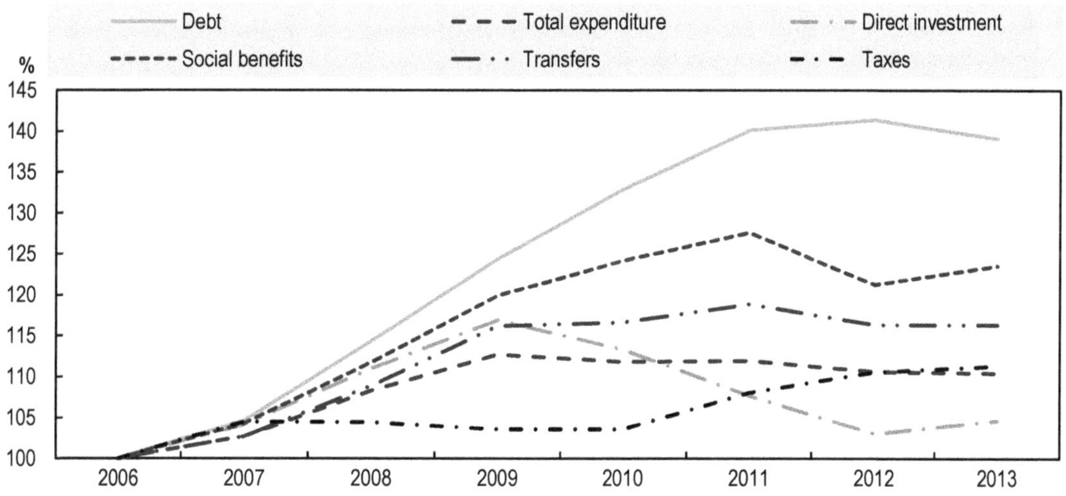

Source: Based on OECD (2015), *OECD National Accounts Statistics* (database), http://dx.doi.org/10.1787/na-data-en.

StatLink http://dx.doi.org/10.1787/888933288620

During the second phase of the crisis (2010-12), as most OECD countries engaged in consolidation plans, SNGs were also requested to contribute to the national consolidation effort (Vammalle and Hulbert, 2013), and SNG total expenditure stabilised. Given the flat growth of SNG revenues (both taxes and transfers) and the persistent growth of social transfer expenditures, the adjustment variable was public investment, which fell drastically. SNG debt levels continued to increase until 2012, and have started to decrease since (Figure 3.2).

Figure 3.2. **Development of SNG debt as a share of revenues from 2003 to 2013**

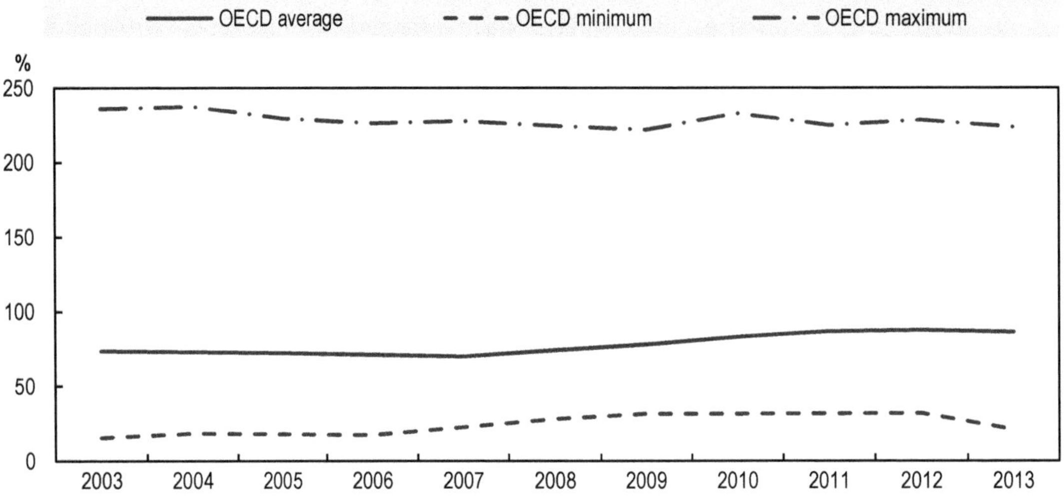

Note: All OECD countries except Chile, Greece, Korea, Mexico, New Zealand, Poland, Turkey. For Australia and Switzerland, data refer to 2012 instead of 2013. OECD average refers to unweighted average. Data consolidated except for Japan, Korea, the United Kingdom and the United States.

Sources: Based on OECD (2015), *OECD National Accounts Statistics* (database), http://dx.doi.org/10.1787/na-data-en and European Commission (2015), *Government Finance Statistics* (database), Eurostat, http://ec.europa.eu/Eurostat/web/government-finance-statistics/data/database.

StatLink http://dx.doi.org/10.1787/888933288633

4. What are the main drivers of SNG debts?

Designing an efficient monitoring and/or control mechanism requires understanding what the drivers of SNG debt are. SNG deficits and debt have three main causes:

- Structural mismatch between SNG spending obligations and allocation of revenues. SNG deficits and debts may be the result of the institutional framework created for fiscal relations across levels of government, where the revenues assigned to SNGs are not sufficient to cover their expenditure responsibilities. This would thus result in structural SNG deficits, or the under-provision of public goods provided by SNGs.
- Economic downturns can also generate temporary SNG deficits, and thus contribute to building up SNG debt. Indeed, SNG spending obligations tend to be rather stable over the economic cycle (even pro-cyclical to some extent, for instance when SNGs have social protection responsibilities), while their revenues are more likely to be more sensitive to the cycle. As growth recovers, these deficits should disappear, and SNGs should regain balanced budgets or even surpluses.
- Finally, SNGs may be subject to soft budget constraints and moral hazard, thus leading them to over-spend and issue debt in the expectation that they would receive increased transfers or be bailed out in case of financial difficulty. In this case, monitoring mechanisms and fiscal rules can be useful to prevent structural deficits and accumulation of SNG debts.

The most appropriate policy action and instruments depend on the mix of causes of SNG deficits and debts. **Rainy day funds** can be an effective tool for smoothing out revenues, thus preventing SNGs from issuing debt to compensate revenue decreases (Box 1.5). Rainy day funds are mainly used in federal countries: Canada (state and local levels), Finland, Germany (state and local levels), Mexico (state and local levels), Sweden and Switzerland (state and local levels) (Table 3.1). The formulas used for **allocating grants** are also crucial, as they can be either pro-cyclical, if they are based on current revenues and GDP growth for example, or on the contrary, they can help smooth the cycle, if they are based on the revenues of several past years (as in Denmark). The **allocation of expenditure** can also smooth the cycle, by granting SNGs the least cyclical expenditures (expenditure on education for example tends to be far less cyclical than that on social protection). Finally, **off-budget funds**, ad hoc increases of **CG transfers** or **cuts in mandated expenditures** are also used (Table 3.1).

Table 3.1. **Mechanisms to protect SNGs against cyclical fluctuations of revenues in OECD countries**

	Rainy day funds	Off-budget funds	Higher revenues from CG compensating for projected fluctuations	Higher revenues from CG compensating for actual fluctuations	Special financial support for SNGs facing budget difficulties	Cuts on mandated expenditures	Allocation of less cyclical expenditures
Australia local			x				
Australia state				x			
Austria local							x
Austria state		x					x
Belgium local							
Belgium state							x
Canada local	x						
Canada state	x	x	x				
Chile					x		
Czech Republic		x					
Denmark			x				
Estonia					x		
Finland	x	x	x			x	
Germany local	x		x	x	x	x	
Germany state	x	x				x	
Ireland			x				
Italy local						x	
Italy state						x	
Korea							
Mexico local	x			x	x		
Mexico state	x			x	x		
New Zealand							
Poland							
Slovak Republic		x					
Slovenia							
Spain local				x			
Spain state				x			
Sweden	x					x	
Switzerland local	x						
Switzerland state	x						
Turkey							x
Total answers	10	6	6	6	5	6	4

Source: OECD (2011a), *OECD Network on Fiscal Relations across Levels of Government Survey on Sub-national Fiscal Rules and Macroeconomic Management*, OECD, September 2011, updated in March 2013.

Ageing and health spending, which impact significantly upon SNG finances in many countries, are areas which have attracted a range of approaches to control costs and introduce efficiencies. Box 3.1 outlines approaches adopted across various countries.

Box 3.1. Reforms to alleviate ageing and health cost pressures on SNG finances in selected countries

- **Austria**: The federal government, *Länder* and social security institutions came to an agreement on a healthcare reform that was approved by the National Assembly in 2013. Targets are set to align health expenditure growth with average GDP growth (+3.6% per year). Agreements with sub-national governments aim to ensure a joint planning of public healthcare spending, increase the binding force of planning at the *Länder* level, and establish joint financing. This reform aims to generate EUR 3.4 billion in savings until 2016.
- **Belgium**: Population ageing should have large repercussions on sub-national finances in Belgium, as local authorities are responsible for a large share of social measures in favour of the elderly – in particular via the *centres publics d'action sociale* (CPAS), who own retirement homes or hospitals. Large investments will need to be carried on in the years to come in order to maintain an adequate provision of public services in this sector, which will induce additional stress on sub-national finances. Recently, the sustainability of public finances regarding costs induced by ageing has become a major subject in Belgium. A long-term strategy based on a reduction of public debt was introduced. The diminution in future interest charges paid should generate extra funding to finance social protection expenditures. However, a recent reform (October 2011) of fiscal federalism in Belgium transferred additional competencies to SNGs in 2014, in particular in the health and social protection (including old age) sectors. These additional competencies granted to regions and communities should induce an increase of 4.4% of GDP in SNG expenditures. In parallel, the fiscal autonomy of SNGs should be reinforced, via an increase in autonomous revenues and the suppression of transfers from the federal government (the equalisation system will be maintained). These new competencies granted to regions in healthcare and social protection could hence generate additional fiscal pressures on sub-national budgets in the long run. Moreover, real growth in healthcare spending has been limited at 3% for 2014 for all levels of government.
- **Denmark**: The increase in sub-national local healthcare spending, together with a political will to provide healthcare services equally across regions, were main drivers of the Danish 2007 territorial reform (see below). The reform was implemented in parallel to the Health Act of 2007, and partly aimed to solve problems faced by the healthcare sector, where new medical technologies increased specialisation and called for larger regions. These problems had already led to a hospital reform in the region of Copenhagen, when several small municipalities merged their hospitals to provide a better service.

Local healthcare expenditures as a share of local revenues in Denmark (1995-2012)

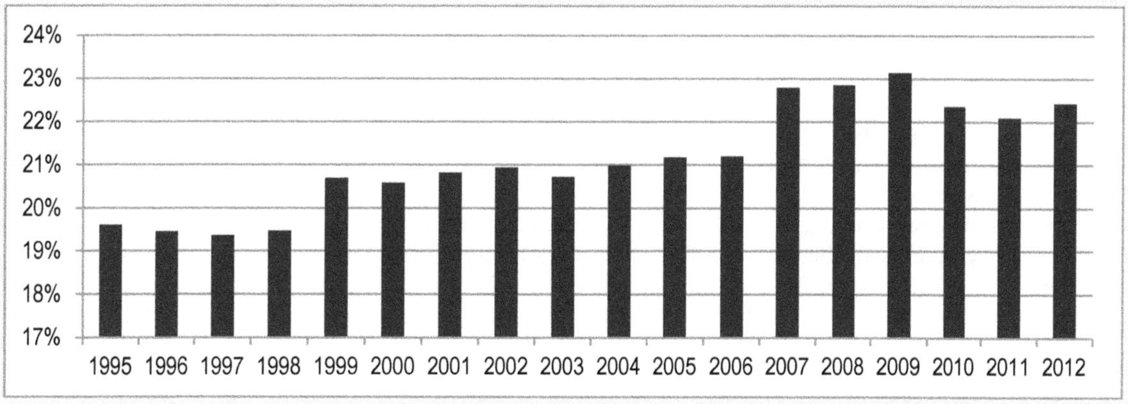

Source: OECD (2015), *OECD National Accounts Statistics* (database), http://dx.doi.org/10.1787/na-data-en.

Box 3.1. **Reforms to alleviate ageing and health cost pressures on SNG finances in selected countries *(continued)***

A main argument in favour of the reform was a potential decrease in bureaucratic costs and taxation levels; decentralised public services in healthcare needed to be designed in a way that could "meet future requirements by creating sustainable structures with a clear responsibility to provide high-quality welfare service to the population" while maintaining democratic accountability. Larger local authorities were seen as a solution to this problem. Although the Danish Government expected to generate synergies and economies of scale in the long run, increased costs for municipalities in the short run were envisaged, and should be borne by municipal authorities. Regions are responsible for all hospitalisation services, while municipalities gained responsibilities in medical prevention and health promotion.

This health reform was accompanied by a reform of the financing of local governments towards less autonomy in spending (the independent taxes levied at the regional level were replaced by a health tax, redistributed as an earmarked block grant from the central government to regions and municipalities. The distribution of grants (which finance more than 80% of healthcare activities in regions) is based on a formula based on the expected need for healthcare (including the distribution of age at the local level). The reform was considered as a structural adjustment towards a sustainable provision of healthcare services by sub-national governments. A major evaluation of its impact on service provision and local finances is currently developed by the central authorities.

- **Finland:** The demographic evolution of Finland is anticipated to drastically affect sub-national finances in the years to come. Finland should experience an earlier and faster increase of its old age dependency ratio, compared to other OECD or European countries; in particular, the share of people aged over 80 will increase from less than 15% in 2000 to around 25% in 2050, when it will be high in the OECD and larger than in other Nordic countries. The financing of pensions, health and long-term care should hence become a major issue. Health and social protection account for nearly 50% of total local spending in Finland, and pressures on sub-national finances are already starting to emerge. The new territorial reform of Finland aims to amalgamate municipalities on a voluntary basis in order to create larger entities which would allow reaching an adequate size for efficient service provision, and benefit from economies of scale. Moreover, the Government and the opposition agreed in March 2014 to centralise most social and healthcare expenditure in five regions (they currently are a responsibility of municipalities); the proposal will be examined by the Parliament in late 2014. Municipalities will still be responsible for financing services. If approved, this reform will come into force in early 2017.
- **Italy**: The Government decided to cut healthcare expenditure by EUR 2.5 billion in 2013 and EUR 5.4 billion in 2014, which will affect SNG spending since most of healthcare is decentralised.
- **Japan:** Local governments in Japan are responsible for a large share of public spending in the health and old age sectors. Municipalities manage the National Health Insurance (*kokumin kenko hoken*), one of the two main health insurance schemes in the nation. Since 2000, they are also responsible for the Long-Term Care insurance (*Kaigo hoken*), which covers public spending for old-age services. The ageing population in Japan is a main challenge for local governments. The old age dependency ratio should exceed 30% in 2030 and threatens redistributive expenditures in Japan. Moreover, the elderly tend to concentrate in regions with weaker economies and tax bases, which generate high pressure on local governments in these areas. The value of long-term care services should increase dramatically, from JPY 5.6 trillion in 2004 to an estimated JPY 19.8 trillion in 2025. In response to this financial pressure, the system has already been revised several times (change in unit prices in 2003; exclusion of some costs from insurance coverage in 2005; introduction of the "long-term care prevention allowance" in 2006).

Box 3.1. **Reforms to alleviate ageing and health cost pressures on SNG finances in selected countries *(continued)***

- **Netherlands**: The Social Support and Long-Term Care Act, planning for decentralisation of responsibilities to municipalities in 2015, is under discussion.
- **Poland**: The government is considering decentralising the National Health Fund (NFZ) in 2014-15.

Sources: Vammalle, C., R. Ahrend and C. Hulbert (2014), "A sub-national perspective on financing investment for growth II - Creating fiscal space for public investment: The role of institutions", *OECD Regional Development Working Papers*, No. 2014/06, OECD Publishing, http://dx.doi.org/10.1787/5jz3zvxc53bt-en; OECD (2013a), *OECD Economic Surveys: Austria 2013*, OECD Publishing, Paris, http://dx.doi.org/10.1787/eco_surveys-aut-2013-en; OECD (2014a), *OECD Economic Surveys: Poland 2014*, OECD Publishing, Paris, http://dx.doi.org/10.1787/eco_surveys-pol-2014-en; National Reform Programme 2014 (Finland, Netherlands).

5. Fiscal rules and SNG finances

An alternative or perhaps supplementary approach to the direct monitoring of SNG debt is a rule-based approach to limit SNG borrowing. Fiscal rules aim to restrain one or more dimensions of sub-national governments' fiscal aggregates. There are three main types of fiscal rules applied in this context: budget balance rules, expenditure ceilings and borrowing limits. These usually involve numerical targets based on ratios using either the level of GDP, of tax or total SNG revenues. This section provides a general overview of the use of fiscal rules for SNG finances in OECD countries, then analyses more precisely the three types of rules mentioned above. Finally, the last section focuses on enforcement mechanisms and consequences if rules are not respected.

Fiscal rules for SNGs have been in place in many OECD countries for a long time, and the recent global financial crisis has triggered several reforms tightening sub-national fiscal rules (Vammalle and Hulbert, 2013). However, the impact of fiscal rules on SNG debt is subject to debate (Box 3.2). The effectiveness of rules depends on the ability of SNG to circumvent them, as well as on the monitoring requirements for SNGs.

Balanced budget rules

As Table 3.2 illustrates, the most common types of fiscal rules in OECD countries are budget balance rules and borrowing constraints rule. Many SNGs are subject to a golden rule, and hence are able to borrow for investment purposes only. Direct expenditure limits are less frequent.

For some EU countries (e.g. Austria, Italy), budget balance rules have been modelled to a greater or lesser extent on the EU-wide economic governance rules which curtail excessive deficits and require a "close to balance" fiscal position. It is notable that the surveillance and co-ordination mechanisms across levels of government in some cases resemble those that apply under the EU Stability and Growth Pact (Box 3.3).

Box 3.2. **Impact of fiscal rules on SNG finances: A debated topic**

Legal borrowing constraints might have opposite consequences on SNG debt levels. On the one side, tight fiscal rules are set to restrain governments from over-indebtedness. The empirical evidence on this matter, however, is inconclusive. Some studies find evidence that balanced budget rules have negative impacts on budget balance deficits. Other literature concludes that fiscal rules do not play an important role in ensuring better fiscal performance. In this case, a plausible explanation is that sub-national fiscal rules might not be sufficient to ensure good performance when spending mandates of sub-national governments are underfunded. In any case, an analysis of the impact of fiscal rules on fiscal balances risks to suffer from a severe endogeneity problem because, as highlighted by the recent economic crisis, fiscal rules are often the response to deteriorated fiscal balances rather than the cause. Other experts get around the endogeneity problem by using the fact that in 2001 Italy relaxed fiscal rules for municipalities below 5 000 inhabitants as a quasi-experimental research design. Their estimates show that, on average, this relaxation of fiscal rules triggered a shift from balanced budgets to a 2% deficit.

On the other side, borrowing restrictions may be easily eluded in a situation where the dependence on transfers is high, responsibilities are not clearly allocated, or accountability levels are low. An illustrative example can be found in Italy. Italian local public finances suffered a deep crisis during the 1970s and 1980s due to a tax reform introduced in 1972-73 that drastically reduced the fiscal autonomy of municipalities and made them extremely dependent on central government grants. In this context, some argue, expenditures kept rising and the inability of local governments to raise revenues and cover expenses led them to borrow large amounts of funds from commercial banks. The consequence was that municipalities approached bankruptcy and had to be bailed out by the central governments through an increase in transfers in 1978 (a measure introduced jointly with stricter debt limits). The unintended outcome was that over-indebted municipalities were *de facto* compensated for their bad financial performance through larger transfers. So, high reliance on transfers might generate a common pool problem as SNGs do not fully bear the cost of overspending and this can translate into high levels of debt.

Source: Ahrend, R., M. Curto-Grau and C. Vammalle (2013), "Passing the buck? Central and sub-national governments in times of fiscal stress", *OECD Regional Development Working Papers*, No. 2013/05, OECD Publishing, http://dx.doi.org/10.1787/5k49dfl kr95l-en.

Table 3.2. **Types of SNG fiscal rules in OECD countries**

Sub-national government	Budget balance rule	Borrowing constraint	Expenditure limit
Australia local		x	
Australia state	x	x	
Austria local	x	x	x
Austria state	x	x	x
Belgium state	x		
Belgium local	x	x	
Canada state	x	x	
Canada local	x	x	
Chile		x	
Czech Republic	x		
Denmark	x	x	x
Estonia	x	x	
Finland	x		
Germany state	x	x	
Germany local	x	x	
Ireland	x	x	
Italy state		x	x
Italy local	x	X	
Korea	x	X	x
Mexico state		X	
Mexico local		X	
New Zealand	x	X	x
Norway	x	X	
Poland	x	X	
Slovak Republic	x	X	
Slovenia	x	X	
Spain state	x	X	x
Spain local	x	X	x
Sweden	x		
Switzerland state	x		
Switzerland local	x		
Turkey		X	x
Total	26	26	9

Sources: Fredriksen, K. (2013), *Fiscal Rules for Sub-central Governments – 2011 Update of the OECD Indicator*, March, http://www.oecd.org/eco/public-finance/Fiscalrulesforsub-centralgovernments2011updateoftheOECDindicator.pdf; OECD (2011a), *OECD Network on Fiscal Relations across Levels of Government Survey on Sub-national Fiscal Rules and Macroeconomic Management*, OECD, September 2011, updated in March 2015.

Box 3.3. **Recent reforms of SNG balanced budget rules**

- **Austria**: In spring 2012, Austria adopted new Internal Stability Pact, which came into force in December 2012. This pact sets new fiscal rules that apply to all levels of government. Concerning deficits, all levels of government must reach a balanced budget in 2016. From 2017 onwards a structural balance rule will be implemented, relating deficits to the output gap. The general government cycle will be used in order to calculate the SNG structural budget requirements (whose target will represent two-ninths of the total cyclical effect, the other seven-ninths being allocated to the CG). Asymmetric SNG shocks are not considered a problem since SNG revenues have little cyclicality: tax-sharing apportionment formulas between central authorities and the *Länder* rely mostly on population (hence are relatively non-cyclical), and local authorities are mainly financed through less cyclical taxes based on real estate. The new rules also include a debt criterion. All levels of government must reduce their level of debt by one-twentieth per year.
- **Belgium**: The Co-operation Agreement reached in December 2013 between the federal government, communities and regions for implementing the Treaty on Stability, Co-ordination and Governance requires the general government budget to be balanced; individual targets in nominal and structural terms for central and local authorities will be defined.
- **Czech Republic**: A proposal under consideration would require local and central governments to balance their budgets if total public debt exceeds 48% of GDP.
- **Denmark**: The Budget Law approved in 2012 introduces a balanced budget rule: structural deficits (on a yearly basis) should not exceed 0.5% of GDP.
- **Estonia**: The State Budget Act came into force in March 2014, and introduces a budget balance rule for the general government, and breakdown by level of government.
- **Germany:** In 2009, Germany introduced a "debt brake" in its Constitution (*Grundgesetz*) to ensure that sub-national budgets are financed without any structural deficits from 2020 onwards, with only a small structural deficit allowed for the federal budget (0.35% of GDP). In addition, a new instrument, the Stability Council, was instituted to survey all public budgets on an annual basis using common benchmarks, to monitor public borrowing and to co-ordinate medium-term financial planning in a multi-level government context.
- **Iceland**: The Parliament passed a new act on local governments in September 2011, which includes two main fiscal rules on local government finances. The first is a balancing rule for current operations of local governments, obliging them to balance revenues and expenditures over a three-year period. The second is a debt rule that limits the total debt and liabilities of local governments to 150% of total revenue. Local governments with debt and liabilities above 150% are required to bring the debt ratio under this benchmark in ten years. Local governments with total debt exceeding 250% of revenue are prohibited from raising new debt except for refinancing.
- **Italy**: The Domestic Stability Pact introduced a budget balance rule for municipalities and provinces. The Stability Law for 2014-16 ease these budget constraints for local governments to exclude capital account payments up to EUR 1 billion and another EUR 500 million to accelerate payment of past-due debts.
- **Japan**: The Fiscal Management Strategy introduced in 2010 includes numerical targets for the short, medium and long term to reduce the primary budget deficit of the central and local authorities.
- **Mexico**: The Federal Budgetary law (*Ley Federal de Presupuesto y Responsabilidad Hacendaria*) approved in late 2013, introduces a structural balance rule; a constitutional reform to limit state and municipal debt is still under consideration.

Box 3.3. **Recent reforms of SNG balanced budget rules *(continued)***

- **Netherlands**: An agreement anticipating the entry into force of the Law on the Sustainability of Public Finances was reached in January 2013 with local authorities; a multi-annual budget balance path will be introduced for local governments. In 2013, a deficit limit of 0.5% of GDP was applied to local authorities as a whole.
- **Poland**: The Public Finance Act (2011) already stipulated to balance local current budgets. In 2014 new rules came into force for local authorities: the debt servicing-to-revenues ratio must remain smaller than the average ratio of current revenues (plus asset sales and operating expenditure) to total revenue over the last three years.
- **Slovenia**: The Parliament approved in 2013 a balanced budget amendment to the constitution that will come into force in 2015.
- **Spain**: An amendment to the constitution was adopted in 2011 to underpin the fiscal consolidation targets for all Spanish administrations, following the EU framework. The main feature of the reform was that neither the central government nor the autonomous communities were allowed to have deficits which exceeded the maximum set by the European Union, and local governments were required to balance their budgets. The maximum structural deficit should be set according to law as a percentage of GDP. This limit will only be in force from 2020 onward. The Organic Law on Budgetary Stability and Financial Sustainability (2012) introduces a structural balanced budget rule for all levels of governments from 2020 onwards. Debt reduction pathways will be revised in 2015 and 2018 to ensure that this objective is met.

Sources: Vammalle, C., R. Ahrend and C. Hulbert (2014), "A sub-national perspective on financing investment for growth II - Creating fiscal space for public investment: The role of institutions", OECD Regional Development Working Papers, No. 2014/06, OECD Publishing, http://dx.doi.org/10.1787/5jz3zvxc53bt-en; OECD (2014b), *OECD Economic Surveys: Czech Republic 2014*, OECD Publishing, Paris, http://dx.doi.org/10.1787/eco_surveys-cze-2014-en; OECD (2014c), *OECD Economic Surveys: Denmark 2013*, OECD Publishing, Paris, http://dx.doi.org/10.1787/eco_surveys-dnk-2013-en; OECD (2013b), *OECD Economic Surveys: Japan 2013*, OECD Publishing, Paris, http://dx.doi.org/10.1787/eco_surveys-jpn-2013-en; Stability Programme 2014 (Belgium, Estonia, Italy, Netherlands); Convergence Programme Poland (2014); National Reform Programme Slovenia (2014).

Expenditure and expenditure-growth ceilings

Only a relatively small number of OECD countries rely on expenditure limits for sub-national governments. Expenditure ceilings aim to restrain SNGs' spending growth over the medium-to-long run, thereby indirectly limiting SNG deficits. Ceilings can be set annually (Denmark, Italy: state and local) or for a multi-year period (Austria: state and local, through calculations based on the EU mechanism). They may be set proportionally to income (Canadian states, Turkey) or linked to an objective needs criteria, such as population growth (Slovenia, Spanish local governments).

In most countries, expenditure ceilings are set for current (operating) expenditures only (Denmark, Estonia, Italian local governments and Korea). For instance, in Estonia, SNG's operating expenditures may not exceed operating revenues. Overall expenditures are limited in Italian regions only; the Internal Stability Pact (ISP) targets both current and capital expenditures (over 2011-13, regional expenditures must not exceed the expenditure average over 2007-09). In Spain, growth in local public spending must not exceed GDP growth (in nominal terms) for nine years; this limit was imposed by the central government, and additional expenditure ceiling were negotiated with Autonomous Communities.

Expenditure ceilings may restrain spending on specific budgetary lines only (Denmark, Italian local governments and provinces, Turkey). This is typically for personnel expenditure (local governments in Italy, Turkey).

Box 3.4 outlines developments in some OECD countries in the context of fiscal consolidation over recent years.

Box 3.4. **New expenditure ceilings for SNGs in selected OECD countries**

- **Austria**: The new Internal Stability Pact signed in May 2012 introduces a limit on expenditure growth of SNGs: aggregate expenditure growth of all levels of government should not be above the average potential GDP growth.
- **Denmark**: a new system of expenditure control was agreed upon in March 2012. From 2014 four-year binding expenditure ceilings for all levels of governments came into force. They cover most public spending with the exception of investments and unemployment outlays. Municipalities and regions have agreed to limit their expenditures; a breach in the ceiling for a given year will have to be compensated in the following year. Moreover, federal transfers may be reduced in case of non-compliance.
- **Finland**: The Basic Public Services Programme approved in mid-2012 introduces a target for municipal expenditure (the average municipal spending growth must be lower than 0.4% by 2020, assuming that local responsibilities remain the same). Moreover, from 2015 local responsibilities will have to match available funding; new responsibilities will have to be financed either through increased revenues or cuts in other expenditure.
- **Slovak Republic**: Since 2014 individual municipal expenditures for one given year cannot be superior to expenditures for the previous year.
- **Slovenia**: The Fiscal Balance Act introduced several measures to reduce the general governments' debt and deficit, which came into force in mid-2012. In particular limits were set in order to limit labour-related costs for public employees (including at the local level).
- **Spain**: The Organic Law on Budgetary Stability and Financial Sustainability (2012) introduces new expenditure ceilings for SNGs. Variations in expenditures should not exceed the medium-term GDP growth (calculated over three years according to EU methodology)

Sources: Vammalle, C., R. Ahrend and C. Hulbert (2014), "A sub-national perspective on financing investment for growth II - Creating fiscal space for public investment: The role of institutions", OECD Regional Development Working Papers, No. 2014/06, OECD Publishing, http://dx.doi.org/10.1787/5jz3zvxc53bt-en; *OECD Economic Surveys: Austria 2013*, OECD Publishing, Paris, http://dx.doi.org/10.1787/eco_surveys-aut-2013-en; National Reform Programme 2014 (Finland); OECD (2014c), *OECD Economic Surveys: Denmark 2013*, OECD Publishing, Paris, http://dx.doi.org/10.1787/eco_surveys-dnk-2013-en; National Reform Programme Slovenia (2014).

SNG debt and debt-service restrictions

It is also open to countries to introduce numerical limits on the debt level, new borrowing, or debt service costs of SNGs. Indeed, limits of this kind are widely used for SNGs across OECD countries. The most common restrictions are limits on the total level of debt and on the emission of new debt (Table 3.3).

Table 3.3. **Debt and debt service restrictions in OECD countries**

	Limits on debt level	Limits on the issue of new debt (caps)	Limits on debt service	No limits	Other
Australia local				X	
Australia state				X	
Austria local	X				
Austria state	X				
Belgium local	X				
Belgium state					
Canada local	X		X		
Canada state					
Chile					
Czech Republic			X		
Denmark				X	
Estonia	X				
Finland				X	
Germany local		X			
Germany state					
Ireland		X			
Italy local			X		
Italy state			X		
Korea	X	X	X		
Mexico local					
Mexico state					X
New Zealand					X
Poland	X	X	X		
Slovak Republic	X		X		
Slovenia	X				
Spain local	X	X			
Spain state	X	X			
Sweden				X	
Switzerland local				X	
Switzerland state				X	
Turkey	X	X			
Total answers	12	9	7	7	2

Source: OECD (2011a), *OECD Network on Fiscal Relations across Levels of Government Survey on Sub-national Fiscal Rules and Macroeconomic Management*, OECD, September 2011, updated in March 2015.

In most cases, limits are expressed as a share of SNG total or current revenues. They are sometimes set as a share of GDP, and in some rare cases, as a ceiling on total debt.

There is an important variation on the ceilings used across countries: ceilings on the overall level of debt vary from 60% to 150% of total revenues, and those on debt service range from 12% to 25% of current revenues (Box 3.5 provides a range of country examples).

Box 3.5. **Debt and debt service restrictions on SNGs in selected OECD countries**

Restrictions on the level of debt

- **Austria:** A debt brake was introduced for all levels of government in 2012.
- **Czech Republic**: The new Constitutional Act (approved on October 2012) introduces new principles for budgetary discipline and accountability. In particular, at the local government level SNG gross debt shall not exceed 60% of a four-year average of revenues.
- **Estonia**: Total SNG debt should not exceed 60% of total SNG revenues from 2012 onwards.
- **Greece**: Total debt should not exceed regular revenues.
- **Iceland**: The Local Government Act introduces a debt rule that limits the total debt and liabilities of local governments to 150% of total revenue. Local governments with debt and liabilities above 150% are required to bring the debt ratio under this benchmark within ten years. Local governments with total debt exceeding 250% of revenue are prohibited from raising new debt (except for refinancing).
- **Poland**: SNG debt should not exceed 60% of GDP.
- **Portugal**: Two recent laws introduced new fiscal rules for SNGs. At the regional level, the law on the Finances of the Autonomous Regions stipulates that the autonomous regions' liabilities should not exceed one-and-a-half times their three-year average net current revenue. At the municipal level, the law on Local Finances introduces similar requirements for each municipality individually (municipalities' liabilities should not exceed one-and-a-half times their three-year average net current revenue).
- **Slovak Republic**: Total SNG debt should exceed 60% of total SNG current revenues.
- **Spain:** The Organic Law on Budgetary Stability and Financial Sustainability introduces overall debt ceilings for all levels of government. Debt should not exceed 13% and 3% of GDP for autonomous communities and local governments, respectively. Moreover, SNGs should no longer be able to borrow in order to finance current expenditures after 2020.
- **Turkey**: SNG debt should not exceed 100% of SNG annual revenues. This ratio is set at 150% for metropolitan municipalities and provinces.

Restrictions on debt service

- **Czech Republic**: SNGs a debt service ratio should not exceed 30% of SNG revenues.
- **Greece**: Debt repayments should not exceed 20% of regular revenues.

Box 3.5. **Debt and debt service restrictions on SNGs in selected OECD countries *(continued)***

- **Italian local governments**: Interest payments should not exceed 12% of current revenues.
- **Italian regions**: Interest payments should not exceed 25% of revenues from taxes, transfers and property sales.
- **Poland**: The sum of loan instalments and interest payments must not exceed 15% of total debt (until December 2013). From 2014 onwards, local governments' debt service should not exceed a three-year average sum of operating surpluses and privatisation receipts.
- **Slovak Republic**: Loan instalments and interest should not exceed 25% of current revenues for the previous year.

Restrictions on debt maturity

- **Mexico**: A bill passed the Senate in April 2013 that proposes a constitutional change to impose stricter controls on SNG borrowing (it still has to pass the lower house to be ratified). If validated, debt would not be used to finance current expenditures, and should be repaid by the end of the contracting administration.

Source: OECD (2011a), *OECD Network on Fiscal Relations across Levels of Government Survey on Sub-national Fiscal Rules and Macroeconomic Management*, OECD, September 2011, updated in March 2015.

Such debt and debt service restrictions are not used by regions/states in very decentralised countries (federal and quasi-federal). However, in federal countries, states/regions often set restrictions for their local governments, thus leading to different situations across the country (e.g. Canada). These limits may also differ among SNGs when they are self-imposed (as in New Zealand).

Enforcement of SNG fiscal rules

Rules and controls are only effective if they are actually enforced, and SNGs that break the rules are in general subject to a range of consequences. In the context of the recent fiscal consolidation plans, several countries have tightened their sanction mechanisms in case SNGs break their fiscal targets (e.g. Spain, Italy). Sanctions and procedures for SNGs breaking fiscal rules must not be confused with the procedures in place for SNGs facing financial difficulties, even if they are sometimes similar.

In addition to establishing new or strengthening existing fiscal rules, some countries have also tightened their enforcement. This has been achieved either by increasing the transparency and reporting requirements, imposing financial sanctions or restructuring plans on SNGs breaking the rules. Some countries have even established new sanctions for political officials responsible for breaking the rules (Box 3.6 provides a range of country examples).

Box 3.6. **Enforcement of fiscal rules for SNGs**

- **Austria**: Austria's new fiscal rules foresee that if a government misses its target, an internal excessive deficit procedure (EDP) will be launched. It will benefit from a tolerance for one year; however, if the target is missed for two consecutive years, sanctions apply. Within the framework of this internal excessive deficit procedure, the government which missed the target is given two months to design appropriate action to restore its public finances. Sanctions are decided by vote in a co-ordination committee between levels of government, where the concerned government level is not allowed to vote (note that this holds even for the central government). Financial sanctions will represent 15% of the deviation, to be deducted from shared taxes.

- **Czech Republic**: In addition to introducing new debt and deficit ceilings, the 2012 Constitutional Act strengthened enforcement mechanisms. If the debt target is not respected, central authorities may cut revenues to a municipality or region by 5% of the difference between its amount of debt and the 60% target. These suspended revenues can only be released to repay SNG debt obligations made before the year in which the suspension occurred.

- **Germany**: The 2010 constitutional amendment included the establishment of a Stability Council to monitor the budgetary developments at the federal and *Länder* levels, and introduced a federation-wide early warning system to prevent budgetary distress. The Stability Council replaces the former Financial Planning Council, and is composed of the federal ministers of finance and economic affairs, as well as the *Länder* ministers of finance. In 2013 the Stability Council was also charged with monitoring compliance with the upper limit on the general government structural deficit under the Budgetary Principles Act twice a year. An independent advisory board was set up to support the Stability Council in monitoring compliance with the upper limit on the general government structural deficit.

- **Italy**: Enforcement of the Internal Stability Pact was strengthened in 2011 by the introduction of a wide range of possible sanctions. For example, regions breaking the fiscal rules may not be allowed in the following year: a) to commit current expenditure (net of health) beyond the minimum commitment of the last three years; b) to hire new personnel; c) to hire external managers; or d) to issue bonds and take out loans, not even for investment purposes. Regions may even experience a reduction or suspension of financial transfers from the CG. Reporting rules have also been tightened, in particular for periods before elections. The audited financial statements of the regions must be published on their websites. If the results are not consistent with the Italian Internal Stability Pact, heavy sanctions may be imposed on the political officers, such as automatic disqualification from office and a ten-year interdiction from office.

- **Slovak Republic**: The Constitutional Act No. 493/2011 on Fiscal Responsibility stipulates that from 2015 onwards, sub-national governments exceeding the debt target will pay a fine of 5% of the difference between the debt level and the target.

- **Spain**: Where the autonomous communities missed their deficit target by a wide margin in 2011, the Organic Law on Budgetary Stability and Financial Sustainability introduces sanctions for governments deviating from fiscal rules: they should submit a restructuring plan and, in the case of repeated deviations, a temporary (partial or total) re-centralisation of budgetary powers could be imposed.

- **Turkey**: The municipal law No. 5393 states that if local authorities do not comply with fiscal rules, the related provisions of the Turkish Panel Code regarding malpractice apply. Hence central authorities may impose sanctions to responsible personnel (local representatives may undergo a trial on Turkish Criminal Code).

Source: OECD (2011b), *OECD Network on Fiscal Relations across Levels of Government Survey on the Impact of National Consolidation Strategies on SNGs and the Strategy of SNGs*, OECD, September-October 2011, updated in January 2012; Stability Programme for the Slovak Republic 2014-17 (2014).

Procedures in cases where SNGs fail to meet fiscal rules range from actions from CGs, or actions taken by SNGs themselves. In many OECD countries, CGs may take action without making any changes to legislation:

- The most common procedure consists of a CG imposing non-financial sanctions on SNGs breaking the rules (either automatic or discretionary), obliging SNGs to offset the breach in future budget, or to take measures so that the rule is respected in the future.
- Financial sanctions may also be applied to SNGs. These can take the form of a fixed fine, or decreases in transfers or shared taxes from a CG. In the Slovak Republic, the Ministry of Finance may impose a fine up to EUR 16 597 to SNGs breaking fiscal rules. The new Austrian fiscal rules introduce possible deduction in shared taxes, proportional to the deviation.
- Administrative sanctions reducing the freedom of SNGs are used in a few OECD countries. Such sanctions often take the form of greater control of central authorities over sub-national finances, through the appointment of a public officer in charge of monitoring to some degree SNG revenues, spending and borrowing.
- Finally, in some countries, sanctions on SNG officials are also possible. These go from their removal (in Poland, local governments' councils or executive bodies may be dissolved) to possible penal sanctions (Italy, Turkey).

Table 3.4 provides an overview of country practices in this regard.

6. Key outstanding challenges for monitoring SNG finances

CGs face a number of challenges when monitoring SNG debts, which can be usefully and concisely summarised under the sections set out below.

Lack of information about SNG budgeting practices

In many countries (particularly in federal and quasi-federal countries), SNGs are free to set their own budgeting laws and practices, and the CG may have little information about these. Canada has recently used the "OECD Budgeting Practices and Procedures Survey" (OECD, n.d.) to gather information about provincial budgeting practices, which were until then obscure for the CG. The results of the survey show a large variety of practices across provinces, with some using more modern budgeting instruments than the CG itself (Rigaud and Arsenault, 2013).

Lack of appropriate and timely information about SNG financial and debt situation

According to OECD Budgeting Principle No. 5, budget documents and data should be open, transparent and accessible. But financial information reported by SNGs often comes with a long time lag, and is often incomplete, thus preventing CG from taking timely corrective measures. Timely information is important for SNGs and CGs to react rapidly to deteriorating fiscal situations of sub-national entities, but also to identify early deviations from fiscal rules, and hence take early correction measures. A recent experience of the OECD Secretariat illustrates this lack of information of CGs on SNG finances: a survey was recently sent out to countries to build a database of financial variables (revenues, expenditures, debt) by region, and only eight countries were in a position to provide such information.

Table 3.4. **Enforcement actions of SNG fiscal rules taken by higher levels of government (without changes in legislation)**

	Oblige SNGs to take measures (raising taxes, reducing spending, etc.)	Oblige SNGs to offset the breach in future budget	Remove, replace of punish officials	Impose financial sanction on an automatic basis	Impose financial sanction on a discretionary basis	Impose administrative sanctions that limit the freedom of SNGs	Make recommendations on corrective measures
Australia local			X			x	x
Australia state							
Austria local							
Austria state							
Belgium local	x (borrowing constraints only)	x (balance budget rule only)					
Belgium state					x (balance budget rule only)		
Canada local			x	x		x	x
Canada state							
Chile							
Czech Republic					x		
Denmark				x (expenditure ceilings only)	x		
Estonia	x			x			x
Finland							x
Germany local		x (balanced budget rule only)			x (balanced budget rule only)	x	x (balanced budget rule only)
Germany state							
Ireland			x				
Italy local	x (balanced budget rule only)	x (balanced budget rule only)	x (expenditure ceilings only)	x		x (balanced budget rule only)	x
Italy state	x	x	x	x		x	x
Korea	x					x	
Mexico local							
Mexico state							
New Zealand	x (balanced budget rule only)						x
Poland			x				
Slovak Republic				x?	x		
Slovenia							x
Spain local	x						x (except expenditure ceilings)
Spain state	x (balanced budget rule only)	x (borrowing constraints only)					x (balanced budget rule only)
Sweden		x					
Switzerland local	x	x		x	x	x	x
Switzerland state							
Turkey		x	x (borrowing constraints only)			x (expenditure ceilings only)	

Source: OECD (2011a), *OECD Network on Fiscal Relations across Levels of Government Survey on Sub-national Fiscal Rules and Macroeconomic Management*, OECD, September 2011, updated in March 2015.

Ensuring reliability of financial information provided by SNGs

Financial audit is necessary to assess the quality of financial reporting and the reliability of financial information. Audits and controls may be centralised at the CG level, or decentralised (with sub-national governments directly in charge of controls). In such a decentralised framework however, the central government still has a major role to play: it should "set the standards and monitor the effectiveness of the internal control systems at the local level" (Baltaci and Yilmaz, 2006). A decentralised control approach may be more adequate in countries where SNGs enjoy a strong degree of financial autonomy, as sub-national governments are directly responsible for preparing and executing budgets. Most OECD countries have introduced some form of auditing of sub-national finances (Box 3.7 provides some country examples).

Box 3.7. **Auditing local finances in Sweden and France**

In Swedish municipalities and county councils, an assembly is granted authority for decision making, while elected representatives (regrouped in committees) are responsible for administration and execution. Following the Local Government Auditing Inquiry (1998), the assembly elects auditors to monitor the financing and executing of policies. All the audits must be carried out independently, in accordance with standards published by the Swedish Association of Local Authorities and the Swedish Federation of County Councils.

In France, the Decentralisation Law of 1982 created the regional chambers of audit. These public bodies are responsible for an *ex post* auditing of SNG accounts, and must also review the management of local governments and related entities. A recent report from the *Cour des Comptes* points out excessive spending and poor management in many French SNGs, with particularly high personal expenses, growing rapidly. Moreover, the court criticises the quality of financial data provided at the sub-national level.

Sources : Baltaci, M. and S. Yilmaz (2006), *Keeping an Eye on Subcentral Governments: Internal Control and Audit at Local Level*, The International Bank for Reconstruction and Development/The World Bank, http://siteresources.worldbank.org/ WBI/Resources/InternalControlandAuditatLocalLevel-FINAL.pdf; *Cour des Comptes* (2013), *Les Finances Publiques Locales*, https://www.ccomptes.fr/Publications/Publications/Les-finances-publiques-locales.

Lack of comparability of SNG data

Financial information provided by SNGs is often not homogeneous across SNGs, and thus, it may be difficult for CGs to compare SNGs' situations, and to assess the sustainability of their debts.

Homogeneity of sub-national accounting rules facilitates the processing of budgetary and financial information. Local governments' accounting standards tend to be more homogeneous than those of regions/states. In federal and quasi-federal countries in particular, a large share of federated entities do not abide by homogeneous accounting rules for budgets. Local governments use the same accounting standards as CGs in 11 countries, while this share is only the case in 3 states/regions.

Ensuring that SNG budgets present a true, full and fair picture of their public finances

OECD Budget Principle No. 7 requires that budgets present a true, full and fair picture of the public finances. In practice, the experience of many countries has been that – partly in response to the rigours of fiscal rules – some SNGs have resorted to "fiscal gimmicks", the use of off-balance expenditure, and other practices that reduce fiscal transparency. Off-budget funds and local public enterprises or agencies are frequently used by SNGs, and should be closely monitored. Box 3.8 provides some relevant country examples.

Box 3.8. **Example of regulation of off-budget funds in SNGs in OECD countries**

Municipal off-budget funds in Portugal

In Portugal, most local governments maintain off-budget funds through municipalised services (*serviços municipalizados*, entities with special statute, created with the aim of increasing flexibility in the provision of public services) and local enterprises. In 2010, the amount of debt of municipalised services and local public enterprises was estimated around EUR 147 million and 1 787 million respectively.

The Local Finance Law (2013) sets new fiscal rules for local governments in Portugal, through the introduction of individual borrowing limits for sub-national entities. The definition of debt considered for the rules have been extended, and includes local governments themselves, municipalised and inter-municipalised services, inter-municipal entities, municipal associations, local enterprises, enterprises owned partly by municipalities, etc. Hence this reform should increase transparency over sub-national finances and limit the use of off-budget funds by local governments.

Reform of the Australian Loan Council

The formal legislation introducing the Australian Loan Council, passed in 1927, was amended in 1936 in order to cover a broader spectrum of sub-national debts.

The 1927 Financial Agreement granted the Commonwealth significant powers over states' debt in terms of management, regulation, etc. However, following this initial legislation, many attempts were made by state governments to circumvent the Loan Council's borrowing limits through the use of off-budget entities. To address this issue, the 1936 reform extended the Council's authority to debt issued by local and semi-government bodies.

Sources: Portuguese Public Finance Council (2012), "Analysis of debt limits in the regional and local finance bills", *Occasional Paper* No. 1/2013; von Hagen et al. (2000), "Subcentral government bailouts in OECD countries: Four case studies", *Inter-American Development Bank Research Working Paper* R-399.

References

Ahrend, R., M. Curto-Grau and C. Vammalle (2013), "Passing the buck? Central and sub-national governments in times of fiscal stress", *OECD Regional Development Working Papers*, No. 2013/05, OECD Publishing, http://dx.doi.org/10.1787/5k49dfl kr95l-en.

Baltaci, M. and S. Yilmaz (2006), *Keeping an Eye on Subcentral Governments: Internal Control and Audit at Local Level*, The International Bank for Reconstruction and Development/The World Bank, http://siteresources.worldbank.org/WBI/Resources/InternalControlandAuditatLocalLevel-FINAL.pdf.

Blöchliger, H. et al.(2010), "Sub-central Governments and the Economic Crisis: Impact and Policy Responses", OECD Economics Department Working Papers, No. 752, OECD Publishing, http://dx.doi.org/10.1787/5kml6xq5bgwc-e*Cour des Comptes* (2013), *Les Finances Publiques Locales*, https://www.ccomptes.fr/Publications/Publications/Les-finances-publiques-locales.

European Commission (2015), *Government Finance Statistics* (database), Eurostat, http://ec.europa.eu/Eurostat/web/government-finance-statistics/data/database.

Fredriksen, K. (2013), *Fiscal Rules for Sub-central Governments – 2011 Update of the OECD Indicator*, March, www.oecd.org/eco/public-finance/Fiscalrulesforsub-centralgovernments2011updateoftheOECDindicator.pdf

OECD (2015), *OECD National Accounts Statistics* (database), http://dx.doi.org/10.1787/na-data-en.

OECD (2014a), *OECD Economic Surveys: Poland 2014*, OECD Publishing, Paris, http://dx.doi.org/10.1787/eco_surveys-pol-2014-en.

OECD (2014b), *OECD Economic Surveys: Czech Republic 2014*, OECD Publishing, Paris, http://dx.doi.org/10.1787/eco_surveys-cze-2014-en.

OECD (2014c), *OECD Economic Surveys: Denmark 2013*, OECD Publishing, Paris, http://dx.doi.org/10.1787/eco_surveys-dnk-2013-en.

OECD (2013a), *OECD Economic Surveys: Austria 2013*, OECD Publishing, Paris, http://dx.doi.org/10.1787/eco_surveys-aut-2013-en.

OECD (2013b), *OECD Economic Surveys: Japan 2013*, OECD Publishing, Paris, http://dx.doi.org/10.1787/eco_surveys-jpn-2013-en.

OECD (2011a), *OECD Network on Fiscal Relations across Levels of Government Survey on Sub-national Fiscal Rules and Macroeconomic Management*, OECD, September 2011, updated in March 2013.

OECD (2011b), *OECD Network on Fiscal Relations across Levels of Government Survey on the Impact of National Consolidation Strategies on SNGs and the Strategy of SNGs*, OECD, September-October 2011, updated in January 2012.

OECD (n.d.), *OECD Budgeting Practices and Procedures Survey*, www.oecd.org/gov/budgeting/39466141.pdf.

Portuguese Public Finance Council (2012), "Analysis of debt limits in the regional and local finance bills", *Occasional Paper* No. 1/2013.

Rigaud, B. and P.-É. Arsenault (2013), "Budget governance in Canada: Comparing practices within a federation", *OECD Journal on Budgeting*, Vol. 13/1, http://dx.doi.org/10.1787/budget-13-5k409g59x7r8.

Vammalle, C., R. Ahrend and C. Hulbert (2014), "A sub-national perspective on financing investment for growth II - Creating fiscal space for public investment: The role of institutions", *OECD Regional Development Working Papers*, No. 2014/06, OECD Publishing, http://dx.doi.org/10.1787/5jz3zvxc53bt-en.

Vammalle, C. and C. Hulbert (2013), "Sub-national finances and fiscal consolidation: Walking on thin ice", *OECD Regional Development Working Papers*, No. 2013/02, OECD Publishing, Paris, http://dx.doi.org/10.1787/5k49m8cqkcf3-en.

von Hagen et al. (2000), "Subcentral government bailouts in OECD countries: Four case studies", Inter-*American Development Bank Research Working Paper* R-399.

Annex A

Budgetary impacts on human resource management in the public sector

In parallel with the Survey of the State of Public Finances 2015, the OECD has undertaken an analysis of Central Public Administration employment has responded to the impacts of the budgetary crisis and how Civil Service HR trends and practices have been affected by fiscal consolidation over the period 2008-13.[1] Compensation of employees accounted for 23.6% of public expenditures on average across OECD countries in 2013, and it is natural that governments will seek to find economies and efficiencies from this significant block of expenditure as part of a broader strategy of fiscal correction.

Across many countries, there has indeed been a renewed efficiency focus within the public sector, coupled in many cases with a broader HR reform agenda, and balanced with the need to have productive, satisfied, innovative and high-performing employees. The OECD analysis indicates that the various HRM responses to fiscal consolidation can be grouped under seven headings or "bundles" (see Figure A.1).

Figure A.1. **Average number of HR reforms by bundle per country, 2008-13**

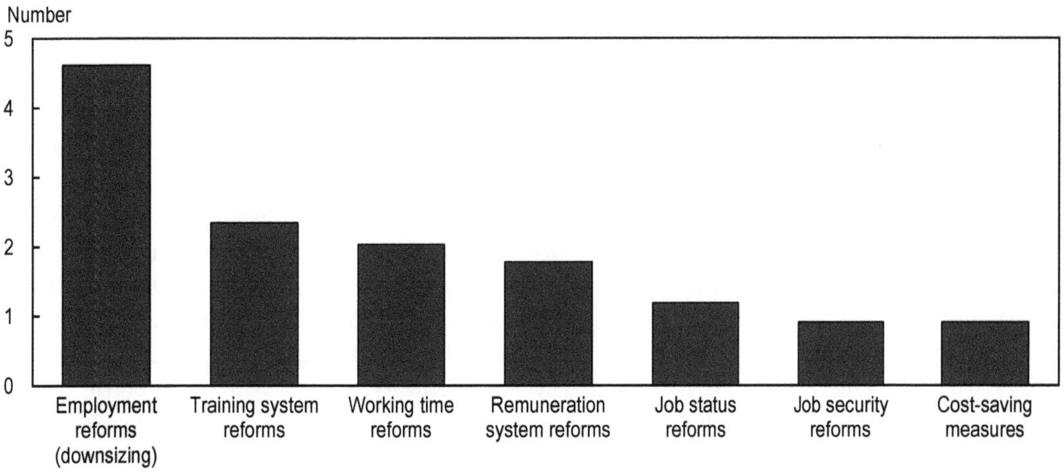

Source: OECD (2014), *Survey on Managing Budgeting Constraints: Implications for HRM and Employment in Central Public Administration*, OECD.

StatLink http://dx.doi.org/10.1787/888933288656

Figure A.2 illustrates that the intensity of HRM reform effort correlates closely with the degree of "fiscal pressure" to which countries have been subject. Of the total range of

50 possible reforms surveyed, the highest numbers of reforms were initiated in Portugal (34), Greece (28), the United Kingdom (28) and Ireland (27), whereas countries with relatively lower fiscal stress undertook fewer reforms: the lowest scoring countries being Norway (3), Germany (3) and Chile (6). The fact that countries like Finland (25) and Switzerland (19) have implemented a relatively high number of reforms, despite being under comparatively less fiscal stress, points to the fact that budgetary pressure is not the sole trigger for reforms. It is notable that the Czech Republic (14), United States (14) and France (13) have not been as proactive in introducing HRM reforms despite difficult budgetary positions, although the "starting position" for these countries may differ.

Figure A.2. **Overview of human resource management reforms, 2008-13**

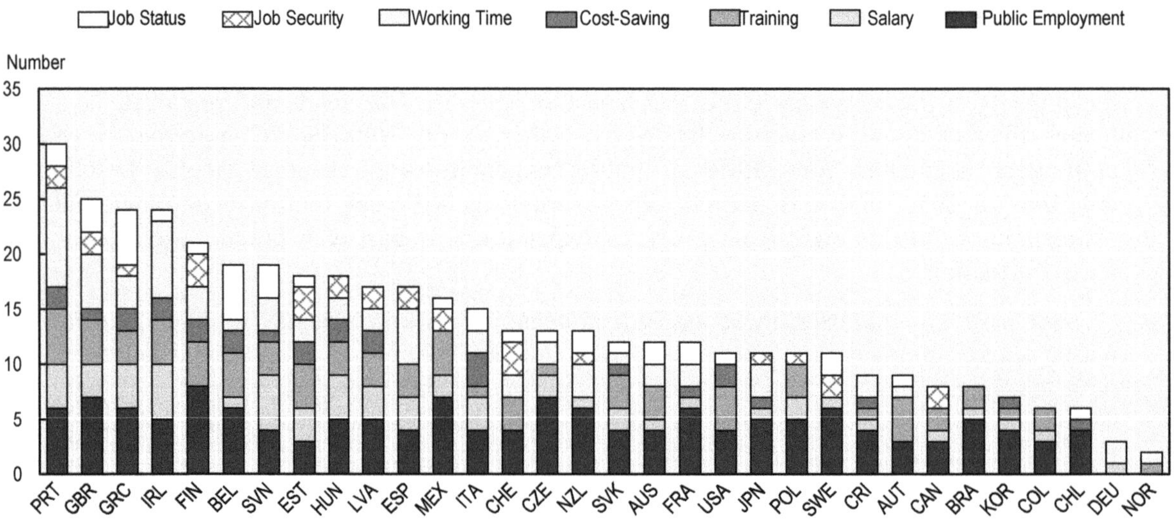

Source: OECD (2014), *Survey on Managing Budgeting Constraints: Implications for HRM and Employment in Central Public Administration*, OECD.

StatLink http://dx.doi.org/10.1787/888933288667

For most countries, the restructuring and downsizing of central public administrations has been a central theme of HRM reform, although there are important differences regarding the targeting of these measures and the choice of instruments. As in the case of HRM reforms generally, the intensity of downsizing of the central public administration (CPA) across different countries (see Figure A.2) correlates well with the level of fiscal stress. Greece decreased employment by 19% from 2010 to 2013, Ireland reduced public service staffing levels from 2008 to Q1 2014 by 10% and Portugal reduced CPA levels by 8.9% between end 2011 and March 2014. As Figure A.3 shows, a number of OECD countries reported a moderate increase in CPA employment over the period, while Norway alone reported a high increase.

Figure A.3. **Changes in central public administration employment levels, 2008-13**

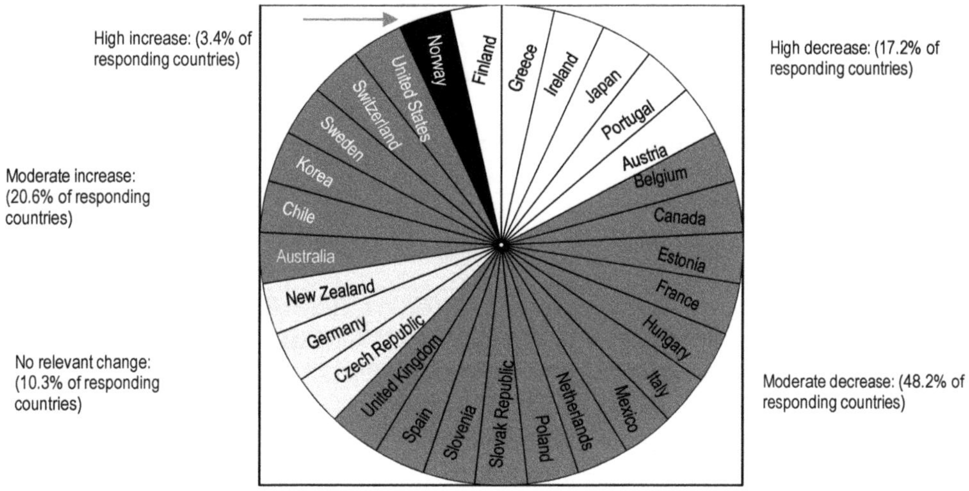

Source: OECD (2014), *Survey on Managing Budgeting Constraints: Implications for HRM and Employment in Central Public Administration*, OECD.

StatLink http://dx.doi.org/10.1787/888933288667

Remuneration systems have also been subject to very strong reform activities in the field of HRM (see Figure A.4). Between 2008 and 2013, 75% of surveyed countries introduced such reforms, with measures ranging from a wage freeze (67% of countries), cuts in allowances and bonuses, through to pay cuts (e.g. Ireland, Portugal, Spain). It is notable that Ireland has recently undertaken to reverse in part the pay cuts to public servants from 2016, in a clear signal that the economy has moved on from the "austerity era".

Figure A.4. **Use of instruments for remuneration reform, 2008-13**

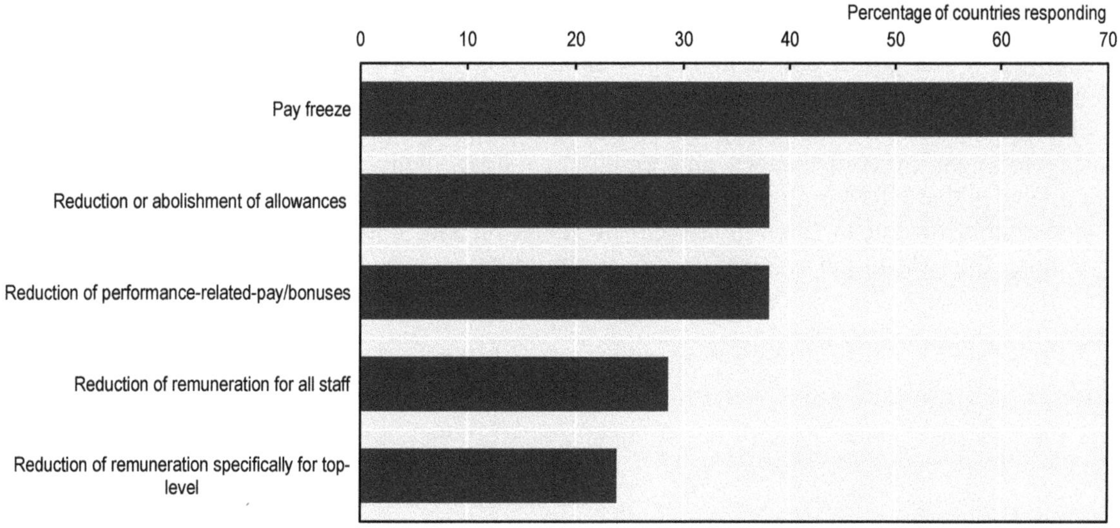

Source: OECD (2014), *Survey on Managing Budgeting Constraints: Implications for HRM and Employment in Central Public Administration*, OECD.

StatLink http://dx.doi.org/ 10.1787/888933288673

The OECD analysis has also examined HRM outcomes and effects on workplace behaviour, and confirms earlier research findings of a strong relationship between: a) the introduction of austerity-related HRM measures; and b) workplace attitudes, notably in terms of job satisfaction and trust in leadership (see Figure A.5).

Figure A.5. **Effects of HR reforms on workplace behaviour**

Since 2008

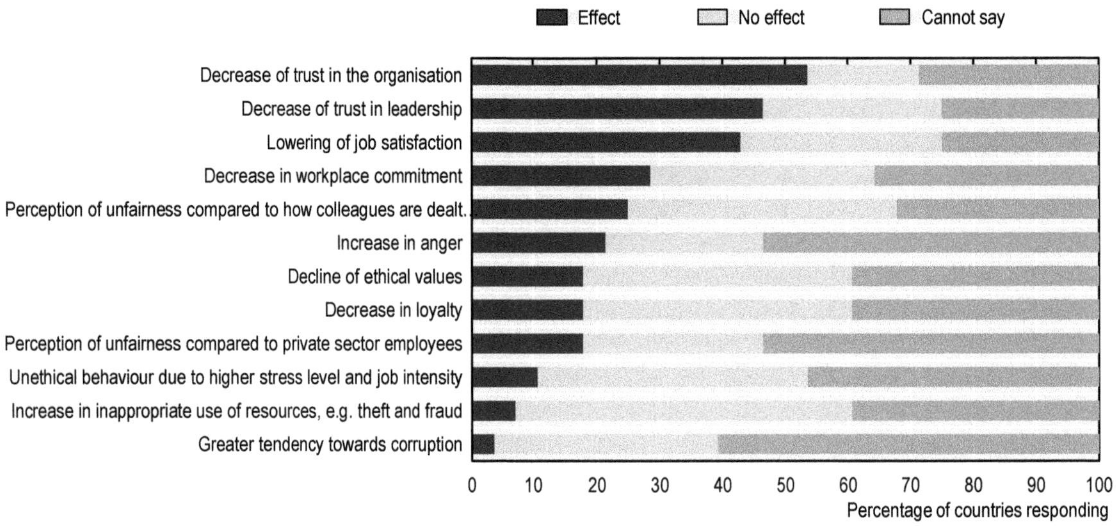

Source: OECD (2014), *Survey on Managing Budgeting Constraints: Implications for HRM and Employment in Central Public Administration*, OECD.

StatLink http://dx.doi.org/10.1787/888933288686

In balance with these findings, however, the analysis pointed to positive side effects of HRM reform, in particular the increased scope to improve workforce planning and the requirement for more strategic HRM planning (see Figure A.6). Overall, the OECD analysis draws policy conclusions for public sector HRM managers that underscore the need for linkages between "technical" HRM approaches (aimed at cost control and reduced operational spending) and "behavioural" HRM reforms (aimed at motivation, development of competences and employee engagement). In particular, the analysis concludes that HRM is an important strategic policy of government; and that if budgetary constraints remain in force as drivers of HRM reform, countries should take action to counter the risks to job satisfaction, job commitment and organisational trust.

Figure A.6. **Positive side effects of human resource reform**

Since 2008

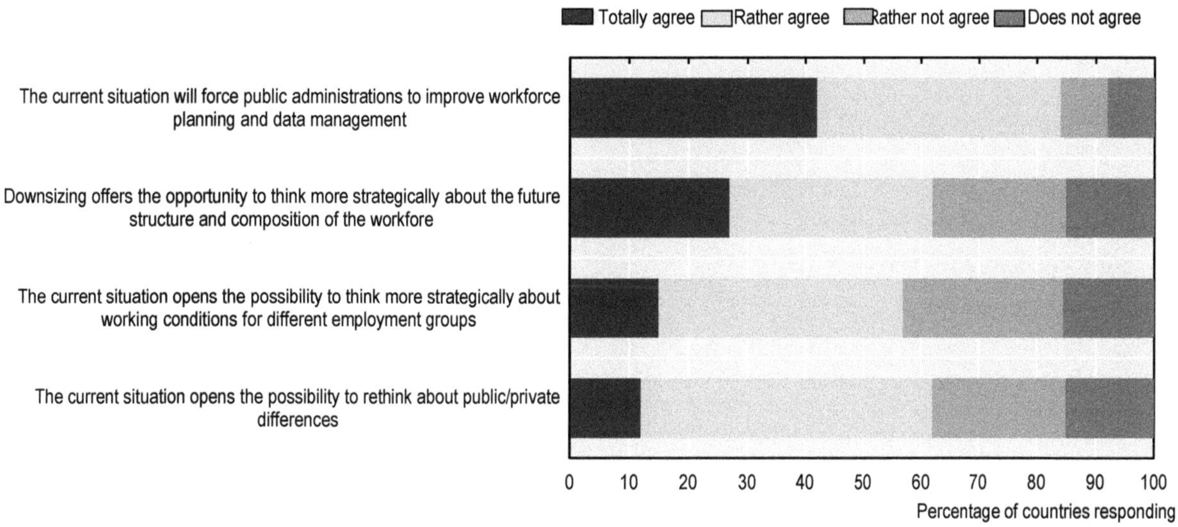

Source: OECD (2014), *Survey on Managing Budgeting Constraints: Implications for HRM and Employment in Central Public Administration*, OECD.

StatLink http://dx.doi.org/10.1787/888933288699

Notes

1. “The Impact of Budgetary Constraints on HRM: Report on Survey Results”, a classified report, was presented to the Public Governance Committee’s *Network on Public Employment & Management,* 20-21 April 2015. Note that the report is based on a survey of 28 OECD countries as well as Brazil, Colombia, Costa Rica and Latvia.

References

OECD (2014), *Survey on Managing Budgeting Constraints: Implications for HRM and Employment in Central Public Administration*, OECD.

ORGANISATION FOR ECONOMIC CO-OPERATION AND DEVELOPMENT

The OECD is a unique forum where governments work together to address the economic, social and environmental challenges of globalisation. The OECD is also at the forefront of efforts to understand and to help governments respond to new developments and concerns, such as corporate governance, the information economy and the challenges of an ageing population. The Organisation provides a setting where governments can compare policy experiences, seek answers to common problems, identify good practice and work to co-ordinate domestic and international policies.

The OECD member countries are: Australia, Austria, Belgium, Canada, Chile, the Czech Republic, Denmark, Estonia, Finland, France, Germany, Greece, Hungary, Iceland, Ireland, Israel, Italy, Japan, Korea, Luxembourg, Mexico, the Netherlands, New Zealand, Norway, Poland, Portugal, the Slovak Republic, Slovenia, Spain, Sweden, Switzerland, Turkey, the United Kingdom and the United States. The European Union takes part in the work of the OECD.

OECD Publishing disseminates widely the results of the Organisation's statistics gathering and research on economic, social and environmental issues, as well as the conventions, guidelines and standards agreed by its members.

OECD PUBLISHING, 2, rue André-Pascal, 75775 PARIS CEDEX 16
(42 2015 17 1 P) ISBN 978-92-64-24424-5 – 2015-18

www.ingramcontent.com/pod-product-compliance
Ingram Content Group UK Ltd.
Pitfield, Milton Keynes, MK11 3LW, UK
UKHW051501290926
15471UKWH00008B/1331